my french connection

Coming to grips with the world's most beautiful but baffling country

SHERYLE BAGWELL

FOURTH ESTATE • *London, New York, Sydney* and *Auckland*

Fourth Estate
An imprint of HarperCollins*Publishers*

First published in Australia in 2006
This edition published in 2007
by HarperCollins*Publishers* Australia Pty Limited
ABN 36 009 913 517
www.harpercollins.com.au

Copyright © Sheryle Bagwell 2006, 2007

The right of Sheryle Bagwell to be identified as the author of this work has been asserted by her under the *Copyright Amendment (Moral Rights) Act 2000*.

This work is copyright. Apart from any use as permitted under the *Copyright Act 1968*, no part may be reproduced, copied, scanned, stored in a retrieval system, recorded, or transmitted, in any form or by any means, without the prior written permission of the publisher.

HarperCollins*Publishers*
25 Ryde Road, Pymble, Sydney, NSW 2073, Australia
31 View Road, Glenfield, Auckland 10, New Zealand
77–85 Fulham Palace Road, London, W6 8JB, United Kingdom
2 Bloor Street East, 20th floor, Toronto, Ontario M4W 1A8, Canada
10 East 53rd Street, New York NY 10022, USA

National Library of Australia Cataloguing-in-Publication data:

Bagwell, Sheryle.
  My French connection.
  ISBN 13: 978 0 7322 8176 2 (pbk).
  ISBN 10: 0 7322 8176 8.
  1. Women journalists – France – Biography.
  2. France – Social life and customs.
  3. France – Description and travel. I. Title.
070.92

Cover design by Darren Holt, HarperCollins Design Studio
Typeset in Bembo 11/16.5pt by Kirby Jones
Printed and bound in Australia by Griffin Press
79gsm Bulky Paperback used by HarperCollins*Publishers* is a natural, recyclable product made from wood grown in a combination of sustainable plantation and regrowth forests. It also contains up to a 20% portion of recycled fibre. The manufacturing processes conform to the environmental regulations in Tasmania, the place of manufacture.

6 5 4 3 2 1   07 08 09 10

To my mother and grandmother,
I wish you were here.
And to Michael,
I'm so glad you are.

Excerpts from *A Moveable Feast/The Sun Also Rises* by Ernest Hemingway, published by Jonathan Cape, reprinted by permission of The Random House Group Ltd.

Excerpts from *French Women Don't Get Fat* by Mireille Guiliano, published by Chatto & Windus, reprinted by permission of The Random House Group Ltd.

Excerpts from *Sixty Million French People Can't Be Wrong* by Jean-Benoît Nadeau and Julie Barlow, reprinted by kind permission of Sourcebooks, Inc.

Excerpts from *France in the New Century* by John Ardagh, 2001, published by Penguin Books Ltd.

Excerpts from *Bonjour Paresse* by Corrine Maier reproduced by kind permission of Editions Michalon.

Excerpt from *Traveller's Prelude* by Freya Stark reproduced by kind permission of John Murray Publishers.

Excerpt by Chris Wilson as published in *The Guardian* reproduced by kind permission of Chris Wilson.

Contents

Prologue 1

1 Destination: Paris 5
2 In Search of a Home 35
3 Settling In 57
4 The Work Ethic 81
5 A Passion for Food 110
6 French Paradox 127
7 Rural Dreams 154
8 *Le Malade Imaginaire* 180
9 Cultural Exception 208
10 Sex, Gender and *La Petite Différence* 236
11 France and the World 267
12 Race, Riots and the Headscarf 291
13 What it Means to be French and a Muslim 315
14 Dogs, Turnips and Other Joys of France 331

Epilogue 354
Afterword 368
Acknowledgments 376

Prologue

THIS IS A BOOK that charts my journey through a country I've come to know and grown to love and admire — France. But this book is not just about me.

Above all, it's a book about modern France, and the glory of its rich culture and history, its quirky politics and its appealing social traditions and mores. With its charm and beauty, its contradictions and conflicting habits, France is a country that manages to both fascinate and frustrate the outsider. It certainly has done all of that in my case. My love affair with France has had its ups and downs, nevertheless I still find myself returning here to live as there is simply no other country like it in the world.

I first visited France — Paris — when I was thirty. I didn't go to write a book, nor was I looking for a Provençal ruin to renovate. I hadn't fallen in love with a Frenchman.

I couldn't speak the language. In fact, I knew little about France back then.

When I was offered the chance to spend a year in France, I simply saw it as a way of being somewhere else for a while.

I'd just wanted to get away from Australia. It didn't really matter where. Paris was as good a place as any. Or so I thought at the time.

Looking back, I can't believe I was so nonchalant about the adventure that lay ahead of me. As it turned out, that year in Paris changed my life. It was there that I met and fell in love with Michael, a Canadian journalist who'd also been drawn to France on a whim. When my time in Paris came to an end, he chose to join me in Australia where we planned to settle down and build a new life together. But we were restless. Paris, it seemed, had spoiled us for the 'ordinary' life.

Within a few years we were back. We scraped together a living in Paris as freelance journalists. We enjoyed the company of new-found friends and the beauty of a city that never seems to change. But we soon came to the conclusion we could never really recapture the past: that one perfect year. We left Paris never expecting to live in France again. Now here we are a decade later, back again in France, this time living in Lyon, a city at the gateway to the Mediterranean south.

And we are still asking ourselves the same question:

should we stay or should we go? And if we go, shall we ever manage to get France entirely out of our systems?

Although in the first few chapters I concentrate on the personal — what it was like to live in Paris in those years, how we managed to survive and why we keep being drawn back to France — this is also the story of an expatriate's life, the exhilarating feeling and heightened senses that come with being an outsider in a foreign country, being in a place far from home. But I didn't want to write just another book about being a foreigner in France. I also wanted to turn my journalist's eye to the country around me: to the customs, habits, traditions and current events that have shaped — and are still shaping — France and its citizens. I wanted to find out what makes the French so French; and what it is about France that manages to keep me — and so many other foreigners — completely in its thrall.

In this endeavour, I've drawn on my own experiences and relationships with the French over the years, as well as hundreds of interviews and encounters with ordinary people, experts, colleagues and friends, locals and fellow expats.

It's not a definitive account of France and the French. Rather, it's an idiosyncratic guide to a country that has fascinated and perplexed me in equal measure over the years, not only as an on-and-off resident, but also a reporter, feature writer, columnist and then as a foreign correspondent based in Europe.

The number of topics that you could cover in a book like this is endless. I've focussed on those which I find the most interesting as a journalist and as an observer. As such, the book is a product of its time, and of my time in France.

At the same time, I've tried to include stories and issues that are in some way emblematic of this unique and splendid country which, after all, has given me some of the best years of my life.

Lyon, 2005.

CHAPTER 1

Destination: Paris

The beckoning counts, and not the clicking latch behind you; and all through life the actual moment of emancipation still holds that delight of the world coming to meet you like a wave.

Freya Stark, *Traveller's Prelude*, 1950

I WAS ABOUT TWELVE years old when my mother first mentioned Paris.

'Imagine walking along the Champs-Élysées and seeing the Eiffel Tower? I'd just love to do that,' she confided one afternoon. 'Paris is one place I'd really like to visit.'

Mum would often talk about going to Paris, but as far as I know she never mentioned it to Dad. As far as I was concerned she could have been talking about Timbuktu, so distant did her dream seem from the reality of our daily life in a working-class suburb of Sydney. It was just her little romantic fantasy. Like mine at the time was marrying Cat Stevens.

Back in 1970, travelling abroad was not really an option in our family. Our summer holidays were taken in places you could easily reach by car — such as The Entrance to the north of Sydney, or Sussex Inlet to the south.

The farthest our family ever travelled was Perth. That was a few years later. As a special treat, my father took Mum, my younger brother and sister and grandparents on the Indian Pacific train.

The journey began at Sydney's Central Station, headed out through the western suburbs where we lived, and eventually continued across the vast Nullarbor Plain into Western Australia. It was about six months before my mother died. By then I was at university and couldn't spare the time for the long train trip. Instead, using money I'd saved up from part-time jobs, I flew to Perth to meet the family when they arrived.

I don't remember much of that holiday now. At the time I was too preoccupied with my new and exciting student life, which in turn allowed me to block out the tragedy unfolding at home.

I do have a photo though of my mother, taken just as she and the rest of the family were about to get on the train at Central Station. Wearing a dark blonde wig to cover what was left of her own hair, she looks gaunt and frail in her ill-fitting sun dress. A handsome woman, Mum always took care of her appearance. But in this photo she looks tired and older than her forty-one years. Nevertheless, she manages a warm smile, even though you can clearly see the pain in her eyes. Perhaps it's because she was finally going on a big trip. It wasn't Paris, but at least she was going somewhere far away.

It would be another ten years before I'd make the journey my mother always dreamed of. But in truth, this wasn't my motivation — despite Mum's yearnings, I was never much interested in seeing Paris myself.

As a teenager growing up in Yagoona, a suburb in Sydney's south-west — my brother and his mates jokingly referred to it as 'Yagoona, the land of meat pies and schooners' — the only travel I was ever interested in was the fast train to Cronulla Beach on hot days.

Yet Mum's musings about Paris had served to sow in me a seed of dissatisfaction and restlessness that I still carry with me today. She made me aware that beyond Yagoona a more exciting life beckoned. It wasn't so much a travel bug that Mum has passed on to me, but rather the feeling that gnawed away at her until she died, that somehow she could be doing more with her life.

That feeling pushed me on to university, a choice which at the time baffled my mother who believed the key to breaking out of suburban drudgery was finding a good job or marrying a rich man. Neither of my parents had ventured past Third Form (Year 9) at High School; consequently, they thought further education was a waste of time.

It also pushed me to seek a job as a reporter with a big Sydney newspaper, and to not give up when my application was rejected time and time again. I had a Bachelor of Arts degree majoring in journalism in my pocket, but in those days, in the eyes of Sydney editors, I was still just a girl from the western suburbs. I hadn't gone to the right schools. I had no contacts in the journalism world that could ease my way.

Despite being burdened with my own insecurities and self-doubt, I wasn't put off. Just months after my mother's death, and after another rejection letter, I left Sydney to take up a cadetship I'd been offered on a country newspaper on the North Coast of New South Wales. That experience gave me my break into mainstream Sydney journalism two years later as a casual news reporter on the Sydney *Daily Telegraph*. Eventually I managed to secure a full-time job as a feature writer on a national business daily, *The Australian Financial Review* (AFR).

Even though I'd secured a plum job, it still wasn't quite enough. By now I'd travelled abroad to various places and had a few interesting experiences in the process — I'd been robbed in Bali, contracted malaria in the Sudan, and spent a year studying at a university in Ohio of all places. Yet that feeling of unsettledness persisted. It was then that a work colleague mentioned a study program in Paris open to international journalists called Journalists in Europe (JE program). It was aimed at mid-career journalists who wanted to deepen their knowledge of European affairs, as well as their reporting skills. Australians were being encouraged to apply.

'I had the time of my life,' said the colleague, who'd just joined my newspaper after returning from the program. Not only did she get the chance to travel all over Europe to investigate stories of her choosing, she'd also hung out with a fascinating bunch of journalists who hailed from all over the world.

'How do I apply?' I asked.

I was ecstatic when I'd got the news I'd been accepted into the coming year's JE program. It was early 1988 and I'd just celebrated my thirtieth birthday. I was in need of a change of scenery. For one thing, my marriage had recently broken down. Andy was a juggler — at least that's how he preferred to describe himself, even writing it down as his occupation on our marriage certificate. An all-round street performer who got occasional gigs at community arts festivals, Andy was an East End Londoner who'd ended up in Sydney. He was about as different as you could get from the boys I'd known in Yagoona, which is probably why I fell for him. But eventually the relationship ran out of steam for both of us. That didn't make the break-up any less traumatic for me.

I'd also needed a new professional challenge. I enjoyed my job on the AFR, mostly because I tended to be left to my own devices. But there was nowhere else on the newspaper I wanted to go, except abroad as a foreign correspondent. As I hadn't come up through the financial reporting ranks, I never seemed to be considered for these few plum posts when they became available.

It was time, I thought, to make my own opportunities; create my own future. Paris, the city of lights, loves and combative locals might be just the ticket, I thought. I asked for a year's leave of absence from my job and signed up for a six-week French language course at Alliance Française in Sydney. I hadn't taken modern languages at school — ever the contrarian, I'd opted for Latin because I liked the teacher. The result was that I could now sing several verses of 'Yellow Submarine' in a dead language — but aside from English I couldn't utter one sensible phrase in a living one. Still, I hoped somehow my Latin studies would give me a head start in learning French.

As my departure date approached, I began to have my doubts about the wisdom of my looming Paris adventure.

I'd heard all the stories about haughty Parisians and their impatience towards foreigners who didn't speak French. On a trip to London with Andy a few years before I'd actually cancelled a side trip to Paris because I wasn't sure I was up to dealing with the locals.

The thought of being away from family and friends — and Australia — for nearly a year was also beginning to fill me with dread. I was about to catapult myself into a potentially hostile environment where I had few contacts and only a smattering of the language. Three months earlier, my decision to up stakes and move to Paris seemed wild and glamorous. Now it just seemed rash.

On the day I left for Sydney airport, I needed two friends to help me carry my giant, overstuffed suitcase to check-in. My father, brother, sister and grandparents had all come to see me off, no doubt fearing from the quantity of my luggage that I might be leaving for good. Fat chance, I thought to myself. I was already feeling terribly homesick and I hadn't even left the departure lounge. The perplexing advice from a friend, who was studying Buddhism at the time, didn't ease my sense of dread.

'Remember, Sheryle, the first person you meet when you get off that plane will be yourself.'

Maybe it was my nervous stomach. Maybe it was the free champagne. But I spent the last half of my flight to Europe throwing up in the aircraft toilet. I was so weak by the time I reached Frankfurt, where I was supposed to change planes for Paris, that I had to be carried off the aircraft. I was taken to the airport clinic where I was pumped with glucose and antibiotics, the all-purpose remedy for stomach bugs in those days. Having missed my connecting flight, I spent my first night in Europe flat on my back at Frankfurt's Airport

Hilton, listening to American music on US Armed Forces radio. Not quite the start I'd imagined.

I pulled myself up from my hotel bed to phone Claudine, who was to be my landlord in Paris. She had been expecting me the previous evening.

'Oh, that's too bad,' Claudine said, in a soft French accent. 'I was wondering what had happened. Just make your way here when you feel better.'

Claudine was a friend of a good friend of mine in Sydney. She'd offered to rent me the spare room in her Paris flat for a few weeks until I could find some permanent accommodation. She wasn't actually giving me much of a break on the rent, but from her letters she seemed friendly enough.

'I'm really looking forward to meeting you. Helen has told me so much about you,' she wrote. 'Helen was so kind and welcoming when I stayed with her in Sydney, I'd really like to return the favour.'

Claudine's apartment was within spitting distance of the lively St Michel area on the Left Bank, one of the few places I'd heard of in Paris. She would be renting me her son's room, she explained; he was apparently now staying with his father, from whom Claudine was separated. 'It will be so nice to have some company at home again,' she wrote.

Claudine was a dyed-in-the-wool Parisienne, so I reasoned she could help me get acquainted with the French capital. It would certainly be better and cheaper (slightly) than staying in a hotel.

I made it to Charles de Gaulle airport the following day. I was still feeling weak and a little sick from my mysterious illness, so I felt no sense of triumph or occasion that I had finally landed in the country that my mother had so wanted to visit all those years ago. All I wanted to do was get through customs, pick up my bags and hail a taxi. After what seemed liked an interminably long time while the customs officer scrutinised my student's visa — 'You have come a very long way, no?' — I wrestled my huge suitcase off the baggage carousel and walked out into the soft sunlight of a warm Parisian August morning.

In an instant, a cab pulled up in front of me. The driver flipped my bag into the boot of his battered Mercedes, then I read him Claudine's address.

'*Quoi?* (What?)' he replied. He looked at me as if I was speaking Swahili.

'*C'est près de Boulevard St Michel* (It's near Boulevard St Michel),' I ventured, using some of the few French words I'd retained from my Sydney language class. Another blank stare, so I handed him Claudine's letter with her address.

'*Ah, oui,*' he said, nodding sagely.

It wasn't until later, after I looked at my Paris map book, that I realised she lived quite a distance from St Michel. No matter. I'd seen two cake shops and three chocolate stores just in the last block before we pulled up in front of her building, a grand-looking place in the 14th arrondissement that had the architect's name and year of construction (1910) carved above the door.

It took the two of us, the driver and me, to lift my suitcase out of the boot and onto the footpath. Then, noticing I didn't quite know what to do next, he pushed a button in an alcove beside the double wooden doors to the building. They immediately swung open to reveal a dark, cool foyer dominated by a wide staircase. After that, he took my money, said his *au revoirs*, and I was on my own.

I knew from her letters that Claudine's flat was on the third floor. But there didn't seem to be a lift. I dragged my suitcase into the hallway and looked up. A casually dressed woman probably in her early forties was looking down from the third-floor landing. 'Hello. Welcome to Paris. I'm Claudine,' she shouted down. 'I saw your taxi pull up.'

'*Bonjour*, Claudine,' I answered. 'Nice to finally meet you … umm … is there a lift?'

'There is — behind the stairs. But I think it will be too small for your *valise*.'

She was right. On inspection, the lift looked like it would hardly accommodate a handbag, let alone my container-like suitcase.

I had no choice but to drag my bag up three flights of stairs. 'Don't worry, I'll be fine,' I shouted up as I began my ascent, not that Claudine was actually offering any help anyway.

By the time I reached her apartment, my face was bright red and I was breathing noisily. 'I better get you a glass of water,' Claudine said, as she ushered me into her living room.

Claudine's apartment was smaller than I expected and it looked like it hadn't seen a coat of paint since Napoleon's time. But it had that shabby chic look about it that some people spend a fortune trying to copy. It had marvellously rich parquet floors, high ceilings and panelled windows that stretched up to the ceilings. The small living room was crammed with old French furniture, potted palms and North African art.

'Morocco is my favourite place in the world. I travel there when I can,' Claudine explained airily as I regained my composure from the stair climb. She took a photo off the hall table and handed it to me: it was of a very handsome, dark-haired young man who looked about twenty-five. 'This is Ahmed, my lover. He lives in Marrakech, but he wants to come and live with me in Paris.'

'How nice,' I said.

We then moved on to what would be my room for the next eight weeks. I didn't have any idea what a Parisian teenager's room would look like, but somehow I didn't expect to see surfing posters on the walls. Under the bed — a single bed to my disappointment — I spied some sneakers. It looked as if her son had only recently departed.

'I'm sure I'll be very comfortable here,' I said politely.

By now I'd been well-briefed about Parisians. On the plane coming over, I reasoned that their poor image in the world was probably an exaggeration; after all, Claudine had been so friendly in her letters. 'There are always exceptions to the stereotype,' I'd counselled a friend who'd recounted her bad experience with an exceptionally rude waiter in Paris. 'It's probably just a cultural thing.'

I didn't expect, however, that I'd be clashing with the culture quite so soon.

Claudine gestured that I take a seat on her son's bed. 'Now, a few house rules,' she said in a tone that had lost all its initial warmth. She then proceeded to list them, one by one, in rapid fire fashion.

Rule 1: She'd prefer if I took my breakfast after her in the morning, once she'd gone to work. 'The kitchen is too small to accommodate the two of us easily,' she said. 'I don't like to be crowded.'

Rule 2: I couldn't use the hot water after 9 am — for what reason, she didn't say.

Rule 3: Under no circumstances was I to leave a tap dripping. (Punishable by what, I wondered, the guillotine?)

Rule 4: No guests.

She then handed me four hangers for my clothes. 'I'm afraid you'll have to use the hall cupboard. There's no room in my son's closet,' she said.

Was this the same woman who had written to me just weeks before about how she was so much looking forward to welcoming me into her home? It became apparent to me a few days into my stay that Claudine was really quite put out by my presence. I would learn later that the French don't readily invite people they don't know well into their homes, and I wondered whether Claudine now regretted her gesture (but clearly not the money I had handed over). But I had no alternative accommodation, and we had a deal. She'd just have to adjust.

Things lightened up somewhat when her son came to visit. A cheery fifteen-year-old, he was outgoing and friendly and unpretentious. (Maybe that was the surfie influence, I thought.) One morning, I saw him sharing a toasted baguette with his mother in the kitchen. 'Come and join us,' he gestured. Claudine smiled wanly: 'Yes, please do, Sheryle.' (Ah, her cold exterior was finally breaking down, I thought.) But the pleasantness was short-lived. Later that day, she came into my room to admonish me for supposedly breaking Rule number 1. 'But I didn't,' I heard myself respond in a tiny voice.

Still determined to make the most of my stay, at least, I thought, I would be able to practice my newly acquired ten or so phrases in French. Claudine spoke fluent, although accented, English. She made lots of small errors, however, some of which were very funny. One night, while telling me how her ex-husband had tried to extract more money than he was entitled to during their divorce, she blurted: 'He tried to take me to the Laundromat!' I wanted to correct her: 'In English, Claudine, you take people to the cleaners, not the Laundromat.' But I didn't. I was hardly one to criticise someone's language skills. Instead, I praised her for her English proficiency. I needn't have bothered — she already thought she spoke better English than I did.

One day, I decided it was time for me to start practising my French, given that I was about to begin a lecture program where half of the seminars would be delivered entirely in that language.

'*Bonjour*, Claudine. *Comment ça va?* (How are you?)' I ventured one afternoon after she returned home from work. '*Il fait très chaud aujourd'hui.* (It's hot today.)'

'Oh please, Sheryle,' she replied wearily in English. 'I'm just too tired at the end of my day to listen to your bad French.'

I immediately decided to bring forward my plans to find a more permanent place to live.

While I searched for a new place to live, I tried repeatedly to engage Claudine in some friendly French conversation. But she would always screw her face up when I spoke, so I eventually gave up (which was precisely what she wanted).

Fortunately, the JE program had enrolled me in an eight-week intensive language course that would run up to the start of the program in October, so at least I was getting some practice.

But the experience with Claudine had rattled me more

than I realised. It was just my luck that the first person I should meet in Paris would be as friendly and helpful as an attack dog. Of course, it didn't take me long to find out that Claudine wasn't necessarily typical of her compatriots. Two weeks into my stay, I started plugging into the JE social network. I'd phoned the JE headquarters shortly after I'd arrived and a friendly woman called Guillmette put me in contact with a few *anciennes stagiaires* (former trainees) from the program who were still in town. It turned out that there were lots of journalists hanging around from previous JE years who were trying to make a go of it in Paris. They were soon inviting me to dinners and parties where I was meeting all kinds of personalities, among them a lot of French journalists and academics who were some of the most charming, friendly and erudite people I would meet during my entire time in Paris.

Yet, on the streets, I seemed to be brushing up against a lot of rude locals who felt compelled to express their annoyance at my earnest attempts at communication. Ironically, they were usually the very people who were supposed to be serving the public — bank tellers, shop assistants, métro ticket sellers, waiters and the like.

'*Je voudrais retirer mon argent*,' I said carefully to the young woman behind the counter at my local Banque Nationale de Paris branch one day.

'You want to take out some money from your bank account? Is that what you are trying to say?' she responded abruptly, speaking so fast I could hardly follow her French. 'I'm sorry — that will be impossible today.'

'*Impossible? Mais, pourquoi?* (Impossible, but how come?)' I asked.

'I haven't got time to explain why's it's not possible,' she snapped. 'Next!'

It took me some time to work out that such exchanges had little to do with my poor French, or the fact that I was a foreigner. This was how all French *petits bureaucrates* spoke to everyone, their fellow Parisians included. To survive in Paris, you had to learn not to take '*non*' for an answer from the bureaucrats, I was counselled by wiser residents. More importantly, you had to master the very useful Parisian art of *s'engueuler* — telling people off. 'If you get good at that, you start to learn how to get by in French society,' an Australian artist and long-time Paris resident would tell me many years later.

But during my first months in Paris, and after my experiences with Claudine, such interactions only served to sap my confidence and dull my bravado.

To learn a language quickly you have to grab every opportunity that comes your way to talk and not give a damn about how you sound and how many mistakes you make. But I found I was only opening my mouth when it was absolutely necessary. I knew other Anglophones back then who spoke worse French than me, or in an impenetrable accent, but they ploughed on regardless, oblivious to the raised eyebrows and pursed lips around them. Not me. I tended to clam up, imagining how bad I must sound to sophisticated French ears.

At parties, I'd become instantly quiet if the language switched to French. Because I didn't speak French very often, I had trouble understanding even simple French words and phrases when they were spoken, even though I knew them when they were written down. As a result, I would miss most of the conversation whirling around me.

Among members of my family back in Sydney, I had a reputation for being outspoken and argumentative. I was always the one who'd talk back to the teachers at school. In Paris, though, I found my personality was changing; I was becoming meeker, more timid. One morning I walked into a shop on the busy Rue de Rivoli near the JE school in search of some batteries for my tape recorder. As I was trying to explain my needs to the shop assistant, I felt a tug on my skirt. I swung around to find a cherubic-looking little boy staring at me. He was no more than nine years old.

'*Oui?*' I asked him, bending my knees to bring my face level with his. '*Madame,*' he whispered. '*Votre accent est terrible!* (Madam, your accent is dreadful!)'

Instead of giving the kid a clip over the ear, I just walked out of the shop mortified.

Still, I was making some progress. Three weeks after I started looking I'd found myself an apartment to rent — a one-bedroom flat on the first floor of a neat building on Rue

Gracieuse in the quieter end of the Latin Quarter, an area in the fashionable 5th arrondissement. I spotted the ad in a French real estate newspaper and asked a former JE journalist still biding his time in Paris to help me with the negotiations.

The rent was high, even by Paris standards — it cost about as much per week as I'd paid per month in Sydney and that was for a much bigger place. It was also completely unfurnished; the owners had even stripped the rooms of their light fittings.

But I grabbed it anyway. The apartment was in a great location. It was just a short walk to all the lively Left Bank cafés I had read about in my Paris guidebook, including one of Ernest Hemingway's reputed favourite watering holes. The flat was also adjacent to a tree-lined square called Place Monge that played host to an open-air farmers' market twice a week selling everything from fresh fish and cheese, to flowers and overcoats. Until my first trip to Paris, I thought all food came in Cellophane packages on supermarket shelves. For a western suburbs girl, French open-air markets were a revelation.

Place Monge would prove to be my best classroom for learning French over the months ahead, for at the market, I had to speak to people — I had no choice.

Bustling open-air markets are the opposite of the impersonalised supermarket where you drop your ready-wrapped food choices in a trolley and trundle along to the check out without ever needing to utter a word.

Now if I didn't talk to the stallholders then I didn't eat. It wasn't as easy as simply asking for a piece of *fromage* either: I had to explain which variety of cheese I wanted (and there are over 300 of them in France), whether it would be eaten tonight or in the next week (so that the stallholder could choose the appropriate maturation), and then tack on something about how bad the weather had been lately.

Once I became a familiar enough face in my neighbourhood, the stallholders at Place Monge market, well most of them at least, even stopped screwing up their brows when I spoke.

'*Ah, voici la jeune australienne* (Here's the young Australian girl),' the cheery fishmonger announced to no one in particular one Sunday morning — to my great surprise as I couldn't remember him ever giving me a glimmer of recognition before. '*Votre accent est très mignon.* (Your accent is very sweet.)'

It wasn't the only time I would win compliments for my language efforts.

As opening lines go, it wasn't as sharp as 'Where have you been all my life?', but for a self-conscious Australian trying to make her way in Paris, it was enough to grab my attention.

It was about a week before the start of the JE program and all the participants were now rolling into Paris. At the

Centre de Formation et de Perfectionnement des Journalistes (CFPJ for short) on the Rue du Louvre in the centre of Paris where our classes would be held, I had just been introduced to one of two Canadian journalists in the program who'd arrived the day before.

'Hi, my name's Sheryle and I'm from Australia,' I said in French, extending my hand in welcome. Then — as was (still) my habit — I immediately apologised for my poor French, explaining that I'd only been studying the language for a few weeks.

'I think you speak French really well for just arriving in the country,' the Canadian replied, giving my hand a strong shake. I didn't believe him. But I thanked him for the compliment nonetheless. It was nice to be flattered for my French for a change. I immediately thought, 'I'm going to like this guy.'

Looking back, I'm not sure why Michael and I clicked so fast. Perhaps it was because we were at a similar hiatus in our lives. Like me, Michael was looking for a change of direction in his journalism career when he grabbed the opportunity of a year in Paris. And like me, he'd just emerged from a broken marriage — although there were no children involved, his break-up had been particularly nasty. He claimed he was in no hurry to start a new relationship, but he clearly liked to have women as friends and felt at ease in their company. I, in turn, liked his wry sense of humour.

Being from Montreal, Michael spoke French fluently, although he was an Anglophone Quebecker, his family having hailed originally from Ireland. As a result, his French was a mixture of North American and Québecois. The French liked to tease him that he spoke French '*comme un canard* (like a duck)' and he'd often get a harder time for his French than I would. But unlike me, he never let the criticism get to him.

'You don't think I have an accent, do you?' he'd tease Paris taxi drivers, who thought he was crazy for asking the obvious. '*Oui, Monsieur,*' they'd respond with a laugh. 'I have to tell you that you do.'

'That's funny,' he'd say. 'Where I come from, we think it's you guys who have the accent.'

With his wispy, shoulder-length blond hair and love for blue jeans and T-shirts, Michael was the North American opposite of the well-coiffed Parisian male of the late–1980s with their velour jackets, silk scarves and penchant for perfumed aftershave. Michael couldn't see the point of following fashion trends — if you held on to your clothes long enough, they'd always come back in style, he insisted. He was still wearing boot-cut jeans when everyone else was wearing stovepipes. 'They'll come back,' he said. (He was right. But he had to wait another ten years.) He did take to wearing his hair in a ponytail in Paris, but that was about the only concession he made to the hip style of the time.

Taken with his lack of pretensions — particularly when everything and everybody around me seemed so intimidating

— I began to seek out Michael's company whenever I could, although in the early days we were usually part of a larger group and rarely alone. The journalists in our program were a particularly social bunch. Most were determined to enjoy themselves in Paris, knowing it would probably be the last time they could act like students and get away with it. Although several of the group already had families, the majority had not yet settled down. Beyond the age of thirty, the serious life loomed; for now, we were living in Paris and we were determined to enjoy every minute of it.

Fortunately, the JE program was not making too many demands on our time and energies — we had plenty of both left over to explore the city and hang out in sidewalk cafés and ponder what our poor working colleagues were doing at that moment back home.

One of our favourite haunts was Les Fourmis café, just down the road from the CFPJ, where Eric, the unusually cheery waiter, was happy to let us sit on one beer or a coffee for most of the afternoon. At Les Fourmis, we'd discuss the morning's seminars on the European Community, then plot our own multinational reunions for the upcoming evening.

Often we'd adjourn to my apartment, which was handy to the cheap Greek restaurants of Rue Mouffetard — places where the proprietors still allowed you to smash the tableware to celebrate a good dinner. We'd then invariably stagger back to my place where we'd continue drinking cheap wine till the early hours, singing rounds of our national songs — one night I taught Jorgen from Denmark three verses of 'Waltzing Matilda'. Such late night karaoke-like sessions didn't actually endear me to the building's concierge, a patience-worn woman who lived just below me.

'This is your last warning,' she'd say, wagging her finger at my face once I'd finally opened the door to her incessant knocking. 'I'll call the police if you don't keep the noise down.' Luckily she never did.

Yet even irate concierges couldn't dent my growing infatuation with my new home. Living in arguably the most beautiful city in the world, without the pressures of a full-time job, and meeting new and interesting people in the process, was having an intoxicating effect. I also had the bonus of being a first-time visitor to Paris, so even the most touristy excursions — taking a lift to the top of the Eiffel Tower, sailing along the Seine on a Bateau Mouche and plunging deep into the Catacombs — were new and interesting experiences for me.

One Saturday, Michael got a group of us together to visit Cimetière du Père-Lachaise, one of the most famous cemeteries in the world where the likes of Balzac, Molière, Proust, Collette and Oscar Wilde are buried. Michael's objective though was to seek out the gravesite of a person who'd had rather more influence on him as a young teenager in Montreal — Jim Morrison, the lead singer of The Doors. When we got there, a young girl dressed in black was kneeling by the graveside, lighting a candle. 'She doesn't look like she was even born at the time Morrison died,' Michael sniffed, as we moved on to find Oscar Wilde.

Mostly, though, I just loved to walk the city streets. Later, I understood exactly why the writer Edmund White described Paris as 'the great city of the *flâneur* — that aimless stroller who loses himself in the crowd, who has no destination and goes wherever caprice or curiosity directs his or her steps'. No matter where I walked in Paris, whatever the district, there was always some beautiful vista or building or person or kissing couple to catch my eye, seducing me to change direction. I rarely took the métro to the CFPJ from my apartment because by walking I'd get to pass by an ancient Roman arena, the botanical gardens, Notre Dame cathedral and the Louvre museum. It was an uplifting way to start the day.

It was also a great time to be in Paris because the city itself was now gearing up for its own big party. I had the good fortune of living in France as it was celebrating a rather big set of dates in its history. January 1989 was the start of a year of street parties, parades and other events to mark the 200th anniversary of the storming of the Bastille on 14 July 1789, the Declaration of the Rights of Man the following month, and the abolition of the monarchy — what *Le Figaro*, France's right-leaning national newspaper, described in an editorial at the time as the most important series of events 'since the birth of Jesus Christ'.

Never mind that there were only seven prisoners in the Bastille at the time of the liberation (there would have been eight apparently but the Marquis de Sade had been moved the month before); that the French revolution unleashed the Reign of Terror whose enduring symbol was the guillotine; and that it ultimately culminated in the installation of another absolute monarch in the form of Napoleon. The French revolutionaries are credited with laying the foundations for modern social democracy, a model that would be eventually exported around the world. And weren't the French proud about that.

Indeed, my year in Paris would give me my first glimpse into the French political psyche, with all its fervent patriotism and nationalism.

At that time, the French economy was about a fifth the size of that of the United States. Yet France liked to stride the world stage as its equal. As I watched and participated in France's bicentenary celebrations, I couldn't help but get the message that France still considered itself a major power in the world — even though I was reading in history books that, in a relative sense, France's power had probably peaked in the late seventeenth century during the reign of the Sun King, Louis XIV.

As far as subsequent French leaders were concerned, the trick it seemed was never to acknowledge as much, but just to assume France still had a major speaking part on the world stage. By booting American troops off French soil and taking France out of NATO in 1966, the then French leader, General Charles de Gaulle, had served notice that France was not a country to be trifled with. He'd helped to restore a sense of power and prestige in the nation after the humiliation of the Nazi occupation during the Second World War by ensuring his country punched above its weight in global political and economic affairs. The late French President François Mitterrand was also determined to continue that Gaullist tradition ... even though he was a Socialist.

For the climax of the bicentenary celebrations in July 1989, Mitterrand gathered around him the leaders of the seven biggest industrialised nations. That same year he also inaugurated several new monuments in a grand artistic and cultural gesture worthy of Napoleon, including the Grande Arche de La Défense, the glass Pyramid at the Louvre and the new Opera House, built on the site of the Bastille prison where the revolution was launched two centuries before. France might no longer command an empire that once stretched from the Atlantic to almost the Urals, but Mitterrand was making it clear — to the French, and to the world — that France would continue to have the architectural trappings that spelt empire.

Or so it appeared in the late 1980s. To me, France seemed to be a country quite sure of its place in the world. That was something to be admired, even envied, when you came from a country like Australia which couldn't seem to make up its mind whether it was part of Asia, Europe or, at times, even the United States.

At first I interpreted French pride as arrogance, as if the French were always looking down their noses at the rest of us. France does have a superiority complex. But I eventually came to appreciate that there are things about France that the French can be justifiably proud of, such as its history, its language, its culture, its food and wine. The French, too, were not blind to the virtues of other countries: I've lost track of the number of French people who have told me how much they admired Australia and would like to visit — if it wasn't so far away.

At that point in time, the full steamrolling force of globalisation had yet to hit France and the French. The French economy was in its best state since the 1970s, thanks to a boom in exports and investment. Although the jobless rate was still in the double-digits, the Socialists in power thought they had it beat, and it certainly appeared to be on the decline. Furthermore, communism had collapsed and all the talk was about German re-unification and a new, more powerful unified Europe with a strong France and Germany at its centre.

The mood was generally upbeat, and to a wide-eyed journalist from Australia, France — and Europe — seemed the place to be. But France was also still a very different, at times difficult, country for a tongue-tied Anglophone to negotiate, with its endless bureaucracy, hard-to-master language and complex social customs.

Nevertheless, the French did know how to throw a party, and that was clear from the number of outdoor concerts, exhibitions, festivals and other events that seemed to be on almost every day during my year in France. On the anniversary of the 200th Bastille Day itself, the whole country seemed to erupt into a giant street party — the biggest since the liberation of France after the Second World War.

Just before that, as a visiting Australian journalist, I'd received an invitation to a bicentennial cocktail party on the roof terrace of the Australian Embassy. While on the JE program, I was also filing articles back to the AFR occasionally and I'd become a frequent visitor to the Embassy. The cocktail party was being held primarily to welcome then Prime Minister Bob Hawke and his wife, Hazel, who, like other national leaders, were making a beeline to Paris to take part in the celebrations.

Although I'd never met Hawke before, I was more excited by the fact that at the last minute I'd managed to sneak Michael and a couple of other JE friends into the party *sans invitation*. (These were far more innocent times, before September 11, 2001, and the Bali bombings, when Australian security had a 'she'll be right' attitude about it.) Hawke greeted all of us — Michael and my JE friends included — with a strong handshake and a friendly, 'How ya goin'?'

From the Embassy rooftop, Fosters beer cans in hand, we gazed out at the breathtaking illuminated nightscape of Paris spread out before us. To our right was the Eiffel Tower, which, with a massive number '200' fixed to its front to mark the bicentenary, shimmered like a birthday candle. Just beyond the Seine, the imposing 1930s architecture of the light-flooded Palais de Chaillot in the Place du Trocadéro dominated the horizon.

'Wherever you go for the rest of your life, it stays with you', Hemingway once wrote of Paris.

The trouble was, those feelings would never stay with me quite long enough. I would always feel the need to return.

My relationship with Michael, despite his initial reluctance, had quickly progressed from friendship to something more serious. Within about three months of our first meeting, Michael had moved into my flat on Rue Gracieuse.

By June the following year, as the JE program was drawing to a close for our group, we were already talking about our future together. Paris had had an intoxicating effect on both of us. Making love with the sound of the métro rumbling underneath our apartment was sweet and hypnotic in a way I'll never forget.

'When we get married, I think we should consider buying a little house in the French countryside,' Michael announced one day as we sped south in our rented Renault towards the fishing village of Cassis, on the Mediterranean coast, where we would spend a romantic holiday in the summer of 1989.

'Should I take that as a wedding proposal?' I bleated as I hugged him happily, causing the car to swerve momentarily off the auto route.

'Maybe we could get married in Paris, at our local town hall, like the locals do?'

This was, of course, a pipedream, as neither of us had yet divorced our previous partners, and anyway, the visa which allowed me to stay in Paris on the program was about to expire.

Both of us would have to return to our respective countries and get our lives in order. Back in Paris, we reluctantly packed our bags and said our goodbyes to our journalism colleagues.

I'd had the most fantastic year in Paris. I'd climbed the Eiffel Tower and seen the Champs-Élysées, as my mother had wished. Now it was time to return to reality and get on with the rest of my life.

CHAPTER 2

In Search of a Home

If you are lucky enough to have lived in Paris as a young man, then wherever you go for the rest of your life it stays with you, for Paris is a moveable feast.

Ernest Hemingway, *A Moveable Feast*, **1964**

I ALWAYS KNEW I'd return to France, but I always expected it would be as a tourist. I never thought I'd live there again. I certainly never anticipated that Michael and I would one day find ourselves living in a French provincial city. But that's eventually where we ended up, in a place called Lyon, France's prosperous second city.

How did we end up here? I've often asked myself that question, particularly when the lift in our old building has broken down for the second time in a week, or when trying for the umpteenth time to make myself understood on the telephone to a French tradesman.

The path to Lyon had been long and circuitous. After we left Paris, it would take another fourteen years, a lot more globe-trotting and even more soul-searching and false starts before we would finally make a serious commitment to living in France. That is, before we started to call France home, or at the very least, our home away from home.

Firstly, Michael and I were still married to other people back in 1989, although getting divorced was not too complicated as neither of us had children. After his divorce papers came through, Michael threw in his job as Montreal bureau chief of a national Canadian magazine and moved to Australia to be with me. We were married in Sydney the following year, in January 1990, at a small ceremony overlooking Sydney Harbour, surrounded by a few close friends and family members. I gave a speech about the wonderfully accidental nature of life: how two people from opposite sides of the world could have met and fallen in love in another place they'd never really planned to visit.

'To serendipity,' I said, and we all raised our glasses to that.

Michael and I then set about building our new life together. It wasn't long, though, before that old feeling of restlessness returned.

Paris, it seemed, had completely spoiled us for the settled life.

At the beginning, we tried hard to adjust. It was easier for me. Sydney was where I was born and I was returning to the bosom of my family and friends. I'd also slipped back easily into my old job as a feature writer on the AFR.

It wasn't quite so smooth for Michael. He'd assured me he was happy to leave Canada and make a new life in Sydney. Yet although he'd gained an instant support group through me, he'd found the move not as easy as he'd expected.

Michael had never considered setting foot in Australia before he met me, and now he was suddenly starting a new life in a country and culture that was similar to his own, but also strangely alien.

Soon after Michael arrived in Sydney, he'd found some temporary work in the newsroom of ABC Radio. Although he was an experienced radio reporter, he was told he wouldn't be able to go on-air. 'Not with that accent,' the news editor at the time had said.

Before long, Michael took a full-time job as a lecturer in journalism at a new university in the west of Sydney. He enjoyed teaching young journalism aspirants the essentials of news writing. Michael's succinct advice at the time to his students to 'just put the new stuff at the top' always brought a laugh. But, never having worked at a university before, he was finding the bureaucratic and administrative demands stifling.

Meanwhile, we pondered whether we should copy our friends and buy a house in Sydney — the property market was heating up and all the advice was to jump in now before it was too late. That seemed the sensible thing to do.

But Michael wasn't sure he was ready to be weighed down by a mortgage in a country he still barely knew (or rather, a country he hadn't quite made up his mind he wanted to live in). I wasn't sure, either, that buying a house was necessarily the answer to our unsettledness.

So when, one day, Michael popped the question: 'Why don't we try living in France again?', I immediately thought: 'Why not?'

Since nearly the moment we'd left we'd thought about going back. Holiday brochures with pictures of the Eiffel Tower triggered pangs of longing. We kept the big brass key to our Paris apartment on the Left Bank on a shelf in our living room. We put up iconic French street posters on our walls.

Needless to say, we were having a little trouble acclimatising — not least to each other. I realised how little we really knew about each other a few weeks after we were married when I announced that I'd decided to dye my hair back to its original brunette colour. (I'd gone abroad a dark blonde, but Paris hairdressers, and their heavy-handedness with the peroxide bottle, had turned me into a platinum blonde by the time I got back to Sydney.)

'You mean you're not a natural blonde?' Michael asked, a little bewildered.

'What do you think those dark roots meant every six or

so weeks? Didn't you notice them?' I cried. Apparently, he hadn't.

Little wonder our thoughts drifted back to Paris. We never actually said it to each other in so many words, but both of us believed, probably naively, that by going back to Paris, maybe we could recapture that special time in our lives. (But not the blonde hair!)

Yet it wasn't just the romance we missed. We also missed the *way* the French lived. Paris is clogged with traffic, the métro is crowded, space is at a premium and the people can be rude, but you can always escape into your own village-like neighbourhood; those marvellous congregations of apartments and speciality shops that are grouped around a square or a market.

Survivors of urban modernisation, these Parisian villages have every service you are ever likely to require — from cheese shops and butchers and bakers to cobblers and seamstresses. Each, too, has its own character and sense of community. These are the things that are missing from the suburbs — the sort of middle-class dormitories where I grew up that lack a heart and a soul.

We also missed the *excitement* of living abroad. In Paris, between socialising and attending lectures, I'd filed articles back to the paper on a whole range of topical stories from various European cities we visited as part of the JE program, like Prague which was in the grip of what became known as the Velvet Revolution, and Belfast which was still weighed down by the so-called 'troubles'. Michael and I wanted to experience that strange exhilaration once again of being an outsider in a foreign place.

So I asked my editor at the AFR for yet another twelve-month leave of absence, and to my amazement, he agreed — but no salary this time. Michael was also granted a leave of absence from his university job.

We both had a year to find out whether we could make a go of it in France. If we could, we knew there was a chance we wouldn't return.

In September 1991, we left Australia for Paris.

In the context of our relationship, Paris seemed to have more relevance and resonance for both Michael and me than either of our home towns. But during our second trip to Paris, we realised that wasn't necessarily enough ground on which to dig deep and proper roots that would grow into something more permanent, like a true home.

The problem wasn't Paris or Parisians. The city was still as beautiful and as sensual as ever. Although Paris is often characterised as a city that doesn't welcome foreigners, I'd come to think of it as a place that preferred to ignore foreigners — and by doing so, it managed to tolerate them. As one journalist from the *International Herald Tribune* had once put it, 'Paris is accommodating in its indifference.' That suited me fine.

I had no pretensions of becoming, or being taken for, French, like a lot of foreigners who have taken up residence.

An Australian friend of mine visiting Paris was once lambasted by a boutique owner for forgetting to say '*bonjour*' — as is French tradition — when he entered the shop.

'In Paris, we expect to be greeted by our customers, because we feel you are walking into our home,' the woman scolded my friend, in heavily accented French.

It turned out the boutique owner hailed from London.

Our problems in Paris, the second time around, were more practical. Like finding jobs that could support the lifestyle we'd left behind in Australia — and enjoyed the last time we lived in Paris. That was more problematic for me than for Michael — despite numerous classes, French fluency still evaded me.

Michael managed to pick up some part-time work at an American news wire service, Bloomberg, which was just starting up at the time in France. He supplemented this with casual shifts on the English service of Radio France International. Meanwhile, I tried to establish myself as a freelance journalist, sending stories back to Australia. Our collective earnings enabled us to rent a tiny apartment in the unfashionable 13th arrondissement in the south-east outskirts of Paris. It was basically one room with a small kitchen at one end, which in turn contained a cupboard that also housed the shower stall. The businessman who seemed to own a chain of these places was charging us

3,000 French francs per month, or about $780 Australian dollars, at the time. Without secure jobs or references, it was the best we could do.

Through a friend, we eventually found a better, more spacious place to live in a funkier neighbourhood. We were actually sharing a large ground-floor flat and garden with its owner, a Parisian civil servant who spent most of his time at his new girlfriend's place and was rarely there. It was a real find. But when Serge announced a few months after we'd moved in that he'd probably have to sell the flat because of his impending divorce, we wondered whether we had the stamina for another property search. Michael's well-paid work at Bloomberg was beginning to dry up and Radio France International was still only offering him shifts on a casual basis. Meanwhile, my freelance work was hardly generating enough income to cover a meal out once a week, let alone the rent.

Perhaps we were unrealistic to believe that we would both be able to find secure, full-time jobs in Paris in the space of a couple of months. You have to be patient, expatriate friends advised us. But I felt we had no more time to waste. I was almost thirty-five and Michael was approaching forty. The door to the period in our lives where we could still take risks and make great leaps was starting to close (or so I thought then).

In a sense, I think I was just chickening out. I'd hoped that somehow we'd be able to recapture that special year in

Paris that had been so full of fun and love and promise. But it quickly dawned on me that those thoughts were naive. Our lives had moved on, as had those of our old friends from JE who were still living in Paris. We were just another couple of Anglophone freelance journalists trying to scrape together a living in one of the most expensive cities in the world. It no longer seemed so glamorous.

While Michael was still wavering, I felt quite certain that it was time to call a halt to our wanderings. We had good jobs waiting for us back in Australia — but not for much longer. Our year's leave of absence would soon be up. Our Australian friends and family were eagerly awaiting our return. Our grown-up lives once again beckoned.

Back in Australia, we tried to make a good stab at the settled life. We bought an old house in Sydney's inner west, renovated it and focussed on our careers. Having a couple of kids would have completed the tableau, but that always seemed a commitment too far away for the both of us. Maybe that was selfishness on our part. Maybe it was just fear. Certainly neither of us felt really able to handle such a responsibility.

But that also meant we had no anchor. I loved my family and missed them immensely when I travelled. I missed the laughter of my nieces and nephew, and the hugs and smiles of my dear grandmother and her unconditional love. But the anticipation of that loss was never enough to keep me at home. I suspect I will regret that when I reach old age. But the temptation to travel, to wash up again on a foreign shore, still had a greater pull.

Five years after returning from Paris the second time, just after my fortieth birthday, the newspaper offered me a foreign posting. I didn't need to check first with Michael to find out whether he was up for another adventure, this time in London. We grabbed the opportunity greedily. And when my posting came to an end two and a half years later, we didn't ponder very long the risks of staying on. I quit my job of fifteen years and opted once again for the insecure life of the freelancer. We were not quite ready for our journey to end. Maybe London, we thought, would be the place we would finally call home.

Then the chance of living in the south of France fell out of the leaden London skies.

'You won't believe this, but I've just got an email from Interpol. They want to interview me for the job.'

I'd been attacking the bamboo that had taken over the small garden of our rented flat in Highbury, north London, when Michael popped his head out the back door with the unexpected news.

It had been about three months since he'd noticed a half-page ad in *The Economist* calling for applicants for the position of chief press officer at Interpol, the international police organisation.

'Wouldn't that be interesting, working for Interpol,' Michael had said at the time. 'Imagine the stories lurking in a place like that.'

Neither of us knew exactly what Interpol did. We knew it had something to do with international crime fighting — maybe even espionage. Mention Interpol and you immediately think of James Bond and 'Mission: Impossible'. It has a brand status on par with the CIA or the KGB. We figured the reality was probably far less glamorous, but the job ad nonetheless tweaked our interest.

That wasn't the only aspect of the job that caught our eye. There was also its location: Lyon, in the south of France.

'Why don't you throw in an application and see what happens?' I said to Michael. Despite our best efforts, Michael and I still hadn't managed to exorcise our wanderlust demons.

Nevertheless, we were hesitant at first. Michael was working as a senior editor on the foreign desk of the Reuters news agency in London. Leaving the independence of journalism to work for an international organisation second only in size to the United Nations would be a leap into the dark for him. As a press officer he would now have to speak on behalf of his employer — a police body no less. Some Leftie friends in London were appalled Michael was even considering doing such a thing.

'He's thinking about working for *Interpol*?' one friend asked incredulously when I told her of our plans over coffee one afternoon in central London. As she spoke, she glanced around suspiciously as if she were suddenly under surveillance. 'But that's the police. He'll be working for an *instrument of the state.*'

Michael had no intention of donning jackboots — just write some press releases about cross-border crime. At least, that seemed to be the job he was being asked to do. He was getting some mixed messages from the people at Interpol who had called him to Lyon for a preliminary interview.

'It's going to be very difficult for you to measure your success in a job like this,' Interpol's tough-talking Secretary-General warned Michael ominously during the interview.

In the end, however, we reasoned that being a press officer at Interpol would have to be less taxing than his current job at Reuters where he worked all hours under intense pressure. We would also have the opportunity to live in France again — and this time with the financial means to make it work.

When the news came through one cold London afternoon that Michael had been chosen for the job, we decided to take the leap. As we'd done so many times now, we began the exciting but onerous task of shifting countries.

We had only experienced Lyon once, and that was at high speed from the auto route as we headed south for a holiday in Cassis that first year we were in Paris.

Our first impressions back then were not good: it seemed to be the place where major roads and rivers came together, and it was also clogged with traffic. At its southern end, oil refineries and petrochemical plants belched white clouds of gas. To the north, high-rise housing estates formed an ugly urban sprawl, testimony to Lyon's ranking as France's second largest city after Paris.

Fortunately, our second experience of Lyon would turn out to be much more positive. After his job interview at Interpol headquarters, Michael spent an afternoon walking around the old city centre. He found the contrast with the dirty, industrial outskirts striking: the city's core was a myriad of narrow, cobbled streets, low-rise Renaissance-era buildings and large statue-filled public squares. The wealth from Lyon's industries — starting with the manufacture of silk in the sixteenth century — had built several museums, a town hall as richly Baroque as that in Paris, as well as a compact, hangar-like Opera House for the enjoyment of Lyon's substantial bourgeoisie.

'Lyon is really quite beautiful. I'm surprised,' Michael said when he phoned me on his mobile phone from a café where he was having lunch. 'It's kind of like a mini-Paris.'

What appealed to me more than any resemblance to Paris, however, was Lyon's location. It was only two hours by fast train from Paris in the north and Marseille in the south. The famous ski fields of the French Alps were a short drive away, as were the vineyards of the Beaujolais and

Burgundy regions to the north, and the lavender fields and olive trees of the Drôme and Provence to the south. Lyon seemed an ideal place from which to explore the rest of France. With its clear skies, hot Mediterranean summers and frosty winters, Lyon would also be an antidote to the monotony of London's endless grey skies.

But our first priority was to find a place to live. This, we found, was no longer a straightforward process in France.

During my first trip to Paris in 1988, finding a place to rent wasn't *too* difficult — even for a foreigner with a limited French vocabulary. At the time, there was an abundance of apartments available for rent. So long as you could prove you had the means to pay the rent — no small feat in itself — you could find a place to live.

This time, in the winter of 2003, we were moving to France when the property market was considered 'hot'. Low interest rate mortgages, population pressures, a lack of new construction and the introduction of the euro had all sent prices soaring for apartments across France, particularly in the main cities of Paris and Lyon. With property suddenly becoming a good investment, renters were being tempted to buy their flats from their landlords. This meant fewer apartments were now available for rent, which in turn was pushing up rents.

Even so, we knew that if we did manage to find a nice place, we'd be secure for our entire stay. Renting is still an attractive option in France, thanks to the paternalism of

French property laws which favour tenants more than landlords. Tenants in France enjoy a degree of protection unheard of in countries such as Australia where landlords get most of the breaks.

Unlike in Australia, where six-month leases are the norm, French landlords offer leases for periods of three years, and often six. In theory, the rent is fixed for the duration of the lease (although there are ways in which a landlord can raise the rent mid-lease, for example, by pleading a never-ending list of extra government charges and taxes).

Once you've signed a lease, it can be nearly impossible for the landlord to break it — even if you decide to stop paying the rent. Under French law, a landlord can't evict a tenant during the winter months, for example — it goes against France's heart-on-sleeve social conscience. To evict a tenant under any circumstances, the landlord has to obtain a court order and give the tenant six months' notice to quit. In reality, court-issued eviction notices can take years to obtain.

Tenants even have the first right to buy a property they are living in, should the landlord decide to sell. If the tenants decline to buy, they still can't be evicted until the lease has ended, even once the property has been sold.

I'd heard stories of landlords offering tenants all kinds of incentives, including offers to pay their moving costs and even their first month's rent in another apartment, to entice them to move out. We later met a Lyon resident who was offered 10,000 euros (around $A16,000) to move out of his grand apartment, which the owner wanted to sell vacant. (He only moved out when the landlord raised the offer to 15,000 euros.)

Others have been less generous. I'd also heard stories of frustrated landlords breaking into their properties when their tenants were away and then changing the locks to prevent them getting back in. This was the method used by one Paris landlord who'd wanted his low-income tenants out so he could raise the rent to what he believed was the correct market value. After three years fighting the issue in court, the landlord decided to take matters into his own hands. His tactic was illegal, but it apparently worked — the poor family never gained access to the flat again, their belongings dumped by the landlord in the building's courtyard.

Such guerrilla tactics, however, are rare in France. Most landlords simply submit to the law — and take extra care when choosing their tenants recognising that the relationship could be a long one. Renting remains the preferred option in France — some 45 per cent of the French population choose to rent their principal residence rather than buy it. Many even live in the same rented property for most of their adult lives. It is quite common for the French to rent their principal residence in town and buy a little weekender in the country, often in or close to the village where they were born.

I remember years ago meeting a Parisian woman who had just moved into a new apartment in the St Germain area and had set about doing some renovations — painting out the rooms, putting in built-in cupboards and shelves, updating the kitchen. I asked her how difficult it had been to find a flat to buy in Paris.

'*Buy*? I'm renting this place from the old woman upstairs — she's a friend of my mother's,' she answered, as if I had asked a really stupid question. She said she fully expected, however, to live in the flat for the next twenty years, at least until her young daughter had grown up and left home.

'It makes sense then to fix the place up a bit, wouldn't you say?'

Her response was so different from the renting culture I knew back home, where if you took the initiative and put a coat of paint on the walls in your flat, the landlord would likely raise the rent because you had made it more attractive (and rentable).

Growing up in the home-owning culture of Australia, renting was something you did while you saved up to buy your own house. Long-time renters generally had a bad name — they were usually the families your parents didn't want you to mix with as kids.

'You can always tell the renters in the street,' John Hewson, the former conservative political leader once pronounced during an Australian election campaign. 'They are the ones who don't mow their lawns.'

So it was refreshing to live in a country where renting an apartment didn't immediately cast you into the ranks of second-class citizenship. But there were some downsides. Being extremely picky about their tenants, French landlords aren't always eager to rent to foreigners who they fear might skip the country without paying their rent — thus putting them out of reach of the slow-moving French courts. (On the other hand, some landlords actually favour foreigners, suspecting — probably correctly — that they wouldn't know their rights as tenants as well as the locals do.)

Nevertheless, we had one obvious advantage in the eyes of Lyon's real estate agencies — Michael would be working for Interpol. I guess they figured if we ever skipped town, Interpol could track us down. Whatever the reason, agencies positively clamoured for Interpol tenants. 'The real estate agents just love us,' said Kate, who worked in human resources at Interpol and was assigned to help us find a place to live.

The Interpol connection, however, didn't bring the costs down. Renting through a real estate agent is an expensive process in France. Aside from paying a *caution* or deposit equal to two months' rent to the landlord, we were also obliged to pay the agent a commission equal to 10 per cent of the full year's rent.

But we weren't too worried about the extra costs. One of our motivations in moving to Lyon was to escape the monstrous cost of living in London. We had been paying 1200 British pounds a month for a one-bedroom plus study in Highbury (about $A3500 at the time) — and that was considered a good deal because we were renting from a friend who was giving us a break. 'Rents in Lyon are a third lower than in London,' said Kate. But first we had to find a place.

I had my heart set on renting an old-style apartment with high ceilings, ornate fireplaces and parquet floors — the kind of classic Parisian apartment that foreigners dream about owning. But Christmas was looming, a time when very few properties change hands. The only place that measured up on the list Kate had put together after she did a tour of Lyon real estate agencies was a flat on the top floor of a newly-built modern block. It was not in the oldest part of town, but was located across the Rhône River from the central peninsula district in a ritzy middle-class area of Lyon favoured by Interpol types. The Rue Massena flat lacked character. But it did have three bedrooms — thus space to accommodate all the friends and family who were threatening to visit — two bathrooms, a large balcony, an underground car park and a place to store bicycles. Older apartments rarely came with a car space, or any extra space for that matter.

We told Kate that we'd take it. As we flew back to London after a whirlwind day of viewing properties, we reasoned we could probably have done worse. We were relieved, at least, that we were able to find a place to live so quickly and painlessly. But we soon learnt things weren't going to be that simple.

All the apartments we'd viewed were described by the agents as 'unfurnished'. We'd rented a few places in our time, so we were pretty confident we knew what that meant — no bed, no dining table and no sofa. Maybe not even a fridge.

Wrong. Unfurnished in France means not only no furniture, but no carpets, certainly no fridge or stove, often no kitchen cupboards and sometimes not even a kitchen sink. By luck, the kitchens in the previous apartments we'd rented in Paris had come pretty much fully equipped, so we weren't aware of this particular definition of 'unfurnished' when, the following week, the real estate agent handling the Rue Massena flat phoned us in London to say the former tenant would be coming around to pick up his things.

'What things?' I asked her. 'The place is empty.'

'The stove and the kitchen cupboards, of course,' the agent replied. She stressed, however, that the sink would stay.

It was now just a few days before Christmas and Kate from Interpol wasn't around to give us any advice. Paranoid foreigners, we instantly took the view we were being conned.

'Nobody strips a kitchen of built-in cupboards. What's the point?' Michael said. 'He's probably left big holes in the kitchen walls.'

Besides, traipsing around Ikea in search of cupboards and bench tops, let alone a cooker, fridge and washing machine, was not exactly what we wanted to do during our first week in Lyon. We told the agent we wouldn't be taking the apartment after all.

Kate later put us straight. 'Sorry, I should have made that clear to you — apartments usually come completely empty in France and in much of Europe as well.'

She explained that owners and tenants tended to take everything they put into a property with them when they left — right down to the light fixtures and kitchen units. It was then that I remembered my experience in Paris when I was renting my first apartment near Place Monge: so that's why all the light fittings were missing? I thought the owners were afraid that I was going to nick them when I left.

Several weeks later, when I raised the issue in my new French class in Lyon as a sort of conversational 'show and tell' exercise, a fellow student from Germany couldn't understand why I was making so much fuss. He said it was normal for new tenants in his country, even if they only intended to stay for a year or two, to fit out the kitchen themselves, to make it their own.

'You mean you would *want* to cook on somebody else's stove?' he said. 'That's really disgusting.' I confessed I'd never thought about it that way.

Meanwhile, having dumped our Rue Massena flat, we were now homeless. We had no choice but to live in a cheap apartment hotel for our first month in Lyon while we searched for another place. With Lyon still deep in winter and snow, the search wasn't any easier. But thanks to Kate, we eventually found a place to our liking, in central Lyon, our original choice of neighbourhood.

The flat on Rue des Remparts d'Ainay had only two bedrooms — one just big enough for me to set up an office so accommodating guests was going to be a problem.

But it did have breathtakingly high ceilings, superb marble fireplaces (that didn't work) and rich parquet floors. And when you stepped out onto the tiny wrought-iron balcony through French doors, if you looked to your right, averting your gaze from the goings-on in the apartment across the street that was so close you could have a conversation with your neighbours, you had a splendid view between the buildings of the shimmering Rhône.

I'd found the *belle époque* apartment of my dreams, even if the claw-footed, 100-year-old tub taking centre stage in our gigantic bathroom meant a proper, stand-up shower was out of the question.

Oh, and yes, the kitchen was an empty shell, except for an expertly tiled double sink.

CHAPTER 3

Settling In

A stay in Lyon is sweeter than a hundred maidens ...

Clément Marot, 16th century French poet

CENTRAL LYON IS PERCHED on a sliver of land between two rivers, the Saône and the Rhône, and two hills, the Fouvière and Croix-Rousse. The city spreads out on both sides of these landmarks, but it's on this peninsula — or *Presqu'île* as it's called — that you'll find the city's shopping and entertainment heart.

It's also where Michael and I were now living — a neighbourhood at the southern end of *Presqu'île* that went by the name of Ainay. Not that it was called that on any map. Ainay had no defined borders so no one could say exactly where the neighbourhood ended and the next one began.

Ainay was simply the name that had been passed down through time for this particular collection of streets, shops and apartments huddled around a square and a medieval church — as if it were some ancient village of urban memory that had long since been subsumed by town planners into the growing metropolis.

Most of these village-like neighbourhoods in French inner-cities were bound together by a specific commercial activity — and in Ainay's case, it was the sale of art and old wares. Within a small radius of our apartment there were dozens of antique furniture and rare book shops, as well as galleries which sold paintings and sculptures of all styles from all eras. There were even a few boutiques selling Lyon's famous embroidered silk.

Each shop seemed like an Aladdin's Cave; their often rather decrepit façades gave few hints as to the value of the clutter within. Not long after Michael and I arrived in Ainay, I ventured into an unremarkable little gallery around the corner from our apartment to take a closer look at a bronze sculpture of a young ballerina displayed in the window. The ballerina's face reminded me of my ten-year-old niece in Australia and I thought it would make a lovely present.

'It looks just like something Degas would do,' I said to the elegantly dressed young woman in the gallery.

'It is a Degas, Madame,' she replied, as if an original sculpture by the famous French impressionist was the most normal thing in the world to find in your local neighbourhood art shop.

'Right, of course,' I said. I didn't bother to ask her the price.

Ainay though wasn't just a *quartier* where Lyon's wealthy came to shop. Sandwiched between the antique stores and art galleries was all the commerce required to support a thriving residential neighbourhood. Within one block of our flat there was a butcher, a pharmacy, a newsagent, a florist and a bread shop. Within two blocks I could get my clothes dry-cleaned, my trousers hemmed and my personality analysed — there was a psychiatrist just up the street. Twice a week there was also an outdoor market at the local square — Place Carnot — selling everything from fruit and vegetables to overcoats and puppies.

There were also about a dozen cafés and restaurants in the immediate vicinity, which meant we would never have to walk very far for a dinner out. This was especially appealing given that our kitchen was hardly big enough to swing a cat in, particularly once we'd equipped it at great expense.

We weren't able to buy kitchen cupboards and appliances in Ainay — there are some things, after all, that you just can't get in a village. For these, we had to travel a few kilometres into Lyon's sprawling suburbs to a *centre commercial*, France's version of an American-style mall where you'll find the superstores and mega-sized supermarkets.

The French might have successfully preserved their inner-city neighbourhoods as remnants of another era, but when they wanted to do some serious shopping, like everyone else around the world, they headed for the suburbs.

It was to one of those malls that we went in search of kitchen cupboards and benches that would provide the finishing touches to our 'unfurnished' kitchen. Against our better judgement, we ended up at Ikea, that Swedish version of shopping hell that is as ubiquitous in Europe as McDonald's restaurants. I've shopped at Ikea stores in Sydney, London, Paris and Moscow and found them all as frustrating an experience as assembling a piece of their furniture. Once you've managed to find a car space miles from the entrance, you are then trapped in the store for hours as you negotiate the maze-like floor plan that ensures you pass by every Ikea item ever made except the one you are actually looking for. In France, the experience was even more nerve-racking because, with no Sunday trading, everybody crams their shopping into Saturdays.

At Lyon's Ikea outlet, we spent an entire Saturday morning in the kitchen cupboard section battling football final-size crowds who, like us, were planning to spend thousands of euros fixing up apartments they didn't own. A few months later I read that Ikea founder Ingvar Kamprad was now snapping at the heels of Bill Gates in the wealth stakes. I wondered how much European tenancy practices had contributed to his fortune.

*

We felt fortunate to have landed in what felt like a genuine and distinctive Lyon neighbourhood, as delightful as any we had experienced in Paris. I'd hoped to settle in quickly to my new home. I knew I'd never be taken for a local — nor did I particularly want to pass myself off as one — but this time I did want to feel more like a member of my local community. Not just merely another expat biding her time until she moved on again.

To improve my chances, I signed up for yet another language course at Alliance Française. It had been ten years since I'd last spoken a word of French so my skills were a little rusty to say the least. When we decided to move to Lyon, I vowed to get on top of my French this time because now I had the time to do so — Michael would be working full-time, but I would not. I was determined to make some French friends and acquaintances within my local community, and not just restrict myself to English-speaking expatriates.

This was easier said than done, of course. I'd met foreigners who had managed to make friends quickly among the French. But they were either parents with young children — the school gate, it seemed, was among the best places to meet and socialise with people of a similar age in your neighbourhood — or those who had jobs in an entirely French workplace. I was neither a parent, nor did I have a local job — worse, I worked from home. I was soon to learn that I had another disadvantage when it came to making French friends. I'd moved to Lyon.

There is a maxim in France that the people became warmer and friendlier the further south you go. It has something to do with the climate, and the distance from Paris. Yet apparently Lyon, at the gateway to sunny Provence, was an exception to this rule. Whenever I asked a French person who was not from Lyon what they thought about Lyon, I was invariably told the place was full of snobs who wouldn't save you if you were drowning.

'Lyon is a beautiful city but you're going to find the people very difficult to get to know,' a French journalist we knew in London told us before our departure.

'The Lyonnais are terribly cold and unfriendly. I've never met one I've liked,' said a French woman from Alsace whom we'd met one summer holiday.

I wondered how the Lyonnais had managed to get lumbered with such a reputation for haughtiness and unfriendliness. It was so entrenched that even the locals seemed to accept the stereotype.

'Do you like Lyon?' one very friendly Lyon-born woman, a friend of a friend, asked me soon after I arrived.

'Yes, I think it's very beautiful,' I said.

'It's a pity the people are so cold, though,' she added.

After some research, I came to the conclusion it probably had something to do with Lyon's complicated history.

Lyon, it seemed, had always had an uneasy relationship with Paris, its historic rival in everything from politics, to religion and economics. It dated back to Roman times when Lyon, known at that time as Lugdunum, was established as the capital of all of Roman Gaul. Lyon then became a powerful religious centre independent from the Kingdom of France, before it decided to switch its devotion to capitalism, where it would eventually dominate perhaps the two most important global businesses of the sixteenth century — silk and printing.

With these industries came the merchant bankers who helped turn Lyon into a financial and trading hub. Renaissance Lyon was apparently the place to be if you had entrepreneurial ambitions. You could hang out at a new institution called a stock exchange — Lyon's was the first in France, predating the Paris Bourse — and double your wealth at the wave of a quill.

But as the city got richer, so its banking and commercial elite became more conservative and inward-looking, claim historians. They sowed the seeds of Lyon's decline when, during the French Revolution, they made the fatal mistake of backing the wrong side. The city stuck with the Royalists, which angered the new leaders in Paris no end. In 1793, revolutionary troops stormed Lyon and destroyed parts of it. Indeed, there are some locals who believe Paris still hasn't forgiven Lyon for its disloyalty; it certainly kept the second city on a short leash for a very long time.

By the nineteenth century, the silk trade had given birth to a chemical industry in Lyon (for dyes, detergents, etc), which in turn attracted rubber and plastics, heavy engineering, petrochemicals and later pharmaceuticals and biotechnology businesses. Yet it wasn't until the twentieth century that Lyon was able to reassert its business credentials and establish itself once again as one of France's wealthiest industrial centres, although it would never again surpass Paris in terms of economic might.

The Rhône–Alpes region, of which Lyon is the capital, is today the second largest contributor to the French economy. Thankfully, the heavy industries have been kept well away from Lyon's attractive historical core, which sits in stark contrast to the ugly factories on the city's outskirts. Living in Ainay it was even possible to forget that the factories existed — except when the winds blew from the south where the oil refineries and their belching chimneys were located.

The locals though seemed to believe that a little air pollution was a small price to pay for the jobs and prosperity that the industries had injected into the Lyon economy. (The environment was never a huge issue in nuclear-powered France anyway.) For one thing, the money had allowed the city to preserve and restore much of its architectural history — some 500 hectares of Lyon's centre, including our neighbourhood, have been classified, like the centres of Prague and Venice, as a UNESCO world heritage

Settling In

site. That, in turn, has lifted tourism numbers, particularly foreign tourists, who previously tended not to include Lyon on their journeys through France despite the city's reputation for gastronomy.

'Lyon is no longer a city that tourists bypass,' the city's tourism chief François Gaillard declared in the local paper. He claimed 40 per cent of Lyon's 5.5 million visitors in 2004 came from outside France.

The city's leaders were trying hard to bury Lyon's reputation for haughtiness and reposition it as a dynamic, cosmopolitan European crossroads which long ago threw off its conservatism and opened up to the world. As proof, they pointed to the election in 2001 of the city's first left-wing mayor in more than a century, and the fact that the city had attracted several big foreign firms as well as two international organisations — the International Cancer Research Agency and, of course, Interpol. These new arrivals had injected a large number of foreign accents into the Lyon population. Indeed, there haven't been so many expatriates living in Lyon since the Gestapo had their headquarters here in the Second World War.

'Before the foreign companies and organisations arrived, Lyon was pretty boring,' one long-term resident who works at Interpol told me. 'Now it's a much more interesting place to live.'

Yet some stereotypes die hard. In our little enclave of Ainay, where time has stood still, strangers still seem to be eyed with a degree of suspicion. Every time I walked into Le Spleen, the café on our street, I was reminded of those scenes in American Westerns when a hush descends in the town's rowdy bar as soon as the bad guy walks in — so it was for me when I entered Le Spleen. For weeks I bought a baguette from the same bakery every morning, but still the young woman serving greeted me in the cool manner of someone enduring a visit from their bank manager.

I was also having trouble getting beyond *bonjour* with the neighbours in my apartment block. Only one of the residents had asked me my name or wondered where I might be from — and she was an Italian woman, 84-year-old Mrs De Marco on the top floor.

That wasn't to say my neighbours weren't polite, even charming, when they met Michael and me on the stairs. But the conversation rarely moved beyond chitchat about the weather, and tut-tuts at the lift having broken down yet again.

If anyone learned that I was Australian, my husband was Canadian and that he worked at Interpol, it was because I'd blurted it out when I ran into someone at the mail box, as I searched for something more interesting to say. The look on peoples' faces was invariably, 'Please, this is too much information', as if I had just launched into a detailed description of my husband's hernia operation.

Even old Mr Rochaix who lived just a few feet away from us across the landing, had never asked me my name —

'*Bonjour Madame*' was as far as it went — although he was a bit more talkative with Michael.

Now if the tables were turned and a French couple had moved in next door to where we used to live in Sydney, I would have had them over for a barbecue before they had a chance to put down their *valises,* curious to find out what had brought them to Australia and what they thought about the country.

But not in Ainay, it seemed. The frustrating thing was that other people we were meeting in Lyon — French and non-French alike — didn't seem to be having the same problems settling in as we were.

Soon after I moved to Lyon I met a friendly French woman my own age at an Interpol party Michael and I had been invited to, who would become one of my closest friends. A bit of an Anglophile, Muriel worked at Interpol as a translator and would eventually come to be one of my guides to understanding the French and what made them tick.

Originally from the Savoy region of France, Muriel had lived in Lyon for sixteen years. A few years ago she'd bought a lovely, airy flat in a modern residential and leisure complex on the banks of the Saône. A short time after I met her, I asked whether she'd had any trouble getting to know her neighbours when she moved into her building. '*Au contraire,*' she replied, adding she was always in her neighbours' flats, and they in hers.

'That reminds me,' she said, 'our building is holding a big party on the front lawns next week, to get to know the new arrivals, and I've promised to make a few salads ...'

Seeing the look of jealousy on my face, Muriel quickly added, 'But I do think my building is quite unusual.'

I'd put the same question to another new friend, a former Swedish police officer whose partner worked at Interpol. Camilla lived in a big flat on the eastern, more modern side of the Rhône and seemed well-settled into Lyon life.

'You have to make an effort with the Lyonnais,' Camilla told me. 'You have to approach them first.'

Camilla explained that about a year after she moved from Stockholm she and her partner Jan held a Swedish Christmas party in their apartment. They'd invited forty-five people, including residents in their building they'd only passed the time of day with before.

'I was really nervous about the whole thing,' she said. 'Jan and I were up till midnight nights before making meatballs, and we had to swap the beer and vodka for wine to cater for French tastes. But it turned out to be a big success.'

Apparently the building was still talking about the Swedish couple and their amazing hospitality. Return dinner invitations hadn't actually flowed in, Camilla revealed, but she had made some firm friends.

'My closest neighbour across the landing told me the other day that I was probably her best friend in Lyon,' she said.

'Gosh, I can hardly raise a smile in *my* building,' I replied.

Perhaps the trick then was to hold an Australian party — although I knew I had little hope of fitting a barbecue on our tiny balcony. I wondered, too, whether my neighbours were the partying type.

'You've moved into a *quartier* which is really old money,' one of my many French teachers later explained to me. Janine's family hailed from Provence but she knew a lot about old Lyon.

'The people in your area are generally the older, wealthier bourgeoisie. They tend to keep to themselves more than most. It's much different where I live.'

I was starting to feel like Judy Garland. 'Somewhere over the rainbow bluebirds fly' — and a friendlier Lyon existed. Such was the downside of living in an old, established neighbourhood, I guessed, even if it exuded beauty and charm.

But I'd been making some progress. The baker said hello to me one day when she passed me on the street, and I was beginning to get nods of recognition from Le Spleen's owner, an unsmiling woman with short red hair who liked to wear red ballet shoes with fishnet stockings and looked a bit like Edith Piaf. Soon after she even ventured an unsolicited comment, aside from 'What do you want to drink?'.

'That's English money, isn't it? What's it called again?' she asked me when I mistakenly pulled out a 10 pence coin rather than a euro from my purse as I searched for change for my morning coffee. I explained that it was British pounds and pence and reminded her that the Brits hadn't adopted the euro.

'They were smart,' she retorted. 'We should never have given up the franc. The euro has only given us higher prices.'

It was then that the penny dropped: in France, a discussion about politics is always a sure way to break the ice.

Now that the owner had become a little friendlier, Le Spleen had become a favourite hangout for me, not least because it served the cheapest coffee in the neighbourhood. It was also a great place to do some people watching and to catch snatches of local gossip.

It was similarly popular with the antique shop dealers who seemed to do a lot of their business from Le Spleen's tables. I could hear them chattering away on their mobile phones, arranging deliveries or searching out the latest deceased estate to plunder, while they scoured the antique magazines. From the few prime tables that blocked pedestrian traffic on the footpath, they could watch over their unattended shops and dash back if a customer entered — which in Ainay didn't seem to be that often. I wondered how these shops survived — there was one shop down the road from us, for example, which only sold paintings and sculptures of animals — dogs, cats, rabbits, even hippopotami. The shops seemed so ancient that I suspected the businesses had been in their families for generations. They probably didn't have to worry about paying the rent.

Like these antique dealers, the activity I most enjoy in France is sitting in a café, sipping a *café au lait*, reading the newspapers and watching the world go by. You can take your coffee quick in France — standing at the bar, gulping down a little espresso in the time it takes to plonk a euro on the counter as payment. Or you can take a table and take your time. I've never been hurried out of a French café. You can sit on one coffee all morning if you like — sometimes, it might take half that time just for the waiter to come and serve you. Café-sitting is for people with time on their hands; it's the opposite of the Starbucks culture with its coffee sold in cardboard cartons and drunk hurriedly on the way to work.

I certainly had a lot of time on my hands in Lyon. I had no work lined up when I arrived, except the vague notion of selling a few stories about France to those who might be interested. Unlike in London, though, it didn't really matter whether I earned an adequate income from my freelancing efforts. We were living in a much cheaper city and Michael's salary more than covered our expenses. This was just as well as Lyon could hardly compare with London in terms of generating legions of stories of interest to Australians. But it also meant my days, at least in the beginning, lacked a certain structure, punctuated only by my visits to Le Spleen and to French class. That was liberating at first, until I found myself spending so much time café-sitting that even the waiters were beginning to wonder whether I had a home to go to.

It was time to explore beyond my little neighbourhood and see what Lyon had to offer. I was surprised to find that there were actually so many things to see and do. On weekends, Michael and I meandered around the city centre where we found traces of Lyon's long and colourful history everywhere, from the ruins of a Roman amphitheatre on Fourvière hill, to the pastel-coloured Renaissance residences of the old city below it.

There were also dozens of churches and art galleries, including one on the city's magnificent main square — Place Terreaux — that had been dubbed the 'Petit Louvre' because of the range and diversity of its collections. But I'd seen inside enough churches and museums in Europe to last a lifetime. What I really wanted to explore was some of Lyon's more recent history.

It wasn't until I moved to Lyon that I'd learned about the city's strategic role in the Second World War. Because of its size and proximity to the Swiss border, Lyon was once a major centre of operations for the French Resistance. Its fighters apparently made good use of the labyrinthine *traboules* or covered passageways in the old city — these are unique to Lyon and were once used by silk manufacturers to move from place to place without damaging their precious fabric — for their clandestine activities. Lyon was once also the headquarters of the German Gestapo, which

Settling In

was sent to the city in 1942 to destroy the Resistance network. Its chief was none other than Klaus Barbie, the German commandant who would go down in history as the 'butcher of Lyon'.

Barbie had apparently set up his headquarters in the city's plush Hotel Terminus, which still survives today. The hotel now houses Lyon's Centre for the History of the Resistance and Deportation. It was established after Barbie's trial in Lyon in 1987, when, some forty years after the war, he was sentenced to life imprisonment for 'crimes against humanity'.

I had some visitors from London staying for the weekend, so I suggested we take a look at the museum, which was just a short walk from our apartment. 'It could be interesting,' I said. 'I've not been there yet myself.'

My guests readily agreed. Sixty years on, the story of the heroic French Resistance fighters still had a certain riveting appeal, even glamour attached to it. Around Lyon, pictures of Jean Moulin, the handsome French hero of the Resistance who was captured in Lyon by Barbie's Gestapo, still popped up everywhere.

Yet there was also the other side of the story, the one which said there were far more Nazi collaborators than Resistance fighters during the German occupation of France. Lyon, despite being awarded the title of 'Capital of the Resistance' after the war by Charles de Gaulle, had a rather more sinister reputation during the conflict. It was a city that was also quite sympathetic to the authoritarian Vichy Regime, the Nazi puppet government set up after France surrendered to the Germans in 1940, and which was led by the French World War I hero Marshal Philippe Pétain.

Moulin had been arrested in June 1943, after an apparent tip-off from a Lyonnais collaborator who had infiltrated Moulin's inner circle, and was brought to the Hotel Terminus where he was tortured by Barbie himself. He died a few weeks later from his wounds while being deported to Germany.

To our surprise, the museum didn't shy away from this dark part of French history. The exhibits highlighted the rise of the Resistance in France and its heroic deeds and successes, but it also recounted the mass deportations of French and non-French Jews, Gypsies and Communists, and the apparent willingness, even zealousness, of the Vichy Government and its supporters, including sections of the Catholic Church, to do the Nazis' dirty work in France.

Nevertheless it was hard not to be moved by some of the testimonies of surviving Resistance fighters, particularly the recollections of elderly French women who had fought to free France but whose role in the movement had often been overlooked.

In one video, a woman called Jeannie de Clarens talked of how she gathered information for the Resistance while working as a secretary for a German officer in Lyon.

'I guess what I was doing was spying,' she said modestly. 'The Germans just saw me as part of the furniture which was my asset.'

Another female Resistance fighter recalled how her fellow compatriot, the Communist activist Emilienne Mopty, was captured while trying to deliver weapons to striking French miners in January 1943. Mopty was deported to Germany where she was decapitated.

'That could have been me,' said the woman, now in her eighties. The look on her face suggested she still couldn't believe that she'd survived the war.

We emerged from the sombre corridors of the museum to the bright light of a beautiful sunny Lyon morning and marvelled at the incongruity of it all. We wondered whether there were people sitting in the little café across the road blithely drinking their coffees, or couples in love strolling the nearby banks of the Rhône, when, some sixty years ago, Jean Moulin and hundreds of others were brought to the basement of the Hotel Terminus for interrogation.

For decades, post-war French governments, for the sake of national reconciliation, had adopted a sort of collective amnesia about French complicity in the implementation of the Final Solution. Events such as the trial of Klaus Barbie in Lyon, however, had forced them to confront some ugly truths.

'No longer could the Resistance be viewed as the sole French role during the Occupation and no longer could its glories serve to shelter France from the shame and guilt of its other past,' wrote one commentator after the Barbie trial.

The Centre for the History of the Resistance and Deportation in Lyon seemed to reinforce that message.

'We will never forget' reads the small plaque outside its door.

Michael and I also threw ourselves into Lyon's nightlife. Like most French cities, it revolves primarily around eating out. The Lyonnais, however, have a particular attachment to their restaurants, some of which are considered to be the finest in all of France. More than in other parts of the country though, the Lyonnais tend to treat the restaurant like their own private dining room — it is the preferred place to entertain family and friends. As a result, Lyon's restaurants — and there are thousands of them — are often full, even on a weeknight. For some of the best restaurants, you have to book weeks in advance or hope for a late cancellation.

The other big night-time activity is hanging out at a trendy bar for a few hours before the sun goes down, perhaps at one of the several located on boats moored permanently on the banks of the Rhône River.

Michael and I also liked to go to the cinema — France is one of the few countries in Europe that has cinemas which show foreign films in their original version, that is, undubbed. As Michael started to get to know his work colleagues at Interpol a little more, we started receiving a few more invitations to parties and dinners at their houses.

In short, our social life was turning out to be not that different to the one we'd left behind in London and Sydney — except for one important difference. The only police Michael and I ever came in contact with at parties before we moved to Lyon were those who turned up at the front door demanding that we keep the noise down. Now we were going to parties being thrown by police — Interpol police officers at that. Not our usual social group.

'Hi, my name's John,' said the tall man whom Michael had ushered me over to meet at one of the first Interpol parties we attended in Lyon. 'I'm from London.'

Michael had clued me up about John before the party. He was a detective-superintendent at Scotland Yard.

'He's a nice guy, really friendly,' said Michael. 'He doesn't seem like a cop from Scotland Yard.' Not that either of us had ever met a detective from Scotland Yard before, or had a clue how one was supposed to act.

John had apparently been seconded to Interpol because of his expertise in credit card fraud, the sort of borderless illegal activity that Interpol was formed to combat. A graduate of the London School of Economics, he'd even written some books on the subject. He'd done no other job though but policing: he'd joined the force at eighteen and had risen through the uniformed police ranks to become a senior officer at Scotland Yard. He was now hoping to see out his last few years until his retirement (at the ripe old age of forty-nine) in Lyon.

'If I go back to London now, they'll probably put me back on the beat catching murderers,' John liked to say.

Both Michael and I took an instant liking to him. Just like us, he seemed to be searching for that special place in the world where he could feel most at ease. Divorced with grown up kids, he wasn't eager to return to London, even though he'd spent his entire career and married life there.

John also changed my rather stereotypical view of cops as pretty one-dimensional types. Like a lot of other police at Interpol, he was smart, well read and philosophic about his chosen profession. He also liked to have a good time, so long as it was within the law of course.

A little while after our first meeting, I went to a David Bowie concert in Lyon with John and some other Interpol acquaintances. (Michael, no fan of Bowie, sat that one out.) Young African guys were selling commemorative concert T-shirts on the pavement after the show. They were clearly forgeries of the official versions being sold for five times the price inside. I was eager to buy one; they were great forgeries! As I picked up a T-shirt and checked it over, Mandy, John's girlfriend at the time, tugged my arm. 'Do you really want that T-shirt?' she asked, gesturing towards John.

'Oh yeah, I forgot — counterfeiting is John's thing,' I replied. I put the T-shirt back and John pretended not to notice what the Africans were doing.

Mostly, though, we tended to forget that the people we were now often socialising with in Lyon were police. They didn't talk too much about their work, at least not with me. They were generally quite discreet, which perhaps wasn't surprising given some of their backgrounds.

At one party I met Geoff, an Australian Federal Police officer from Canberra who'd once been a part of Prime Minister John Howard's personal bodyguard detail. Unfortunately, Geoff didn't have — or wouldn't reveal — any interesting titbits about John Howard's habits. 'You're a journalist after all,' he'd say with a laugh.

Michael had also met an American police officer who used to be part of the Secret Service protection team for Bill Clinton when he was US president. 'I've seen some things,' the American would say, tantalisingly, like the time he had to sit outside Clinton's hotel room all night while the president played poker with members of the Rolling Stones.

'One day, I'll give you the full story,' he told Michael. He never did.

For most of the police officers sent from their home countries on assignment to Interpol, Lyon was a lovely place to get away from it all for a time, away from the daily rigours of their often more dangerous jobs at home, while still trying to do their bit to fight international crime.

Lyon was hardly a hardship post — the closest most Interpol officers came to criminals was when their pictures or fingerprints flashed up on computer screens. Contrary to popular opinion, Interpol officers were not a roaming global police force. They weren't heavily armed agents who hunted down and arrested international crooks and terrorists, as portrayed in a James Bond film. Their jobs were in fact far less glamorous. Most of their work involved helping national police forces put the pieces of a cross-border investigation together using Interpol's vast criminal databases, or analysing patterns of modus operandi, or simply calling upon a network of contacts around the world.

That was fine by them. Most, like John, were in no hurry to return to their street-cop jobs back home. In a way, the social group we were becoming part of reminded me of the journalists on the JE program I'd met in Paris on my first trip to France. They'd found themselves serendipitously — at mid, or even late, career — in a beautiful city on the other side of the world, with interesting new work to do and new people and new relationships to enjoy, and they were determined to make the most of it.

For us, that meant we were rarely short of an invitation to a party.

CHAPTER 4

The Work Ethic

What you do ultimately means nothing and you could be replaced tomorrow by the first passing cretin . . .

Corinne Maier, *Bonjour Paresse*, 2004

AFTER A FEW MONTHS of acting the tourist in Lyon, I decided to turn my attentions to finding a job, something that would supplement my meagre freelance journalism earnings and get me out of the apartment and into a new circle of people.

I was under no illusions that this would be a simple task.

I'd moved to a country with an unemployment rate that hovered around 10 per cent, one of the highest in Europe; some 2.5 million people were out of work.

France is a great place to live if you have a job — there is the government-mandated 35-hour week, the long holidays (under French law, citizens are entitled to five weeks' annual leave, plus eleven national public holidays a year), the generous sick leave, and the rigid labour laws that make it extremely difficult for your boss to fire you. Indeed, it is one of the last countries in the world where you can pretty much hold on to your job for life if you want to.

It isn't such a bad place either if you are unemployed — state benefits are relatively generous and easily accessible, at least for citizens and legal residents, foreigners like me included. Medical care is also free.

But the French system isn't so helpful if you desperately want to find a job. French employers regularly complain that the high cost and complicated regulations associated with hiring and firing in France discourages them from recruiting new staff.

As a result, public universities, such as the famous Sorbonne in Paris, are literally crammed with aging students who prefer to prolong their studies rather than face the cruel realities of the French labour market, which has a poor record of hiring young people. Nearly one in five young people are unemployed in France — one in two in the run-down migrant housing projects that ring major cities.

Government attempts to inject some flexibility into the job market, like winding back complicated redundancy laws that make it extremely difficult for employers to fire staff, and thus discourages them from hiring new workers and creating jobs in the first place, nearly always hit a brick wall in France. Such 'Anglo-Saxon style' reforms are generally greeted with contempt, as in March 2006 when an estimated three million people took to the streets to protest a new job contract for young people that would make it easier for employers to fire new recruits during a two-year trial period. It was the biggest day of strikes and demonstrations that France had seen in more than a decade.

Young people were rightly angry that they were being asked to bear the brunt of labour market reforms when their parents and older people still enjoyed jobs for life — particularly the five million or so, or one quarter of the workforce, who hold jobs in the public service, the most protected and generously paid sector in France. (Little wonder that most people dream of becoming civil servants.)

Yet for French youth who do want to work, the status quo isn't that appealing either. A majority of young people are trapped in an endless cycle of back-to-back short-term work contracts — about the only way to get into the workforce in France when permanent jobs are like hen's teeth. Others are willing to work for nothing just to get their foot in the door of a desirable company — French workplaces are filled with these young, highly qualified students on low-paid or no pay internships. Yet here they were on the street fighting riot police and tear gas over a new labour contract that offered them the possibility of full job protection after two years. Sometimes you wonder whether the French are simply addicted to street protests.

Soaring unemployment isn't just a problem for the young either. At the other end of the age scale, workers barely past the age of fifty are being enticed into early retirement schemes in the hope that it will free up jobs for others. The chances of someone over the age of sixty-four still being in work is next to zero — President Jacques Chirac seems to be the only elderly Frenchman holding down a regular job.

Little wonder I often struggled to get a table at Le Spleen. With so many students, early retirees, unemployed artists and the like with free time on their hands, hanging out at a sidewalk café is a French national pastime.

I was also one of these under-employed café-sitters. But I had no shortage of suggestions as to how I could better fill my day.

'Why don't you come and help out at the Interpol shop?' one American woman married to an Interpol officer had suggested soon after I arrived. Apparently it was a bit of a tradition for spouses of Interpol officers to give up their spare time for the shop, a sort of souvenir store for visiting police and dignitaries, which sold Interpol-branded scarves, mugs, wine and the like. Not being the ladies auxiliary type, I begged off. Besides, I was hoping to find a paying job, something where I could use my skills.

It was then that I remembered the suggestion of a

colleague in London that I try my luck at EuroNews, a multilingual pan-European 24-hour television news channel that happened to have its studios in Lyon.

Owned by a consortium of nineteen European public broadcasters, EuroNews was Europe's answer to America's CNN. It provided viewers with round-the-clock coverage of world affairs, although its prime focus was on European news and current events. To enhance that European perspective, EuroNews broadcast simultaneously in English, French, German, Italian, Spanish, Portuguese and Russian. It employed a team of journalists for each language broadcast.

'But I've never worked in television before,' I'd told my colleague Annalisa, an Italian radio reporter who'd worked at EuroNews before moving to London.

'Don't worry about that,' she said. 'They are usually so desperate for staff, they'll take anyone.'

'Gee, thanks a lot,' I said.

Although its location in the south of France was a drawcard, the pay was so low and the reporting opportunities so limited that few qualified journalists stayed at EuroNews for long, Annalisa explained. Running a 24-hour news channel in seven languages was an expensive task as well as a logistical nightmare. To save costs and to keep things simple, the channel rarely sent reporters out to gather the news, but instead relied on wire agency copy and images flowing in, which the seven teams of journalists then reassembled for broadcasting in their own language.

Thus the primary task of the desk-bound EuroNews journalist was to rewrite wire copy into television prose, and then voice and mix the report over the news images in a do-it-yourself digitised studio. On air, the journalist was never identified, nor were there any on-air presenters. The result was a kind of radio with pictures, with the news broadcast updated and repeated around the clock.

As such, it wasn't exactly riveting viewing, although I was told the English broadcast was a big hit with European viewers who spoke English as a second language — the simple presentation helped their comprehension. But its bland style had its critics.

'After 30 minutes you begin to wonder if a neutron bomb has gone off at HQ, leaving the technical equipment functioning but killing its entire staff,' one TV critic, Thomas Sutcliffe, wrote of EuroNews in *The Independent of London*.

'You would have to be very passionate about the décor of Strasbourg meeting rooms to find it compelling. Such viewers exist; EuroNews gets bigger audiences than CNN in Germany, France, Spain and Italy.'

The lack of on-air presenters, however, suited me fine. I probably would never have gotten past first base if I had to look the part as well. In London, I'd been a regular on a 'meet the foreign press' type of show on BBC World TV, but that was as far as my television experience stretched.

That seemed to be enough, though, for Niall, an affable Irishman who I'd contacted about working at EuroNews.

Niall was the editor of the English language broadcast. He agreed to give me a few days' training and then start me out on a few night shifts to see how I went.

'If anything, you're probably overqualified for this place,' he joked, as he looked over my résumé.

'The only problem I think we'll have is with your Australian accent. Can you tone it down?'

When it was launched in January 1993, EuroNews had to scramble for staff. Operating a news service 24-hours a day in several languages required a lot of labour, and the channel would often fly in reporters from Paris, Rome, Madrid and even London to do shifts in Lyon. I knew of one Australian journalist living in Paris during EuroNews' start-up days who'd managed to pick up work there despite her accent.

These days though, EuroNews could be more picky. It was now an established TV network that boasted an audience of 154 million people worldwide. To maintain what it called its European identity, it liked to use 'European' voices on-air wherever possible, Niall explained. On the English team, that meant speaking with a British accent. Irish voices were acceptable as Ireland was part of the European Union. Voices from the colonies, however, just wouldn't do. Australian and New Zealand accents were only tolerated if they were toned down to the point of being unrecognisable. Americans had no chance.

It seemed to be the same with the other language groups. The Spanish team rejected Latin American accents, while the French seemed loath to use French speakers from its former colonies in Africa. I had an Irish passport by virtue of my marriage to Michael — he'd had an Irish-born grandparent, which allowed him to take out Irish citizenship — which in turn allowed me to live and work in the European Union. But my accent was undeniably antipodean. Living in London for five years had knocked off some of the rougher Australian edges, but at EuroNews the way I spoke was a cause for concern.

'We're trying to set ourselves apart from the BBC,' Niall said. 'They use loads of Australians and New Zealanders, even Americans these days. We can't really do that. If you had an American accent, I don't think we could use you at all.'

It seemed ironic that the person sitting across from me, telling me I had the wrong accent, was himself speaking in a heavy Belfast brogue. I wondered whether it might make more sense for EuroNews to demand clarity and precision in their broadcasts rather than merely the correct European accent.

But then I remembered: this is Europe, where multiculturalism is a dirty word, and newcomers are expected to blend in with the dominant culture. The French Government didn't tolerate Muslim girls wearing the Islamic headscarf at school. A French-based TV station wasn't going to allow Aussie-accented presenters to deliver the English news on their box either.

Not surprisingly, I got little sympathy from my European colleagues. 'Well, it is a European channel after all,' sniffed one Spanish woman in my French class after I explained my predicament. 'The news should be delivered by people speaking in an accent that all the population can identify with.'

I was now beginning to understand why I rarely saw or heard minority faces or voices on the European media. It seemed to me the only time a person of colour got on the prime time 8 pm French news was when he or she was in the company of the gendarmes.

But I wanted the work, and there weren't many other paid work opportunities for English-language journalists in a city the size of Lyon. So I tried to oblige the accent police at EuroNews by toning down my Aussie twang wherever possible. Against the counsel of my own Strine-speaking father back in Sydney ('don't bend to those bloody Poms'), I also tried to sound British. But I was no Nicole Kidman, and I found my acting efforts just sounded artificial and confused. One minute I sounded like a character from 'East Enders', the next a posh twit from the Home Counties. It didn't work.

So I gave up affecting a British accent and decided instead to concentrate on improving my TV news writing skills, as well as delivering my scripts in as clear and authoritative manner as I could manage. I hoped to win over management with my journalistic credentials. As no one mentioned the accent issue again, I assumed I'd succeeded until I noticed I wasn't being called in to work as regularly as the British freelancers on EuroNews' books.

I asked Niall whether this had anything to do with my nationality. He claimed there had been no complaints from management about my Australian accent, but he'd decided to act pre-emptively. He thought it best to limit my EuroNews appearances so as not to risk having me banned altogether. He thought it was the best strategy.

'But I'll always give you the work before flying someone in from London,' he added, trying to make me feel better. It didn't.

Given that the bosses at EuroNews were Spanish and Italian, I wondered just how vigilant they were likely to be about my accent. I'd met few Europeans on my travels who could tell the difference between an Australian and a New Zealander. It all sounded English to them.

I did think of confronting the EuroNews management and putting this theory to the test. But I didn't have the nerve — after all, I wanted to hang on to the precious shifts I still had at the station. I figured I was lucky I wasn't American — their accent had a worse time abroad than mine did. No Americans worked on air at EuroNews.

But the experience did get me thinking about accents. Unless you are a master of disguise, your accent tends to travel with you even if you try to deliberately leave it behind. Some people I know say they feel their accent becomes even broader when they're out of Australia — maybe that's because foreigners always seem to want to point it out. I certainly couldn't shake off mine, try as I might. I could dress like the French and live like the French, but my voice always gave the game away.

I didn't quite realise this until I fronted up for work at EuroNews. It's funny how you think everyone else has an accent — not you. If anything, I thought the years of living abroad had rendered mine unidentifiable. Not so.

'Of course you still have an Aussie accent,' a friend back in Sydney said when I told her about my EuroNews experience. 'You might have been away for a few years, but you still sound like us.'

It was then that I thought: why fight it? To hide your accent is to deny your identity. What I enjoy the most about living abroad is being an outsider — to be that person outside the glass looking in is a privileged, indeed, revelatory position to be in.

In France, my accent continued to underline my outsider status. It said to my new home that I was not from here; that I was a traveller. And that was fine by me.

On the other hand, my accent was doing me out of work at EuroNews. My shifts were becoming so few and far between, I could hardly even call it a part-time job. Padding around our apartment in the same old pair of jeans and worn sweater day after day, I found myself yearning to get dressed up in a business suit and to go into an office again. After years of dreaming of escaping the daily grind, I now wanted to get back in the working mainstream where I could contribute to a common purpose and draw a weekly salary for my efforts.

It was then that I realised how out of sync I was with my surrounding culture. I was yearning for a full-time job again. But most French people, or those in work, seemed to be looking for ways of dumping theirs, or at the very least working less.

I was living in France during the enormous success of a little book that urged middle managers — France's legion of *cadres* — to rise up against the drudgery and indignity of their corporate workplace by doing as little work as possible.

Bonjour Paresse: De l'art et la nécessité d'en faire le moins possible en entreprise, or *Hello Laziness: Why hard work doesn't pay* (its English language title), denounced corporate culture as rigid, empty-headed, avaricious and ruthless. The advice of the book's cheeky author Corinne Maier was to actively disengage from it. 'Just play the part of the model worker, say the right words and do the right things, but without actually getting involved,' wrote Maier, a senior economist who worked part-time at the French electricity company EDF (which preferred that she didn't).

'Work as little as possible, and spend some time (but not too much) on "marketing yourself" and "building yourself a personal network" so that you will have the support and be untouchable (and untouched) when the next restructuring comes around.'

At a time when the rest of the world — and French business leaders — was castigating France for not working hard enough, *Bonjour Paresse* had become a runaway bestseller. Only *The Da Vinci Code* had sold more copies in France during the summer of 2004.

The French thrived on such contrariness. That was something I'd come to understand about my new home. Work — whether to do more of it, or not — had become a particularly fertile subject for debate in France in recent years.

French employees already worked less hours, took more holidays and enjoyed greater social benefits and job security than workers in most Western nations. Now, more than ever, this relaxation addiction was being blamed for France's continuing economic woes.

It was true the French economy was stagnating while its jobless rate was climbing. Only Germany and Belgium had longer unemployment queues. Meanwhile Britain, demonised by everyone from the French president down as a bastion of Anglo-Saxon-style free market capitalism, had managed to push unemployment below 5 per cent, less than half the French rate.

Commentators and economic experts alike were crying out in unison: things have to change. The International

Monetary Fund was urging France, and its equally leisure-loving neighbour Germany, to abandon its old ways. If it wanted to compete more effectively with the United States and Asia in the coming years, its citizens would have to work more and longer.

'French voters are trying to preserve a 35-hour work week in a world where Indian engineers are ready to work a 35-hour day,' wrote American columnist Thomas L. Friedman in the *New York Times* in 2005. 'Good luck.'

But the French preferred to ignore such arguments. I was astonished at how little outcry there was in the community, for example, at the chronic levels of unemployment in France. Instead, people seemed to prefer to make a folk hero out of a part-time economist who was advocating even greater disengagement from the workplace.

I'd thought no one embraced leisure more than Australians until I moved to France. Since the 1970s, the French, along with other Western Europeans, had been willing to accept slower growth in wages as the price for shorter working hours and longer vacations. It was a trade-off that the French had readily accepted. Americans now worked 20 per cent more hours than they did in 1970 while the French were working 24 per cent less.

But you didn't need the statistics to realise this. You just had to live here. On any given weekday there seemed to be a lot of people hanging out in cafés and shops — and they weren't just the masses of unemployed.

They were people merely taking advantage of their time off. There was not only the sacrosanct month-long summer break in August (spreading increasingly into July) when the whole country pulled down its shutters and headed to the beach or the mountains. There was also the numerous and strategically placed public holidays that allowed workers to take regular long weekends thanks to the accepted practice of taking '*le pont*' or the bridge — that is, taking-off the day (or days) in-between the public holiday and the weekend.

Since 1 January 2000, the French have also enjoyed a statutory 35-hour working week brought in by the then Socialist Government in the hope that it would encourage employers to hire more workers.

Under the phased-in law, the official French working week was cut from 39 to 35 hours, although employers were required to keep paying the same salaries. Anyone who worked more than 35 hours could claim overtime payments (the amount of which was capped), or add the extra hours to their annual leave.

Many working mothers, however, preferred to take Wednesdays off, to fit in with the French school week which gave many children a day off mid-week that was then made up with a half day of school on Saturdays. The only group of workers who were exempted from the law were managers or executives who were still expected to work a normal (by international standards) working week.

For the rest of the working population the 35-hour week was mandatory — and as such, extremely popular, even though there was little evidence that the law was helping to create more jobs. Employers, not surprisingly, hated it, even though they had used the introduction of the shorter working week to extract considerable concessions from unions in other areas. They widely welcomed the Chirac Government's move to reform the law in March 2005 — which the government believed was causing consumers to spend less — to make it easier for employees to work longer hours (and earn more money to spend) if they wanted to.

Workers though were not amused. In a time-honoured tradition, thousands took to the streets across France to protest the Chirac reforms (just as they would a year later when the same government tried to introduce new youth job contracts). No one wanted to go back to a longer working week, and who could blame them? In 2003, French employees clocked up an average of just 1,453 hours of work, or about 400 hours less than the average worked the same year in the United States and Australia. And the French economy, although not booming, hadn't fallen into the abyss as many economists had feared.

Some French though do worry about the effects of the 35-hour week on the economy, and the country's general disinclination towards work, particularly as more and more French companies relocate to Eastern Europe, China and

India where labour costs are a fraction of those in Western Europe.

As one French journalist living in America commented in *Le Figaro* in 2004, 'During our annual holidays in France, we notice that ... holidays occupy such importance in French life that work is denigrated and devalued.' France's finance minister Thierry Breton summed up the changing mood about work within the French governing elite when he told the French Parliament in June 2005: 'To finance our model, we need to work more. We have to work more to create growth. We have to work more throughout our lives.'

Yet most French people I've met are unapologetic about their love of leisure time. They believe they have a much more civilised attitude to work compared to Anglo-Saxons, even if it means less material wealth at the end of the day.

'In France, we work to live,' explained my friend Muriel. 'In Britain and America, people seem just to live to work.'

It was hard to argue with her. I always thought that as nations got richer, they were supposed to have more leisure time at their disposal. The future was supposed to free us from the drudgery of the long work day. Remember George, the father in that interplanetary cartoon show 'The Jetsons'? He only worked a three-hour day. Now we were being told that the French and their 35-hour week belonged to the Stone Age. No matter that so many of us Anglo-Saxons travelled to France — even bought farmhouses and lived here — just so we could watch the French relax and share in their glorious lifestyle. In the eyes of the twenty-first century world France had got it all wrong.

As one of those people who moved to France to enjoy the lifestyle, I am much more partial to the French social order of things. The French seem to have things in perspective. I always remembered that old adage that was cited often during my time as a financial journalist in Australia: 'I've never heard of a businessman on his deathbed who wished he'd spent more time at the office.'

Nevertheless, some habits die hard. Although no one would describe me as a workaholic, I had to adjust to the French way of life. It wasn't just the French phenomenon of the 4 pm rush hour (thanks to the 35-hour-week) that I found such a novelty. More problematic was the absence of Sunday and public holiday shopping.

In theory, I was all for giving citizens a day off from consumerism, but in practice it could be downright inconvenient. I'd come from a culture where shopping at any time of the week was considered a basic human right. What, no Boxing Day sales? It took time to adjust.

I still found myself absentmindedly walking to my local Printemps department store on Sundays only to find the doors firmly closed. My only choice then was to head to the river and the open-air food market, which operated on the banks of the Saône River on Sunday mornings. Buying lettuces, however, was not quite the same as browsing a book store or trying on shoes — my favourite Sunday afternoon pastime in Sydney. But it was better than watching football on TV, which is what the French loved to do on Sundays.

I eventually grew to love the quiet and cleaner air of Sundays and public holidays in France. Sunday became a true day of rest in our household, rather than just another day of the week. And while fewer shopping hours might not be good for the French economy, it didn't do my personal finances any harm.

There were other adjustments. In France, people don't tend to wrap their identity up in their work — like we do in Australia and elsewhere. At dinner parties, at least at the few non-Interpol functions I was attending, the main topics of conversation were usually about the food being served, upcoming holidays or relationships gone wrong — but rarely what happened at work that day.

In contrast, I always seemed to be explaining my professional credentials to total strangers. 'Well, actually, I used to be the full-time correspondent for a large, well-known Australian newspaper and now I still contribute to several media outlets,' I'd say, until I realised that no one was actually asking me what I did for a living.

Posing the Anglo-Saxon conversation opener, 'So, what do you do?', tends to be met with silence and a change of topic in France. Discussions about salary would certainly ensure you are never asked to a French function again.

'You never ask someone what they do for a living or where they studied — that's extremely impolite,' author

Corinne Maier once explained in an interview with an American journalist.

'At a dinner party, you are supposed to just hint, with little impressionistic touches, about where you work. And gradually, during the course of the evening, you might reach the point where you say it. It's an indirect approach.'

I wondered why the French are so reluctant to talk about work. Indeed, anything to do with making money or business seems to be frowned upon in France. French corporations keep such a low profile that you could easily forget how powerful they are, particularly behind the scenes of government and in global markets (think perfume, handbags, insurance and cars). Business developments in France are largely ignored on the main nightly television news shows. This is in sharp contrast to Australia where business leaders are often treated like heroes and are quoted by the media on everything from the economy to government policy.

As I began to do some research, I found that French attitudes to work and business have been moulded by several factors, among them France's revolutionary past, its social welfare traditions, and in particular its disdain for the Anglo-Saxon model of free market capitalism. The Catholic Church, dominant in France, had also played its part. The message from the pulpit was that work, and the making of money, was a means to an end, more a necessary evil than a calling. According to the French social historian Patrick Fridenson, work was often viewed as a punishment, in contrast to Protestant countries where people believed that work provided an individual with backbone.

'The Catholic Church in France has played a considerable role in defending free time for workers because this means ... people have more time to go to Mass and to take part in community fellowship,' Fridenson said.

The other sector demanding shorter hours and greater leisure time was, of course, the unions, themselves heavily influenced by both Catholic and Communist ideals.

After moving to Lyon, I was surprised to learn how un-unionised the French workforce actually was. French union membership had fallen by half in the two decades to 2004 to just below 10 per cent, the lowest level in Europe.

Yet this had made no real impact on the amazing French tolerance for strikes and protests. I did hear French people grumble about the number and frequency of strikes that regularly shut down their cities and disrupted public services. In the summer of 2003, a new group called *Liberté Chérie* emerged on the French landscape to express its discontent at what it saw as uncontrolled union power: it organised anti-strike protests that drew tens of thousands of participants during a French rail strike in June that year. (Most unionised workers are in the public sector; at large concerns like the government rail company SNCF, which are responsible for about a quarter of all strikes in most years.)

But the majority still seemed to accept regular worker revolts as a part of the fabric of their culture. The French saw their democracy as more vibrant and participatory than that of Anglo-Saxon countries, where union power was hobbled a long time ago, and where workers' rights have had to take a backseat to company profits and shareholder dividends.

I suspected, too, that the frequency of strikes and protests in France had dulled their impact. People were always going to the barricades over some problem or another. In the week that the French learnt that unemployment had hit new highs, ambulance drivers were on strike; France Inter, the government radio station, had gone to Muzak due to action by technicians; and high school students were staging sit-ins around the country (backed by their parents and unions) because of proposed government reforms to the French school leaving certificate known as the *baccalauréat*, or just plain *bac*. This was a normal week.

But I thought even the French might have drawn the line at one particularly harmful union campaign that raged in the summer of 2003.

Part-time theatrical performers and backstage technicians had decided to go on strike in protest at government plans to trim France's unique unemployment fund for artists.

In France, performing artists were entitled to twelve months of unemployment benefits if they worked 507 hours a year, which was equal to a bit over three months of full-time work. Such levels of welfare support underlined the high priority France accorded its cultural sector, which it considered to be precious and fragile and thus in constant need of protection (from marauding Americans in particular).

But with a weakening economy and lower tax receipts, the problem for the current government was how to continue to pay for this protection. Perhaps unsurprisingly, given the level of state benefits, the number of part-time artists in France had more than doubled over the past decade. The government said the artists' unemployment fund now had a shortfall of 1.3 billion euros. To make that up and ensure the survival of the fund, it proposed some minor reforms. The upshot was that artists would now have to work 507 hours over ten months, instead of one year, to receive unemployment benefits for eight months.

I imagine that to performers in Australia who drive taxis and wait tables when they can't find work in their chosen field, such a system of support would be seen as paradise and they'd accept the reforms as a reasonable compromise to ensure that the system survived. But French artists were having none of it.

With the support of their Communist-backed union and millionaire celebrities, such as film director Bertrand Tavernier and actor Gérard Depardieu, the performing artists took to the streets, forcing the cancellation of many summer events across the country, including Avignon's famous theatre festival and France's biggest musical festival in Aix-en-Provence. It was an unprecedented action — not even during the turbulent days of May 1968 when students and workers went on the rampage against the de Gaulle administration, were arts festivals closed down. The strikes resulted in the loss of millions of euros in tourist revenue for those towns.

'I don't get it,' I said to a French acquaintance. 'If culture is so important in France, shouldn't artists be trying to do all they can to make sure the festivals, their long-term livelihood, are protected at all costs? Shouldn't the show always go on?'

The woman just shrugged her shoulders, 'That's just how it is in France. Everyone's used to doing without things because of strikes.'

As often happened with union negotiations in France, when the protesters vowed to block the Cannes film festival the government blinked and moved to soften the reforms.

At Interpol, there always seemed to be a bit of debate raging around its corridors about national workplace practices and customs.

'The only people who seem to work past 5 pm or come in on Sundays to finish some job that might be due the next day are the Anglos,' complained one American officer to Michael. 'Most of the French wouldn't dream of working overtime.'

The French, of course, just saw this as typical French-bashing on the part of the Anglo-Saxon officers. If Anglos gave up their Sundays to meet some unrealistic deadline imposed from on high, more fool them, the French said.

'The Americans think you should work every day of the week,' one French woman at Interpol told me. 'But everyone knows working longer doesn't necessarily make you a better worker. It just makes you a more tired one.'

If you tell a French man or woman they don't work long enough, they'll likely respond that when they do work, they work harder than anyone else.

They'll point to surveys which show that in terms of productivity rate per hour, the French beat their American counterparts hands down. Economists say this is because the French squeeze their work into a shorter period of time thanks to the 35-hour week and extended holidays. The people who tended to be out of work in France — the very young and the old — are also those who would mostly be below average productivity anyway.

'The French are much harder workers than Australians,' declared Thierry, a young French winemaker I was interviewing one day for a magazine article. He'd just returned from a stint working in the vineyards of South Australia.

'Australians just seemed to take ages to do work that we'd do in half the time.'

'Oh really,' I replied. 'But what about all that hand-shaking, and kissing and coffee-drinking and cigarette breaks that the French engage in at work? Not much work seems to get done then.'

Indeed, Michael was having his own problem with one of these ubiquitous French customs at his own workplace. At first, he'd been charmed at how everyone greeted each other in the office each morning with either a kiss on each cheek or a hand shake. No matter that you only last saw each other the day before, a new work day could not begin without another complete round of hand-shaking and cheek-pecking.

But after a few months, the novelty began to wear thin.

'It takes up so much time,' Michael said one evening. 'By the time you shake hands and kiss everyone's cheeks, and everybody's had their coffee and cigarette breaks, half the morning is gone.'

Never one for physical contact with workmates anyway — he was a Canadian after all — Michael decided, as a personal efficiency measure, that he would drop the ritual and keep his hands in his pockets. From then on, he would offer a cheery Canadian 'hello' each morning to his twenty-odd staff. The French eventually adapted, but I always thought his office lost some of its warmth after that.

Changing French workplace customs though was the least of Michael's problems. The biggest adjustment he'd have to make was to his new job. A few days after he'd started at Interpol, his immediate boss had resigned and Michael was asked to take over as the organisation's director of communications. This was a much more senior and demanding role: much of Michael's time would now be spent managing a mostly French staff and dealing with endless administrative tasks.

At the same time, he was expected to do his old job, juggling media inquiries from around the world until he could hire a new press officer. Since the attacks in New York and Washington on September 11, Interpol was getting a lot of requests for information related to global terrorist activities.

Sometimes, though, the requests were of a much different nature.

'You'll never guess who phoned me today — a Hollywood producer by the name of Jerry Weintraub,' Michael said after he'd returned from work one evening.

'Apparently he made that movie with George Clooney in the lead role — *Ocean's Eleven*. Anyway, he plans to make a sequel and he wants to film some of it at Interpol.'

Michael was only a few weeks into his job, but he was learning quickly about the pull of the Interpol brand. Most people, it seemed, had heard of Interpol even if very few actually knew what it did. Some thought it was a cross between Scotland Yard and the CIA.

Interpol's profile had been lifted even higher with the publication of the Dan Brown bestseller *The Da Vinci Code*. Soon after, Michael's office began receiving a steady stream of requests from people asking Interpol to track down a loved one or a colleague who'd gone missing in Europe. This was because Brown in his book had accorded Interpol Orwellian surveillance powers.

'On any given night, all across Europe, Interpol officials could pinpoint exactly who was sleeping where,' he wrote. 'Finding Langdon at the Ritz had probably taken all of five seconds ...'

This, of course, was nonsense. Interpol didn't keep records of hotel guest lists. It didn't even have a police force (the entire staff at Lyon only numbered 400 people). Yet there was no point telling *Da Vinci Code* fans that. The requests just kept on coming.

Now a Hollywood producer wanted to make Interpol the backdrop for his next movie, to be called, not surprisingly, *Ocean's Twelve*. 'This is the plot in a nutshell Mike,' Weintraub explained breathlessly. 'Catherine Zeta-Jones will play the part of an Interpol police officer. She'll track the *Ocean's Twelve* guys all across Europe. It will all revolve around the theft of the Fabergé egg. I'm right now getting permission to use the real Fabergé egg in the film from its owner ...'

Michael, ever the journalist, tried to set Weintraub right. 'But that's not what Interpol does. We don't have any armed officers,' he said. 'We also don't normally allow filming inside the building. I'll have to get back to you about that.'

Weintraub was unfazed. 'George let us film inside the CIA, I'm sure your people will allow us into Interpol,' he said, in an apparent reference to George Bush Senior, the former American president and CIA director. 'But let's do lunch next week in Paris to discuss the whole thing. I'll bring along my director Steven Soderbergh.'

'You should have said yes immediately,' I snapped at Michael that night when he told me about his Hollywood call.

'A few weeks of film cameras inside Interpol are a small price to pay to get to see George Clooney. Can I come to the lunch, too? I'll pretend I'm your secretary.'

In the end, neither of us got to do lunch with Jerry. A few days later, his secretary called from Los Angeles to say the deal was off. Weintraub had decided to film at Europol instead, which was based at The Hague and was Interpol's police agency rival in Europe.

It appeared the people at Europol hadn't hesitated about building access or story lines when Weintraub had put a similar call through to them. Catherine Zeta-Jones would now be a gun-toting Europol officer in the film. And I'd never get to meet George Clooney.

It was bitter blow to the women in Michael's office as well. 'You said no to George Clooney?' cried one. '*Mon Dieu!*'

For the next few weeks there would be no morning cheek kisses for Michael even if he had wanted them.

CHAPTER 5

A Passion for Food

Lyon is a place where one is fed so prodigiously well that one can barely gather the courage to leave ...

**French writer François-René
de Chateaubriand, 1895**

I FIRST STEPPED INTO a French restaurant when I was a teenager.

I'd been invited by some friends who were studying French at my high school to join them for dinner one Friday night at what was considered at the time to be Sydney's best French restaurant. A timid girl from the western suburbs, I remember feeling mortified when the waiter scolded me for asking that my steak be well-cooked (and certainly not running with blood).

'We don't do well-done steak here, Miss,' the waiter said

in an accent that was straight out of *The Pink Panther*. 'If you want over-cooked food, please go elsewhere.'

Not wishing to clash with France's famous culinary superiority complex again, I gave French restaurants a wide berth after that. Even when I lived in Paris, where the daunting figure of the French waiter was hard to avoid, I tended to stick to cafés and unpretentious bistros where I could slip in and out with not much fuss or expense.

But now in Lyon I was much older and certainly more assertive when it came to ordering a meal in a fine restaurant. I'd also moved to a city whose main preoccupation seemed to be food; about the only thing I knew about Lyon before I arrived was that the French considered it to be the country's gastronomic capital. The famous French food critic Curnonsky (the pen name of Maurice Edmund Sailland) gave it that title when he emerged from one of Lyon's grandest restaurants in 1934 and declared: 'Lyon cooking has reached the supreme pinnacle of art: simplicity.'

The first modern food critic, Curnonsky was the man they called the 'Prince of Gastronomes'. At the height of his fame in the 1930s some eighty restaurants around Paris were said to hold a table for him each night just in case he showed up. Not surprisingly, Curnonsky became a rather big man and in his later years his widening girth made it difficult for him to walk — legend has it that he had to be carried by six friends to his favourite restaurants. In July

1956, at the age of eighty-four, Curnonsky leaned too far out of his window and fell to his death.

Michael and I had no intentions of mimicking Curnonsky's gastronomic feats, but given his high praise for Lyon's cuisine, we felt it was our duty to try as many of the city's restaurants as we could.

This would be a tall order. There were said to be more restaurants in Lyon per head of population than in Paris. I'd counted thirty within a two-minute walk of our apartment alone. As a travel writer from the *London Times* once put it, 'Whereas the rest of France has a healthy respect for food, in Lyon it is an obsession.'

There seem to be several reasons for this, but the prime one is Lyon's location. The city is surrounded by some of the best produce in France. In Lyon, you can eat succulent milk and corn-fed chickens from Bresse, freshwater fish and frogs' legs from the Dombes and tender Charollais beef and black truffles from the Beaujolais. You can follow this up with rich cheeses from Jura and Isère, notably Comté and Saint-Marcellin. Lyon also floats on a veritable wine lake that stretches from the Beaujolais in the north to the Côtes du Rhône just south of the city.

This abundance has inspired a legion of local cooks, some of whom have risen to become the most renowned and celebrated chefs in France, and the world. Perhaps the most famous among them is the man other French chefs simply refer to as 'Monsieur Paul' — Paul Bocuse.

The original celebrity chef, Bocuse was one of the inventors of French minimalist cooking in the 1970s, better known as *nouvelle cuisine,* which de-sauced and generally lightened up the heavy, cream-drenched French cuisine of old. *Nouvelle cuisine* would later descend into a parody of itself — 'small portions on big plates, inevitably involving raspberry coulis and fanned kiwi fruit', as one food writer from the London *Observer* put it. But Lyon-born Bocuse would go on to become an institution, dominating French and Lyonnais cooking for four decades and exporting his cooking style all over the world. In 2005, he celebrated his fortieth year as the holder of three Michelin stars, the highest ranking given by the *Michelin Guide*, the French food bible.

About a year after we moved to Lyon, Michael and I had the opportunity to sample Bocuse's legendary *haute cuisine* at the place where it all began. We were guests at an Interpol function which was being held at L'Auberge du Pont de Collonges, Bocuse's gaudy restaurant-cum-residence on the northern outskirts of Lyon. The three-star service began with a welcome at the Auberge's entrance by the Maitre d'hotel, and ended with a warm handshake at the same door from the master chef himself, who makes it a policy of personally seeing off each and every guest from his restaurant when he is there.

'*Bonne soirée,*' a still sprightly 78-year-old Bocuse said to Michael and me as we headed to our car around 11 pm. 'I hope you enjoyed your meal.'

'Yes, we did, thank you. It was fabulous,' we replied in unison.

Actually, we lied. The meal, in fact, was a bit of a letdown.

Our group of about fifty had taken over the restaurant's private dining room, which was decorated with photographs of Bocuse with various world leaders, including Jacques Chirac and Bill Clinton, and resembled a sort of opulent library from the Roccoco era. We were served a four-course set menu on Bocuse-monogrammed plates starting with a lobster salad and followed by filet of beef, then a platter of local cheeses, and a dessert of crème brûlée. It was all served with a flourish by a team of impeccably dressed waiters who seemed at times to outnumber the guests. The food, too, tasted great, particularly when it was accompanied with a glass of fine Burgundy red.

For Michael and me, it was our first three-star restaurant experience. Yet we couldn't help wondering later what all the fuss was about. If Bocuse made his name as the chef who'd injected creativity into French cooking, he certainly was the king of conservatism now. Many of his dishes wouldn't have looked out of place on the menu of the first French restaurant I'd entered in Sydney back in 1977. His famed sea bass in puff pastry dated from the 1960s, and his black truffle soup was first created for the Élysée presidential palace in 1975.

Bocuse, though, made no apologies for being a throwback to another era. 'Yes, sure, my cuisine is square,' he told a French journalist on the day he learned that the *Michelin Guide* had awarded him three stars for the fortieth year in a row. 'This is a restaurant of classical tradition because that is what I designed it to be. I love classical music but that doesn't stop rap existing.'

In truth, Bocuse has his foot in both camps. He presides over an international food empire, which includes a French cooking school, a wine label in the United States, a frozen food line in France and delicatessens in Japan. In Lyon, aside from his Michelin-starred restaurant, he also owns five brasseries where the food is not only much cheaper — 38 euros a head (about $A60) versus on average 178 euros ($A290) at L'Auberge du Pont de Collonges — but also more modern and open to foreign influences. At Ouest, Bocuse's Asian-influenced French brasserie, for example, you can eat tuna sashimi and frogs' legs in tempura.

Yet French food lovers — often wealthy American and Japanese tourists — still seek out his Michelin-starred temple to loftier traditional cooking north of Lyon, probably because they know they can eat exactly the same dishes they served on previous visits. Certainly, I've found that's what many foreigners like about France, the fact that the architecture, the streets, the monuments, the people, their favourite restaurants, never change. Bocuse understands that better than most.

'We ought to make him a historic monument,' quipped a former *Michelin Guide* restaurant inspector, Pascal Lemy, who in 2004 lifted the lid in a book on Michelin's secretive star system. According to Remy, Bocuse was one of a group of top French chefs whom Michelin regarded as 'untouchable'.

Not all top chefs in France, however, occupy such a privileged position as Paul Bocuse, or feel immune from the vagaries of the restaurant star system where getting one and then additional stars can create legends, but losing a star can cause heartbreak.

Bernard Loiseau, a celebrity chef who owned the legendary three-starred La Côte d'Or restaurant and hotel in the Burgundy village of Saulieu, was a good friend of Bocuse and had a similar style of cooking. Loiseau's signature dish was another classic: frogs' legs in parsley juice and garlic purée. Former French President François Mitterrand was said to have been so taken with the frogs' legs he'd eaten at La Côte d'Or that he awarded Loiseau the Legion of Honour in 1995, France's most coveted national award.

Like many perfectionists, however, Loiseau also suffered from bouts of depression. And on one cold February afternoon in 2003, after only twelve guests had showed up for lunch at La Côte d'Or, Loiseau ended his life. His widow, Dominique, blamed his suicide on overwork and his massive mood swings. But the issue that was thought to have pushed him over the edge was speculation in the French press that

Loiseau was about to lose one of his three Michelin stars. Just days before, Michelin's main rival in the food guide business, *GaultMillau*, which awards France's best restaurants points out of 20, had downgraded La Côte d'Or from 19 to 17. It described Loiseau's cuisine as 'hardly dazzling, just simply well-prepared'.

It wasn't the first time a French chef had killed himself over a bad review. In 1966, Alain Zick shot himself in the head when he learned his Paris restaurant had lost a Michelin star. And Vatel, the master of seventeenth century French cooking, also killed himself after a delivery of fresh fish apparently didn't arrive on time for a banquet he was preparing in honour of King Louis XIV.

It could only happen in France, the country that invented the restaurant and the whole idea of *haute cuisine*. Or could it? In other countries where restaurants are also big business and chefs have been elevated to celebrity status, such as in Australia, the Loiseau suicide was big news. Within days I was contacted by a Sydney editor I knew asking whether I could follow-up the story for her magazine.

I knew immediately that it would be essential to talk to Dominique Loiseau. She'd been inundated with requests from the French media since her husband's death, so it came as a surprise when I received a message from her assistant that she had agreed to meet me the following week.

I made the two-hour drive north to Saulieu and met Madame Loiseau in the restaurant's library. It was the same place where she'd faced the world press just twenty-four hours after her husband's death to primarily dispel rumours that it was financial problems (and the promise of a healthy insurance payout after his death) that had actually driven him to suicide.

'People couldn't believe that I could do it,' she told me of that press conference. 'But I'd seen my husband the night before, after he had shot himself. I couldn't make him alive again. He worked twenty-seven years to build this business. I couldn't allow [the press] to write something that was untrue.'

Dominique Loiseau, herself a former journalist, went on to recount the events leading up to her husband's suicide; how he'd become exhausted by his relentless work schedule, and how he'd been in a deep depression for months — how deep, she hadn't realised until it was too late.

She also spoke about how he'd been worried that his style of cooking might be going out of fashion. He feared the empty seats in his restaurant signalled that his patrons — particularly the wealthy American and Japanese tourists that his business relied upon — were going elsewhere, and that the reporters and food guides he'd long cultivated were now turning against him.

'All the critics were interested in this crazy style of cooking that was coming out of restaurants like El Bulli in Spain,' Madame Loiseau explained. 'Bernard was quite anxious about that. He told me, "I have my own style. I can't change it for the critics".'

Although none was to react as violently as Loiseau, other French chefs were also worried about the new wave of 'crazy' cooking emerging from Spain.

The leader of this new culinary movement was Ferran Adria, who owned a small restaurant called El Bulli on the Costa Brava coast near Barcelona. Adria was determined to break all the accepted rules and traditions about food, namely what it should look like and how it should taste.

He first came to the attention of the trade more than twenty years ago when he began serving his 'foams', the result of an experiment in his kitchen laboratory involving gelatine and a nitrogen-dioxide canister used for whipped cream. Adria's tomato, shellfish and potato foams proved to be a big hit with El Bulli diners and critics, who described them as a taste explosion that melted away in the mouth. Encouraged, Adria continued his experimentation, coming up with new dishes that challenged conventional wisdom about taste. He'd encase quails eggs in sugar and turn out ice cream flavoured with parmesan cheese.

International food journalists soon clamoured to interview Spain's Salvador Dali of the kitchen. Adria obliged by making some rude remarks about French cooking and declaring that its dominance of the culinary world was now 'finished'. *The New York Times* backed up this judgement in a lengthy article in 2003, stating that French innovation had congealed into complacency.

'You can still eat very well in France, as you did 20 years ago,' Arthur Lubow wrote. 'The problem is that almost everywhere you eat in France, it could still be 20 years ago. Nothing has changed.'

Lubow came to this conclusion after talking to Marc Veyrat, perhaps France's most exotic and innovative chef, who had long complained about the staidness of French chefs, and after dining at El Bulli himself, which Lubow described in glowing terms as 'a gastronome's once-before-you-die Mecca'.

Indeed, Ferran Adria's fame has spread so far and wide that you would now be lucky to get a table at his restaurant once before you died. Only American journalists and the rich and famous seem to be able to secure a seat at El Bulli, which opens for only six months of the year — the rest of the year, Adria and his chefs are supposedly holed up in a laboratory creating new and challenging recipes. I once tried in May to get a table in October but was told the whole season had already been booked out. El Bulli could seat 8,000 people during a six-month season, yet it typically received requests to seat 400,000, the restaurant explained.

These days, Adria is no longer the only exponent of what the food media has now come to call 'molecular gastronomy'. The spotlight has shifted to other innovators in the field, such as British chef Heston Blumenthal, whose signature dishes include snail porridge and bacon-and-egg flavoured ice cream. His Michelin three-star restaurant, The Fat Duck, in Bray, England, was named the world's best restaurant by a panel of international food judges in 2005, pushing El Bulli into second place. Sydney's own Tetsuya's restaurant came in fourth.

France had to be content with sixth place in the poll, which went to Pierre Gagnaire's eponymous restaurant in Paris. Himself a convert to molecular gastronomy, Gagnaire has joined forces with French chemist Hervé This and the two conduct food experiments in the laboratories of the College de France in Paris.

It seemed it had become fashionable in the gastronomic world to regard French chefs — Gagnaire and a few others aside — as culinary has-beens, beaten at their own game by more creative upstarts in Spain, Britain, the United States and even Australia. Critics laid the blame on the failure of traditional French chefs to innovate, to reach out to the world and to keep in touch with the changing tastes of a younger generation. Marc Veyrat, who owns a pair of three-star restaurants in the French Alps, told *Time* magazine that the reason France had fallen on its face was because '95 per cent of French chefs are conservative'.

'It's no accident if Spain and Italy are on the rise, and New York is the city where you eat better than anywhere in the world,' he said.

Yet after a few months eating out in Lyon, I began to wonder whether this criticism had become somewhat overdone.

It was true that traditional French dishes still dominated menus in France, and no more than in Lyon where the most popular lunchtime destination for office workers was the old-fashioned *bouchon*, or bistro, which can be found everywhere. For centuries *bouchons* have served up the same simple Lyonnais fare of seasonal vegetables and offal — things like tripe, chicken gizzards and liver. I was never one for organ meats, but the food at a *bouchon* is always hearty and generous and the atmosphere convivial. Might it be just another handy stick with which to beat the 'arrogant' French?

Indeed, France's main national newspaper, *Le Monde*, thought as much in 2003. It came out with its own magazine piece on El Bulli after Lubow's *New York Times* critique, suggesting that Lubow's 'diatribe' against French cuisine was just another example of American vengeance against France for not supporting its 2003 invasion of Iraq.

'First our wine, now our gastronomic reputation is being challenged,' *Le Monde* wrote.

Contrary to what the critics were saying, Michael and I were finding Lyon to be a great place to sample a different kind of French cuisine, one which seemed less tied to the past and increasingly more open to new influences from abroad, particularly from Asia or Africa, both in the ingredients used and style of cooking employed.

One of our favourites in this category was a restaurant named for its young chef, Nicolas Le Bec. Le Bec had already travelled the world in search of inspiration and was considered one of the up and coming stars of French *haute cuisine*. He'd managed to garner a Michelin star just two months after he opened his new restaurant in Lyon in 2004. He'd written cookbooks and appeared regularly on TV. He was still only thirty-three.

Needless to say, getting a table at Le Bec was no easy task. The restaurant was often booked out weeks in advance. Once, Michael had managed to get us in there for my birthday in the middle of the week, but only after a last-minute cancellation. Lunchtime though was always an easier bet, so one Friday, Muriel, Rachael and I headed there for a blow-out, end-of-week lunch. The attraction of eating in a top-scale restaurant at lunch in France is that it usually offers a scaled-down version of the night fare for often half the price. At Le Bec, they did a three-course 'business lunch', which at 45 euros (or $A75) was exceptional value. But then the drinks cart came around.

'Would you like to start with an aperitif?' the waiter asked.

'Why not?' said Rachael. 'I've taken the afternoon off.' So had Muriel, and I certainly had no pressing engagements. We opted for glasses of champagne all round. When the bill came, we realised we'd mistakenly pointed to the Krug on the cart instead of the cheaper house champagne. Our budget was well and truly blown. No matter — the food was well worth the drinks bill.

What I liked about Le Bec was his penchant for turning traditional French recipes on their head. He would add, say, poached rhubarb to his signature starter of grilled duck *foie gras*, and then serve it with a warm fruit jelly. A tomato purée would come with a dollop of Greek taramasalata, while his breast of duckling would be served in a light brown sauce flavoured with something exotic like gentian (a herb that hails from Turkey). He'd even added English Stilton to his cheese cart, which took guts in a country that hardly ever recognised that foreign cheeses existed.

So I decided to return to Le Bec to ask the chef himself whether he thought French cuisine had lost its way. I was greeted by an energetic young guy with messy hair whom I'd mistaken at first for the kitchen hand.

'So much has changed in France in the past three to four years,' Le Bec told me over coffee in the restaurant's upstairs lounge area where diners were politely asked to move to if they wanted to smoke. Uncharacteristically, the dining area was non-smoking.

'It's just wrong to say all French chefs are all conservative and staid,' he said.

Le Bec turned out to be no fan of Spanish-style molecular gastronomy, which he saw as just another food fad. 'The most important thing in my kitchen is not chemistry or deconstruction — it's the produce itself,' he said.

Yet he was also no automatic knee-jerk cheerleader for French cuisine either. He said it was nonsense to describe French cooking as the best in the world because these days you could eat well all around the world. There were simply good chefs and bad chefs, good restaurants and bad restaurants, he said. Where they were located was no longer that important in a globalised cooking world.

Having said that, though, Le Bec believed that the basics of French cooking — the traditions, methods and skills that good French chefs learned nearly at birth, and which gave French cuisine what Le Bec called its 'backbone', such as how to make the lightest of sauces — remained relevant today even as conventional views of food and taste were being challenged. He pointed to the number of aspiring chefs who still came to France to gain work experience. In fact, about 70 per cent of his own kitchen staff came from abroad — from Japan, China, Britain, South America and Australia.

French cuisine may be *passé* to some, but for most French diners, there is simply no other. Everything else is derivative, a pastiche of what was first created in the grand kitchens of France's best chefs.

Even Arthur Lubow of *The New York Times* admitted that French cooking rested on an enviable base, with more solid, mid-level restaurants than in any other country. You can find excellent restaurants not only in the cities, but in the smallest country towns and villages. As a result, France probably has one of the most discerning restaurant-going publics in the world. Even the most scathing of France's critics respect the taste of the French populace.

'They have the best public,' Spain's powerful food writer Rafael Garcia Santos told Lubow, even if they don't have chefs anymore 'who want to change the world'.

In Lyon, everyone seems to have an opinion about food and wine. At Le Bec, I watched as one diner debated with the waiter about whether it was better to grill or poach a breast of duck. At the next table, an elderly man sent back his bottle of Pouilly-Fuissé, declaring the wine '*bouchonné*' or tasting of cork. 'Ah, the Lyonnais,' said Le Bec.

At dinner parties, guests proudly announce the providence of every morsel of cheese they place in their mouth — and there are 365 different kinds of French cheese — or debate the impact of the heat wave on the following year's vintage of wine. Little wonder that meals can sometimes stretch for hours.

'I'll taste the wine. I'm the French person here,' Muriel informed the waitress during one of our restaurant outings in Lyon. Muriel didn't mean to sound like a smarty-pants. She actually thought she was doing me a favour.

CHAPTER 6

French Paradox

*Until now, I humbly submit, one glorious triumph
[of French civilisation] has remained largely
unacknowledged, yet it's a basic and familiar
anthropological truth: French women don't get fat.*

French Women Don't Get Fat, Mireille Guiliano, 2004

IT WAS ABOUT SIX months before the alarm bells began to go off. While dressing one morning, I realised that I no longer needed a belt to hold up the loose-fitting jeans I'd bought in London a year before. And the folds in my favourite skirt — well, they weren't there any more.

'Do you think I'm getting fatter?' I asked Michael one day.

'Ah … no … not at all, sweetheart,' he replied, trying to sound convincing. 'Those jeans fit you perfectly now.

I never liked the way they used to bunch up in folds across your stomach.'

It was then that I went out and bought some bathroom scales. The news was not good.

In six months I'd put on approximately 6 kilograms. Two months later, my weight had ballooned by another 2 kilograms. I seemed to be adding a kilogram for every month I was living in Lyon.

I've never been a really thin woman, but I wasn't a terribly overweight one either. I dabbled in diets like everyone else, and had even signed up once to a Weight Watchers' program in Sydney where I managed to lose 10 kilos. I'd felt fabulous. I eventually put on half of that weight again, but I didn't really mind. My weight always seemed to hover within a 5-kilogram zone and I felt reasonably comfortable with that. My friends always told me I looked right in my clothes. I had my mother's meaty build. You can't beat your genes, she always said.

True, we were now eating out often, tempted by all the restaurants in our neighbourhood. But not that much more than when we lived in London. I also thought I was eating much healthier than in London, where I'd developed a taste for roast beef dinners with Yorkshire pudding accompanied by a pint of London bitter.

It seemed we'd moved to the land of the great food paradox: where the people ate fat but remained incredibly thin. In Lyon, restaurants are nearly always filled with locals

— men and women — who were eating exactly the same food as Michael and me. Everybody tucking into three courses, sometimes even four. I'd long ago noticed how small the portions were in restaurants, but what the French lacked in size, they made up for in the number of courses. Most French restaurants offer a three- or four-course set-meal deal that is always better value than ordering à la carte. A typical meal might include a salad to start, then the main meat dish, followed by cheese and then a tart for dessert.

Yet while the French ate all of this and stayed thin, it was having the opposite affect on me. I was eating like the French but gaining weight like an American. (Michael was gaining weight too, but at a far slower rate and amount than me, which only made me more anxious.)

It then dawned on me that it wasn't enough just to live in France to benefit from the French food paradox, you also had to *be* French. Other Anglophone women who had recently arrived in Lyon told me their weight had ballooned too.

'It's definitely something in the water,' said Rachael, who hailed from Manchester. A successful graduate of the Atkins diet, she said she'd put on 3 kilograms since moving to Lyon despite limiting her intake of baguettes and croissants.

'I can't bear to look at myself anymore in photographs,' said Camilla, who was equally perplexed about her weight gain since moving from Stockholm.

So were the French really missing the fat gene? This of course had become the $64,000 question in the diet world.

How the French can gorge themselves on a high-fat diet of buttery sauces, triple-fat cheeses, goose liver pâté, chocolate mousse and red wine and remain thin and relatively healthy compared to the rest of us has been the subject of thousands of scientific studies, newspaper articles and bestselling books.

There are overweight people in France, and more fat people in France than ever before. But walking around the streets of Lyon, I still find fat people a rare sight, at least compared to Sydney or London.

Dr Atkins, the pro-fat, anti-carbohydrate diet guru, had drawn his own conclusions from this phenomenon, making a fortune along the way. He told his fellow Americans that if they wanted to stay thin, they had to eat like the French. The doctrine according to Dr Atkins said there was no French food paradox; it was the rest of us who had gotten fat all wrong. The Atkins' manifesto argued that the best way to loose weight was to adopt a low-carb, high-protein and fatty diet like the French. How else had they managed to stay so thin, he asked?

The good doctor conveniently overlooked the fact that France was also a country of carbohydrate lovers. French men and woman eat on average 59 kilograms of bread per year, compared to 24.5 kilograms for Americans. In France, Sunday morning wouldn't be the same without a trip to the bakery for a bag of freshly baked croissants. This might explain why Atkins' diet books didn't sell that well in France compared with the rest of the world. Any diet that banned bread from the dinner table had little chance of succeeding here.

Yet, when it came to food and weight, I was finding France a rather schizophrenic place.

In one way, moving to France could be a liberating experience for the weight-challenged. Here, you are thrust into an unfamiliar, quite pre-modern society where fat — the kind found in cheese not on waistlines — is not a dirty word.

It is possible to find low-fat dairy products in French supermarkets, but you really have to go looking for them. In my local supermarket, they are usually stacked on the very top shelf of the refrigerated section and thus out of the direct line of sight. At eye-level are the vast bulk of fatty products — the full-fat cheeses, the creamy desserts and yoghurts. Weight Watchers' products, at least when I first moved to Lyon, just didn't exist.

Most people buy their cheese from specialty shops anyway where the powerful odour of unpasteurised milk can make you giddy if you have to queue too long. Here, the main concern is whether the cheese will be ripe enough to eat that evening. The fact that their Camembert or Brie is 55 per cent fat is of no concern. To the French, it is pointless eating cheese without fat.

On the other hand, French nonchalance about fat in food is also a bit of a charade. French women are as worried about getting fat as the rest of us, although they tend to be more discreet about their fears. You rarely hear a French woman talking about how she's lost weight on such-and-such a diet, or complaining about the extra kilos she's put on over Christmas. As the French-born American resident Mireille Guiliano wrote in her 2004 bestseller *French Women Don't Get Fat*, women in France never talk about diets and, 'certainly not with strangers' — unlike her American friends who talked about nothing else.

I, too, was like the Americans now and talking about my rapid weight gain with virtually everyone including my (skinny) French gynaecologist. She immediately handed me a diet that she said was a favourite with her patients. It limited your food intake to 1200 calories per day — I couldn't stick to it.

Yet French women did diet, even if they didn't talk about it publicly. I'd met a few French women who regularly resorted to crash diets to bring their weight down quickly. One of the most popular methods of losing weight in France is to skip a meal. In France, that usually means replacing lunch with a cigarette. Cosmetic surgery is also said to be booming — among French men as well as women.

If that is too drastic a remedy, women can always seek help from their local chemist. The shelves of French pharmacies are stacked with all manner of slimming aids — from water-elimination and fat-burning pills, to appetite-control potions and anti-cellulite thigh creams.

Slimming products are big business in France, as they are

in other parts of Europe, such as Italy and Spain, the theory being that in countries where food is a central part of the culture, people are less willing to change what they eat and are more likely to opt for a slimming aid.

This certainly seems to be the case in Lyon where weight-loss products often outnumber the cosmetics and perfumes sold in most chemist shops. At one major pharmacy in the centre of Lyon, a whole floor is set aside for slimming aids. La Boutique Minceur, or the Slimming Shop, as it is called, is staffed with young, female assistants in white lab coats, giving the place the air of a medical clinic.

I went to La Boutique Minceur one afternoon not to search for a magic bullet to fix my problem, but to find out whether the main reason French women remained so slim was because they took loads of laxatives — at least that was the explanation put to me by my new (male) French teacher in Lyon.

The assistant at La Boutique Minceur was horrified.

'I've never heard that theory before,' she said 'We'd certainly never recommend laxatives for weight loss.'

Water-elimination tablets maybe, but never laxatives.

France is clearly not the only country in the world where the diet aid industry has gained a foothold. The United States is the home of the quickie weight-loss remedy, but it hasn't done much to stem the rise of obesity there.

Something else had to be going on in France. Take *foie gras*, for instance, which is full of saturated fats. The French consume about 9,700 tonnes of goose and duck liver pâté each year. Yet in the heart of *foie gras* country — the Gascony region of south-west France where locals typically consume *foie gras* as an appetiser at almost every meal — the coronary death rate among middle-aged men is about half that for the rest of France. Researchers from France's National Institute of Health and Medical Research (INSERM) surmised that there was something different about the fats in duck and goose liver, and in cheese, that made them less damaging and possibly even protective of the heart. A Canadian pharmaceutical company agreed and, in cooperation with INSERM, was reportedly conducting further studies about what made the fats in cheese and *foie gras* so special.

The rest of the scientific community, however, remain sceptical. No diet rich in saturated fats can be good for your health, they argue. But you only have to visit France to wonder: have the scientists got it all wrong?

For me, arriving in Paris as a reasonably svelte young journalist in 1988, it was like looking at one of those trick mirrors at a funfair, except everyone else appeared skinny. And yet there they were in their many fine restaurants, enjoying their meal, including dessert. They didn't even seem to work out. I never saw a French woman jogging during my whole time in Paris. Perhaps it was because they wouldn't be seen dead in track pants.

It's true that the percentage of slender and chic tend to diminish the further away you travel from a big city. But even in the countryside, the French haven't gone to fat despite eating it in copious amounts every day of their lives.

Pharmaceutical makers have apparently noticed this too, and like the Canadian firm investigating the special properties of *foie gras*, over the years several others have dispatched a small army of researchers to France to study the phenomenon. They were no doubt motivated by the knowledge that if they could come up with a drug equivalent to the French food paradox the pay-offs would be enormous. A drug that lowered cholesterol and heart attacks and kept people thin at the same time would be an instant success, bigger than Viagra.

One American company has already come up with a pill which it says contains the same chemicals found in red wine. The French drink up to four glasses of wine a day, making them the biggest consumers of wine per capita in the world, and for years some scientists thought that this might be the reason the French suffer fewer heart attacks and strokes.

The Bordeaux-based epidemiologist Dr Serge Renaud first went public with the theory in 1991 when he released his famous study which claimed that moderate but regular red wine consumption helped flush damaging cholesterol out of the arteries, thus protecting the body from cardiovascular disease and stroke. He also ventured that moderate wine consumption might even help prevent some cancers and dementia. After Dr Renaud first revealed his findings on US television, red wine sales in America soared.

Yet, the jury is still out on whether moderate red wine consumption actually improves a person's health over the longer-term. Sceptical scientists have said other aspects of a wine drinker's lifestyle could be contributing to their longevity, such as exercise or healthier eating. They also point to the fact that wine consumption has been declining in France — over the past four decades, the amount of wine drunk has dropped by 25 per cent. But that hasn't been matched by a corresponding rise in mortality rates. In fact, the death rate is still falling in France.

Many doctors now point to France's more Mediterranean diet, considered the second healthiest diet after Japan's, as the real explanation for the French food paradox. The French diet is rich in fresh fruit, vegetables, salad, olive oil and fish — although it has to be said, this is more prevalent in the wealthier south than in the poorer north where the diet is starchier. But overall, scientists believe the sheer variety in the French diet is the key to the country's relatively good health.

More recently, though, a more prosaic explanation has also emerged to explain this Gallic food and health enigma: the French simply eat less than the rest of us. A couple of years ago, French and American researchers analysed portion sizes in a range of restaurants in both Paris and Philadelphia and found them to be, on average, 25 per cent bigger in the United States. Even a medium serving of French fries weighed 65 grams more in a McDonald's restaurant in Philadelphia than one in Paris. (That's about thirty-five extra French fries per portion: I checked.)

One of the scientists on the project, Paul Rozin, a professor of psychology at the university of Pennsylvania, explained: 'While the French eat more fat than Americans, they probably eat slightly fewer calories which, when compounded over years, can amount to substantial differences in weight.'

American tourists often said they'd managed to lose weight just by routing themselves through France. One hefty American couple told a British journalist that they'd lost between 3 and 4.5 kilograms each by simply abandoning their usual diet and eating their way around Paris restaurants during their two-week holiday.

That was good news for them. But it didn't explain why I was gaining weight at a rapid pace. Having eaten my way around Lyon's best restaurants, I could certainly attest that the portions were generally smaller than in London, let alone the United States. Yet I was no lighter for the experience.

Rather than search the scientific journals, I decided to seek some advice from the locals. What, in their view, was I doing wrong?

Michael said he'd put the question to his barber, who usually had an opinion on everything around the town. Despite his slight build, he was also a bit of gourmand, as most people are in Lyon. He was not surprised at all to be asked about food and weight gain; the French pretty much see themselves as experts on the subject.

'Tell your wife to eat goat's cheese and to stay away from cooked cheese,' the barber advised. He explained to Michael that cooked cheeses are those with a 'shiny' surface, such as Emmental. The problem with his theory, however, was that Emmental was the most popular cheese in France, ahead of Camembert and Roquefort. It didn't seem to be doing the French any harm.

I then turned to a vigneron for advice. We were visiting Burgundy and had stopped off at a cellar to buy some Aligoté white wine, which is what the French use in their Kir aperitifs. The woman behind the counter was, of course, very slim. She, too, wasn't surprised by my questioning.

'Since I've moved here, I've been putting on weight at an alarming rate,' I told her. 'What do you suggest I do?'

I expected her to reply that I should drink more wine and less shiny cheese, but instead she advised me to refrain from drinking coffee, which in France is usually drunk with several lumps of sugar.

'It's the sugar that does it,' assured Madame Gerbet.

'But I don't take sugar in my coffee,' I thought.

I then turned to Interpol, not that weight gain was

actually an international crime (well, maybe among some police). Interpol, though, has lots of young French women working there who are very slim. I talked to 29-year-old Sandrine who worked in the Secretary-General's office, and loved to eat cheese. Indeed, it was Sandrine's favourite food. She could name any cheese placed in front of her, and tell you where it came from. Yet Sandrine remained relatively thin, although she admitted her weight often fluctuated and that she had a tendency to go on crash diets. Nevertheless, she was happy to give me her dieting tips.

'Don't eat croissants. They are way too greasy,' Sandrine said. 'No one eats croissants in France. They are only there for the tourists.'

'Really?' I replied in disbelief.

'Well, you never see French women eating them,' she said.

It was true. I'd never seen a French woman — or man for that matter — ordering a croissant at my local café, Le Spleen. If people wanted something with their coffee in the morning, they generally ordered a tartine, a piece of baguette that comes buttered or perhaps with jam. I seemed to be the only person who liked a croissant with my coffee. But a preference for tartine over croissants couldn't explain the relative slimness of an entire nation. I decided to dig deeper.

The next stop was my local gym. 'Maybe the French are working off their extra calories behind closed doors,' I thought. Yet at 10.30 one morning, I found the place virtually empty, aside from a packed yoga class in an adjacent room, which seemed to me to be just a bend and stretch work-out. Ashtanga devotees they were not.

In the main gym, a few women — all reed thin, of course, one dressed in a gleaming white track suit and gold jewellery — were giving the bike machines a go. The woman in white put in about ten minutes before returning to the changing rooms without having even worked up a sweat. The others lasted not much longer. I saw maybe half a dozen men and women come and go during my 45-minute workout, where I desperately tried to burn off the previous night's meal. I was the only one in the changing room later with unsightly sweat stains on my T-shirt.

The French are not obsessed by exercise. Gyms seemed to be patronised more for the classes they offered — Salsa dancing was a popular choice — rather than the exercise equipment. Indeed, the Lyonnais in particular seemed to prefer to do things in groups. On Friday nights in summer, for example, hundreds of Lyonnais would take to the streets for a mass, but well-organised, rollerblading session around the city, which could be frustrating if you were trying to cross town to get to your favourite restaurant.

Yet seasonal rollerblading couldn't be the answer either. I decided to head back to Interpol, and talk to Laurence, a 31-year-old public relations consultant and mother of one, who was working in Michael's office for a while.

Laurence was married to a chef, yet weighed in at a slight 50 kilograms. Over lunch in the Interpol cafeteria, she told me she didn't miss any meals. Her days started with a tartine (of course), which she dunked in her morning coffee. On this day, we both ordered a hot meal — she beef, me fish, with a ladle of fresh steamed carrots on the side. I passed on dessert, but she chose an apple tart. At 6 pm, when she returned home, she said she normally had a quick bite of cheese and bread, before enjoying another hot meal of meat and vegetables for dinner. Laurence even admitted to the occasional visit to McDonald's on the insistence of her young daughter.

This was hardly a strict dietary regime, I told her. But perhaps it was what Laurence didn't eat that made the difference. Like most French, she rarely snacked between meals. No chocolate bars, no potato chips, no Coca-Cola, no slurping of milky coffee from a cardboard cup as she hurried to work.

In France, meals are usually eaten at the same time every day, as anyone who has ever tried to get into a restaurant outside the country's limited serving hours can attest. Restaurants usually serve lunch from 12 noon to 2 pm, and dinner from 7.30 pm to 9.30 pm. The meal table is not treated as a filling station, but as a place to come together with family, friends and work colleagues to enjoy — slowly, without the pressure to order and eat quickly so the restaurant can turn over the table once again — the wonderfully fresh and varied produce that is plentiful here.

Laurence said she rarely ate processed foods, and limited her restaurant outings, now she had a child, to perhaps three times a year. 'But when we do eat out, it's always to somewhere special like Chez Paul Bocuse or Georges Blanc,' she said.

It seemed to me that the French simply understood the meaning of moderation. At restaurants, I usually scoffed down the lovely fresh bread brought to our table while I waited for my first course to arrive, whereas the French would only nibble theirs. And because a bottle of good wine can be expensive in a restaurant (there's no such thing as BYO) — and wages are not high in France — most people would drink their wine slowly with their meal, savouring its flavour and aroma with small sips. Indeed, French diners, it seemed to me, rarely finished their bottle of wine, preferring to leave the remnants behind rather than gulping down the last glass after their coffee, as we Australians tend to do. Waste not, want not, I say.

Some anthropologists believe the reason for all this moderation and discipline at the dining table is because historically there has never been a prolonged famine in France. There was little genetic pressure to eat or drink more than was necessary, they'd reasoned.

I put this theory to Dominique Loiseau, whom I'd interviewed after the suicide of her husband, celebrity chef

Bernard Loiseau, in February 2003. Twelve months on, she was now running her husband's restaurant and food business.

I wanted to ask her about the French food paradox because I knew from my research that before she married Bernard, she'd been a journalist specialising in health and nutrition.

Madame Loiseau said she thought the answer lay in the French meal culture, which had infused in the French an appreciation of a balanced and healthy diet and the discipline to consume smaller portions of food.

'The first thing, the French don't eat all day,' she told me, 'We eat at fixed times: morning, noon and then in the evening.

'Unfortunately, snacking is on the rise among children, but up until now, we haven't really been a snacking country.'

She also said that thanks to the availability of fresh produce in the cities, salads, freshly cooked vegetables and fruit have always been a staple part of French mealtimes.

'In Germany, the accompanying vegetables with meat and fish are nearly always potatoes,' she said. 'In France, it's considered bad food preparation to always cook with potatoes. You must have a variety of vegetables. It's not just a question of nutrition, it's knowing how to live and enjoy life.'

The central place of food in French culture helped explain why France hadn't struggled with a weight problem like the rest of the rich world. Madame Loiseau, who occasionally received complaints from her American guests ('only those who don't travel often') that the portions served at La Côte d'Or were too small, believed the French had a different attitude to eating compared to most Americans.

'In America, people expect value for their money above all else when they go to restaurants. If they aren't served large quantities of food, they think something is wrong. Quantity is more important than quality.'

Yet even Madame Loiseau admitted that attitudes to food were now changing in France. She lamented the arrival of Tex Mex style restaurants on French soil that served giant-sized pizzas 'the same as in the US'. In fact, a popular little bistro around the corner from our apartment now boasted its 'generous servings' on its blackboard menu. *Mon Dieu*! What next? Starbucks? Actually, yes. Several outlets had opened in recent years in Paris.

Nobody was yet presaging the demise of the French café, but food habits — and even body shapes — were already beginning to change in France. Scientists were predicting that the French would eventually catch up with British and American rates of heart disease as their diet became more Americanised. In 2003, INSERM said that if the current rate of weight gain was not arrested, the proportion of the French population classified as overweight or obese could match that of the United States in a couple of decades.

I found this hard to believe, until I had a chat with the woman who ran my favourite clothing boutique in Lyon. I shopped there because it was one of the few places in the city that stocked my size.

'I suppose most of your clientele take a size 36? [Size 8 in Australia/UK],' I asked as I plonked down the trousers I planned to buy, an unlovely size 42 (size 14).

'Not at all,' she replied. 'Sizes are getting bigger, particularly for young women. I'd say the average size we sell these days is around 40–42. It's been going up for the past decade.'

Perhaps French women do get fat after all. Or at least some do anyway.

It was ten o'clock on a cold February morning in Lyon, yet there was hardly an empty chair to be had at Espace Conseil Minceur, the aptly named meeting place for the Lyon branch of the American slimming programme Weight Watchers.

I'd been to Weight Watchers' groups in Sydney and London before, so I knew the drill. After paying my nine-euro fee, I joined the lengthening queue for the scales — the public nature of this embarrassing weigh-in process being a central part of the Weight Watchers' philosophy.

I'd expected to find others like me here: Anglophone expatriates who hadn't adapted too well to French cuisine and were now seeking help from a familiar source. There were two Danish women in the group, but the rest were all locals, mostly older women, a few young mothers with young children in tow, and one man. The festive season now over, they were all expressing a gritty Gallic determination to shed a few kilos after the ritual gorging of *foie gras* and *gateaux*.

After the weigh-in — the news was even worse than that delivered by my own bathroom scales — I took my seat just as our svelte team leader, Brigitte, was beginning her morning lecture.

In London, where I last ventured into a Weight Watchers meeting, hardly anybody stayed for the folksy advice session after the weigh-in. Most simply turned up, got weighed and went home. In Lyon, however, everyone stayed to hear Brigitte tell us how 'we must keep an image in our minds always of how we want to look'.

For the French, this had become a surprising, new challenge. INSERM in their 2003 survey had found that the number of obese people in France — considered to be anyone with a body mass index (BMI) above 30 — had risen by 5 per cent a year since 1997. (BMI is calculated by dividing the person's weight in kilograms by the square of their height in metres.)

The institute estimated that 11 per cent of the French population was now obese, compared with 8 per cent six years previously. Some 30 per cent of the population were also considered to be overweight. The Institute also said the problem affected all ages and social groups.

Overall obesity levels were still lower than in the United States, where 31 per cent of the population was estimated to be obese and 61 per cent were classed as overweight. (In Australia, obesity levels had hit 20 per cent and were continuing to rise.)

But the sudden sharp rise in numbers in France had set off alarm bells in a society which had prided itself on its reputation for thinness and elegance.

The government immediately declared childhood obesity a major national problem, and launched a five-year plan aimed specifically at promoting good eating habits at school and in the home. Besides giving away free fruit at school, the program also pledged to create 850 new posts in hospitals for dieticians and doctors specialising in nutrition.

In case this didn't work, the government was also funding a new National Sizing Campaign — across the country, the French would be measured so that clothing sizes could be adjusted to better reflect the slightly fuller French figure.

I decided to contact INSERM to find out why obesity levels were rising so rapidly in France. Marie-Aline Charles, an obesity researcher at the institute, told me that changing eating habits were the major culprit. As in other parts of the world, the traditional way of eating had given way to the pressures of modern life.

Charles said the French no longer had the time for their traditional 90-minute lunch at the local bistro where they would eat a balanced meal. Now they tended to eat on the run and, as a result, more often snacked between meals.

Working mothers, too, had less time to prepare an elaborate family meal at home and were opting for more convenient, processed food. Children, more interested in TV and computer games than playing football, weren't getting as much exercise as previous generations.

'In France, obesity levels suddenly started to rise in the mid-90s. Before that they had been stable,' Charles told me. 'In Great Britain, the same rise started in the 1980s. In the US, it probably began back in the 70s. So all we can say conclusively is that it's something coming from the West.'

That 'something coming from the West' was of course fast and convenience food, which has exploded onto the French market in recent years. McDonald's and Kentucky Fried Chicken might be struggling in their home markets, but they were continuing to open new outlets in France where demand was rising. By 2004, there were almost one thousand McDonald's restaurants across France, nearly double the number of five years before. This was despite the popular view of the French as the world's leading connoisseurs of fine cuisine and haters of American-style fast food. Yet it seemed the French were munching away on Big Macs as much as the rest of us. In Lyon, there are McDonald's outlets at every big métro stop, and they are filled with young people at most times of the day. Indeed, there are now more McDonald's outlets in France than in any other European country aside from Britain.

Snack food, too, is everywhere. A decade ago, when I first lived in Paris, it was almost impossible to find a packet of sugary biscuits in the local supermarket. Now there are whole aisles dedicated to 'American-style chocolate-chip cookies' and similar items at my local store. The refrigerated sections have also been expanded to accommodate the growing demand for frozen pizzas and other prepared foods.

It seemed that the French were suddenly overdosing on convenience food. According to one French doctor, there was a reason for this. Dr Jean-Michel Cohen, a nutritionist and author of *Understanding Eating*, told the *International Herald Tribune* that the French were particularly susceptible to the invasion of fast food because their culinary traditions had insulated them from it for so long.

'The rise in obesity is probably the result of the fact that the French don't understand how to eat properly with commercial food, since they have never had to do it before,' he said.

But Marie-Aline Charles said it was too simple to blame the arrival of American fast-food chains for France's emerging weight problem.

'Modern societies need to have fast food,' she told me. 'We just have to find different ways to meet that need.'

In the meantime, slimming groups like Weight Watchers have been stepping into the breach. A woman at their head office in Paris told me that the company had begun to notice a rise in membership in 1997 when the first reports about the increasing girth of the French began to emerge. In 2003, Weight Watchers France claimed a total national membership of more than two million, with 45,000 of those devotees attending 1,300 meetings across the country each week. This was just a fraction of Weight Watchers' nine-million-strong membership in the United States, but it wasn't bad for a weight-loss scheme that didn't hide its American accent, particularly its emphasis on the group confessional — which is so not French.

Sales of Weight Watchers' products, which were introduced into France in 1992, were also said to be booming. According to a report in the *International Herald Tribune* in 2005, Weight Watchers now sells 3,000 tonnes of frozen food in France annually.

'The market in France is growing and we believe it has an excellent future,' Michael Mullen, European product manager for Weight Watchers, said.

They were certainly taking the issue seriously in Lyon. I was now being confronted with the anti-fat message everywhere I went. One day at my local gym, I was handed a frightening leaflet, sponsored by the pharmaceutical giant Roche, warning me that excess weight would not only wreck my 'silhouette', it would also damage my knees, bring on diabetes and hypertension and raise my cholesterol levels. I was urged to talk to my doctor at the first sign of any of the above.

It seemed a strange place to distribute this message, though, given that everyone at my gym seemed underweight to me. I was beginning to wonder where all these fat French were hiding. It was hard to know whether young women were getting fatter, as the clothes shop owner claimed, given their current penchant for wearing baggy jeans. To my eyes, the slim still heavily outnumbered the overweight on Lyon's streets.

It was then that I realised that everything was relative, even weight gain. Obesity rates might have topped 11 per cent in France, but they were still way behind the United States and Australia. I read in *Le Figaro* that between 1997 and 2003, the average French person had gained 1.7 kilograms, while another article claimed the average French woman regardless of age, and with a height of 162 centimetres, now weighed 63.5 kilograms.

Big deal. It's been some time since I've seen the sunnier side of 65 kilos.

Even my *confrères* at Weight Watchers didn't appear to be that overweight to me. In fact, they were the slimmest bunch of people I had come across in my international weight-watching travels. No one here could be described as obese. They were, like me, just a little meaty around the waist (and legs and arms).

'My problem is chocolate,' one woman in the group told me. 'I love it. I don't want to give it up. I just want to learn how to avoid it from time to time.'

What I like about the Weight Watchers' program in France is that they have adapted it to French tastes. They don't tell people to abandon their chocolate mousse, their brie, or their baguettes. There are no American guilt-trips about food and abstinence here. Instead, the message is to eat traditional French food in moderation. This is something that the French, of all people, can understand.

Which makes me think that they will probably win their battle of the bulge in the end. The French still eat better quality and more diverse produce than the rest of us. Their portions in restaurants are still smaller. And the culture still dictates restraint at the dinner table.

Also, any country that has as many lingerie shops as patisseries is not going to turn to fat without a fight. The French spent $A3.8 billion on lingerie in 2003, more than any other country in Europe.

'For French women, pretty silky lingerie is a next-to-skin constant reminder to make the choices that pay off in slimness,' wrote Anne Barone, author of the 1997 book *Chic & Slim: How Those Chic French Women Eat All That Rich Food and Still Stay Slim*.

Perhaps there lies the nub of the French food paradox. The French gain weight like any other group, but social norms encourage them to lose the excess kilos. According to an article in Israeli newspaper *Ha'aretz*, some scientists believe that it isn't the physical attributes of the French that should be admired, but their mental capacities.

'The American wants to be thin, but eats in secret,' said the article. 'The French person wants to be thin, and is.'

Maybe that is the root of my problem. I just don't have that gritty Gallic determination when it comes to dieting. My fatal flaw is that I'll always opt for a three-course meal accompanied by a glass of Côte du Rhône over a gift of sexy French underwear.

CHAPTER 7

Rural Dreams

Living in the French countryside is like being transported back to the 14th century without any of the good bits of that era. The people are suspicious, lack social skills and dislike anyone who is not a white Catholic.

French resident Chris Wilson writing in *The Guardian*, **2004**

'WHAT ARE YOU DOING THERE? Don't you know you're on private property?'

The young, shirtless man glaring at us through the bushes looked a little menacing. In one hand he held a lead which was connected to a growling Alsatian. I half expected to find a hunting rifle in the other.

'It's OK. It's OK,' Michael answered immediately, his

Rural Dreams

hands slightly raised. 'We're just looking around. The real estate agent said we could.'

At this, the man huffed, and then started to walk away, slowly. As he did, he threw us suspicious glances over his shoulder. The dog on the lead was straining in the other direction, towards us. We scrambled through the bushes and back onto the road. We should have known better than to venture into a backyard without a local guide. We were in the French countryside, where the locals didn't always take too kindly to strangers, particularly foreign ones.

We had come to a little village called Menas in the Drôme region, a two-hour drive south of Lyon, to look at a house that was up for sale. It was a two-bedroom stone cottage in the middle of Menas. Like most French village houses, it had its idiosyncrasies. The bedrooms were on the ground floor, while the kitchen was upstairs and you had to cross a small street to get to the piece of land that came with the house. The real estate agent had to leave to meet some other clients but he told us to take our time and have a second look around the property.

'You could build a swimming pool on that land,' the agent suggested.

We were considering what it would be like to cross the road from your house to the swimming pool when the menacing man who would likely be our neighbour broke our concentration. Suddenly the Menas house no longer seemed the place for us. It wasn't just the thought of having a menacing Alsatian-owner as a neighbour. It was also the price tag. For a 70 square metre stone cottage with rooms in the wrong places and with a backyard across a dirt road, the owners were asking 175,000 euros or around $A280,000. It was hardly the bargain that was promised by all those TV programs and real estate magazines aimed at people like us who dreamed of owning a little cottage in some out of the way hamlet in the French countryside.

Ever since Peter Mayle wrote about his long lunches and renovation misadventures in *A Year in Provence* in the late 1980s, hordes of Anglo-Saxons have fantasised about owning their own rural idyll in France. Michael and I were no different.

We enjoyed being expats in France, unburdened by heavy mortgages and lots of possessions. But another part of us also wanted to dig some roots, to have a place where we would always be able to leave the few things we owned.

Given our long affair with France, owning a house in or near a French village seemed just the ticket. The rural life here had attracted me in a way that it had never done in Australia. Perhaps that's because the French countryside is so accessible, and so full of people and buildings. In France, you can't drive more than 10 kilometres outside a major town without coming across an appealing little village or hamlet that boasts a history stretching back to Roman times.

Houses may have been cheap before Peter Mayle came along, but no longer — at least not in the more charming parts of rural France where foreigners wanted to live. From the time *A Year in Provence* hit the bookstores, the British — and much of northern Europe for that matter — have been buying up any structure they could get their hands on so long as it was old and made of stone, and prices have risen as a result. This is despite Mayle having long ago sold up and moved out of his Provençal village, sick of the curious tourist hordes who would peer in his window.

Still, it hadn't dampened our yearning to own a piece of rural France for ourselves. We knew what we wanted. In our mind's eye, the cottage of our dreams would have thick beamed ceilings and a large open fireplace. It would come with a small parcel of land enclosed with an ancient stone wall, and maybe a barn that had probably fallen derelict.

If we were lucky, the house would also have a terrace that commanded a view to the south, perhaps over some vineyards. The kitchen would be spacious and functional, with a deep marble sink and a dark flagstone floor, the sort of place where a matronly cook might have rustled up a steaming *pot au feu* in centuries past when she wasn't knitting at the foot of the guillotine. And if you weren't feeling inclined to cook yourself, you could always pop out to that charming *auberge* down the way offering regional dishes and delicacies.

On market days, you could fill up your empty plastic Evian bottles with more-than-drinkable table wine from the local vigneron for little more than the price of a cup of coffee. You could spend part of your time converting the old barn into a self-catering *gîte* that you could let out to help fund your rural lifestyle, and then write a bestselling account of the experience. You would make friends with the ruddy-faced, barrel-stomached locals who would tip you off about where in the woods to scrounge the best truffles during the season.

Ideally, this little piece of rural France wouldn't cost an arm and a leg — about as much as a garage in the better parts of Sydney or London.

Once, when we were still living in London, we thought we'd found our rural dream nest. We had travelled to the Languedoc region of southern France where some British friends had managed to buy a small cottage with a large terrace for the princely sum of £33,000 or $A70,000.

In a hamlet near the tourist town of Minerve, we were shown through a two-storey former schoolhouse that was in need of some work, and it got our hearts racing. It had a pot-belly stove, beamed ceilings, a marble sink and even an old well in the garden that was dominated by a massive plane tree. The hamlet had no shop or even a café, but it was only a short bicycle ride away to the next town that at least had a bakery.

It was exactly what we were looking for in a country cottage, although some rooms were a little dark, and it had no terrace or a view to speak of. 'If you could just crop those trees, then we'd get a view over the vineyards from here,' said Michael, standing at the window of the upstairs bedroom.

The house seemed to us to be dripping with charm and the price was right. The owners were asking only 70,000 euros, or about $A120,000.

Back at the real estate agency in Olonzac, we kept our sang-froid. We told the agent we would think about it over coffee in the café next door. Michael told him he had noticed some troubling plug holes in the staircase which he thought signalled that the house had once been treated for termites. He thought we should take a second look at the property so he could inspect the holes more closely.

The agent merely shrugged his shoulders. A small, thin man who seemed new to the real estate game, he didn't seem to care whether we bought the house or not. But as we walked out the door, he did nod towards his female colleague at the next desk who was showing an elderly Belgian couple some photographs of houses.

'Beatrice is going to take them to see the same property this afternoon,' he whispered as he handed the house keys to his colleague. 'They seem very keen to buy something.'

We pondered the agent's warning, but then decided to continue our search. We'd lined up some other houses nearby for inspection, via the Internet from London, and wondered whether they might offer more space and views than the schoolhouse, with its mildly troubling termite-like holes. By the end of the afternoon, we'd realised that nothing matched the schoolhouse, either in charm or price. Most turned out to be derelict barns.

'I really think the Minervois house is the one for us,' I said to Michael that evening. 'I have a good feeling about it.'

Michael agreed. He decided to put aside his termite fears — after all, most villages in the south of France were riddled with them, and it looked like the current owners of the property had already dealt with the problem. Asbestos was another problem in French villages, although owners were obliged under French law to tell buyers about it, even though they didn't have to remove it. Leaking roofs and waterlogged walls during major downpours, not uncommon in the south, were another bothersome but hard to fix problem with 300-year-old houses.

Michael and I returned the very next morning ready to make an offer. Our agent was standing on the pavement outside the office smoking a cigarette.

'*Aah* ... sorry,' he said after we'd exchanged *bonjours*. 'But those Belgians I mentioned, they bought the house yesterday.' He shrugged his shoulders in that French manner that was now really irritating me. It seemed those damn Belgians, with their better-nuanced French and better understanding of the property market, had snatched the house from under our noses not long after we had left the agency the day before.

Just then the woman who had sold the Belgians the schoolhouse came out of the agency on her way to another inspection.

'Sorry,' she said, not meaning it. 'But my client had a

good feeling about that place. They made an offer on the spot.'

'But I had a good feeling about it too,' I retorted, now close to tears.

In the hot French rural property market, the Belgians had known better than to dawdle over coffee. They also knew something we didn't know at the time: in France, after you make an offer and it is accepted, and you hand over your 10 per cent deposit, you still have a week to change your mind about the property without any penalties. During this cooling-off period, the house is safely off the market.

It seemed we needn't have dallied over coffee at all; we could have made an offer and investigated the termites issue later. Devastated, we told the agent we would offer the property owners more money than the Belgians. But French law forbids gazumping — unlike in Sydney where, ironically, we'd been gazumped before.

The Belgians went ahead and bought our little schoolhouse at the end of the cooling-off week, and since then prices for similar houses have doubled. If you think buying a house in Sydney or Melbourne can be tough, try competing with the British, the Belgians, the Dutch, the Germans — basically every cashed-up northern European looking for their place in the sun.

*

At less than a tenth the size of Australia, you can't really describe France as a huge country. But it certainly has a varied geography: high mountain ranges, arid plateaux, volcanoes, lakes, long rivers, beaches and rainforests, not to mention beautiful, urban architectural gems, such as Paris. This diversity helps explain why France is still the world's most visited country, welcoming around sixty million tourists each year. It also has rich agricultural lands and a moderate climate, necessary foundations on which to build an enviable gastronomic reputation.

In Europe, only Italy rivals France for gastronomy and geographical diversity, but for northern Europeans seeking solace from their long winters, France is always the first — and for a majority of them the most favoured — stop.

The Germans long ago expressed their preference for the Gallic lifestyle with the saying *Leben wie Gott in Frankreich* — Living like God in France. They had once rolled into France with their tanks; now they came with their caravans and trailer homes, allowing them to bring some of their creature comforts should the Gallic culture prove too overwhelming. During the summer months, the Germans conquer entire camping grounds in southern France, as do the Dutch, who tend to seek out sites favoured by their fellow countrymen, ensuring that they were only likely to fly into another Dutchman on the way to the toilet block. So much for greater European integration.

The French I knew were not so much annoyed as

bemused by these tourism convoys. My friend Muriel told me how she'd once stumbled into a designated 'Dutch' camping ground near her hometown of Annecy in the Savoy region one summer's day in August.

'I felt like I'd crossed the border into a foreign country,' she said.

'They seemed to have brought everything with them from Holland — even their own bread.'

The northern Europeans, though, must enjoy their vicarious Gallic experiences because many have returned to put down more permanent roots, buying up village houses across France as holiday homes. So too have the British, and many other nationals with a middle class that yearned and had the means to own a piece of the French countryside.

But it was the British who seemed to be arriving in the greatest numbers. Decades ago, it was the British nobility who sought out refuges amid the familiar clipped hedgerows and jagged coastlines of Normandy and Brittany. These days, it is middle-class Brits who are doing the buying. They are also heading further south to warmer areas, their favoured destinations being the rolling hills of Dordogne, the vineyard-rich region of Provence and the glitzy Côte d'Azur.

That trickle has turned into a flood in recent years and has spread out across France, as the strong pound and rising property prices in Britain made the acquisition of relatively cheap property in France affordable even for families with modest incomes. The arrival of discount airlines meant cashed-up Britons could now also access their French dream nests even more cheaply and quickly.

'It took us one hundred years to get rid of them,' one villager in the Lot region complained to a British-based French property magazine, in a reference to the Hundred Year's War. 'And now they are coming back.'

Estimates vary, but banks and real estate agents have claimed that about one million Britons now own property in France, from cow sheds to chateaux. Most only use them on holidays, although at least 300,000 Britons — retirees, professional couples, families with young children — are thought to have moved to France permanently. The trend was expected to continue. A 2004 survey found nearly a quarter of Britons approaching pension age planned to retire abroad, with France being the third most favoured destination behind Spain and Australia.

The departing Britons cited rising crime at home and better weather and healthcare system abroad for their reason to up stakes. Also, moving to France was not too much of a wrench — homesick Britons could always pop back across the Channel to see family and friends.

Most French seemed to be remarkably sanguine about foreigners buying up their rural heritage, even if only for the money that they brought in. Unlike in some other European countries, there was no law against property ownership in France by non-nationals.

Indeed, local mayors welcomed the flow of foreign cash which was helping to revitalise otherwise dying village economies where unemployment and poverty still remained the number one problem. They appreciated the fact that foreigners were restoring and renovating thousands of village dwellings that would otherwise have fallen derelict.

That was certainly the plan of Bruce Leonard, a New Zealander I'd met who'd retired from his executive job at the age of fifty-three to move to France. He and his Australian wife Claudine had run a bed and breakfast operation in Provence, and when I met them in late 2004, they had just finished the renovations on a large property they had bought in Chaudenay in Burgundy and had opened it as a B&B.

'There is this whole image of the French being arrogant, disinterested, and not liking foreigners, yet nothing could be further from the truth in our experience,' said Bruce.

'People liked the fact that we were from Australia and New Zealand. They seemed genuinely intrigued that we would come from such lovely countries, as they saw them, to live in France. They would always say to us, "It's our dream to live in Australia and New Zealand."'

Yet not everyone was pleased about the foreign rush to own property in France, particularly with the accompanying rise in prices. With a French country cottage still costing on average half the price of a one-bedroom flat in London, few Britons in particular felt the need to haggle over prices —

to the delight of local real estate agents, but to the dismay of some locals who now found themselves being priced out of the market.

Well-off Parisians and other city dwellers buying up second homes in the country have also been blamed for rocketing rural property prices. But at least they spoke the language.

Locals complained that the British made little attempt to learn the language or to integrate into village life when they arrived.

'Some of the foreigners who come to settle here form a somewhat closed group and that acts as an obstacle to their integration into the local community,' the mayor of Gaillac, a bustling town in the Midi-Pyrenees, told the *Financial Times* in 2004.

Their sheer numbers, and the tendency among expats to buy in areas favoured by their fellow compatriots, had turned whole hamlets in popular areas into French-free zones. There were now villages in the Dordogne where up to 80 per cent of the resident population were foreigners, the majority of them often being British, and included an assortment of British tradesmen who had set up shop there to serve them.

We stumbled across one of these expat towns a few years ago while on a Sunday lunch restaurant hunt. As we walked around the pretty Perigord village of Ribérac, we saw a sign pinned to the local community board calling for players for the local cricket team and an advertisement for the next performance of the Ribérac English dramatic society.

No wonder they called this region 'Dordogne-shire', we said. But our good humour was soon tested when we were served our midday meal. We had chosen a restaurant in the main street that was overflowing, usually a good sign. It was also in the heart of one of the best food regions in France — Perigord was known for its fine *foie gras* and tasty duck dishes. But what we were served for Sunday lunch was neither fine nor tasty; it was an unidentifiable piece of meat drowned in a stodgy sauce, the sort of meal you might have got at a British Rail canteen twenty years ago. The only thing missing was a tin cup of steaming tea.

We thought things couldn't get any worse until the cheese plate came out — we were offered triangular portions of the supermarket cheese *La Vache Qui Rit* wrapped in tin foil. It's what mothers often put in their children's lunch packs in France.

Normally a restaurant as bad as this would not survive in France, but in Ribérac this hot Sunday afternoon, it was doing a roaring trade. The diners were mostly British, cheery souls who were having a gay time despite the 35-degree heat. That may have had something to do with the fact that the restaurant owners had cleverly included a free carafe of wine and an aperitif with the meal, something you rarely see in French restaurants. The free wine and the heat meant a large part of the restaurant was now so tired and emotional, they didn't really care how bad the food was. As the noise increased around us, for a minute I thought I was back in a London pub.

The expatriate mentality is a queer thing, and I can't say I have been immune from it. Abroad, expats often hang around together and do things which they say they would never have dreamt of doing at home — in my case, once watching an Australia versus England rugby final in a Lyon pub called Ayers Rock with a whole bunch of chanting Brits. In France, the resident Britons search out cream teas and sign up for cricket matches and whinge about how difficult it is to get a good cup of tea. Abroad, expats tend to cling, desperately in some cases, to their own fragile sense of nationality — the thing that reminds them of who they are and where they came from.

By failing to learn the language and respecting local customs, however, they end up doing the very same things for which they often criticise immigrants to their own countries. Culture migrants, like those who have sought out the tranquil French countryside experience, face a further dilemma: by following their dream, they risk killing, or changing forever, the very thing they came in search of. And so it seemed to be happening in French-free zones such as Ribérac.

Locals were increasingly not amused by the rising number in their midst of '*les rosbifs*' (the roast beefs) — as the French called the British — particularly those French not sharing in the new wealth brought by the foreign influx of house-hunters. They also abhorred what they saw as the Brits' famed lack of self-control when it came to drinking. Some had even begun to call the British '*Les Fuck-Offs*', on account of a perceived British bent for booze-fuelled aggression.

Villagers also complained that rising rural property prices would make it even more difficult for their children to make their own way on the land.

That frustration was beginning to find expression across the countryside. In February 2005, in a little village called Bourbriac in Brittany (population 1200, of which 700 were British), local residents waving Breton flags held a demonstration in the main square to protest the number of foreigners buying up houses in the area. The year before, the walls of the office of a notary who handled home sales for British buyers had been daubed with the words 'Brits out, stop speculation'.

'If it carries on like this ... there'll be no French people left here at all in ten years' time,' one young Bourbriac resident complained to a British journalist in 2005.

'Why would a French person living in his own country want to live in a village where 99 per cent of the population are foreigners?'

Of course, there would be no buyers without willing sellers, and many French farmers have done well out of the foreigner-led rural property boom, selling off buildings and farms that had become too small or inefficient to be economically viable.

The French themselves have also been doing much of the buying. Poverty and economic decline forced many people to leave the French countryside for the cities in the 1960s and '70s. Now families, couples and professionals were returning to the villages, particularly those within 100 kilometres of major towns.

They were being drawn by the quieter lifestyle, the promise of the Internet — France Telecom had pledged to provide broadband services to 95 per cent of the French population by the end of 2005 — and emerging business opportunities in rural tourism. Some had bought properties which they used only on weekends or for summer vacations: owning a *résidences secondaire* in the countryside had become something of a cult among middle-class Parisians and other city dwellers. According to historian John Ardagh, who has written extensively on France, only the Scandinavians now beat the French in the world record for owning second homes. Ardagh says Parisians and Lyonnais will quite happily drive hundreds of kilometres each weekend, braving the legendary weekend traffic jams in the process, just to take advantage of their rural 'dream nest'.

It's hard to overestimate the attachment the French have to their countryside. I've found this relationship to be one of the most fascinating — and the most baffling — things about the culture. Half the surface area of France remains farmland, making it more rural in appearance than any other country in Western Europe. Yet only about 3 per cent of the population actually still work in farming — compared to 20 per cent four decades ago — despite the influx of a new class of 'neo-rurals' to French villages.

Like Australians, the majority of French live in cities and work in either industry or the service sector. But unlike Australians, the French retain a physical, even spiritual bond with the countryside — through their second homes, their family ties, and their cultural connections with regional areas that are the sources of their food and wine. Most French city dwellers I've met prefer to identify with the region from where their family hails — for example, Beaujolais, Perigord and Aveyron — even if it has been several generations since their ancestors actually worked the land.

Understanding what a potent cultural force *la France profonde*, or deepest rural France, remains for the population, French politicians have always been particularly attentive to preserving it, and the last two French presidents, François Mitterrand and Jacques Chirac, have been no exception.

To ensure easy access to the countryside, governments have built a superb road and transport system. You can get almost anywhere in France by train, sometimes even by TGV (*Train à Grande Vitesse*) which has a top speed of around 300 kilometres per hour.

Successive French governments, too, have steadfastly defended the system of European Union (EU) agricultural subsidies which has underpinned the European farming sector for decades — and delivered vast amounts of money to French farmers in particular. The so-called Common Agricultural Policy or CAP was set up after the Second World War, when food rationing was still a reality, to guarantee minimum levels of production so that Europeans would never have to go hungry again. The CAP was also established to ensure a fair standard of living for European farmers.

The CAP has certainly achieved those goals. Despite a decline in farming as an economic activity across Europe, the EU produces more food than it can consume — selling much of the excess cheaply to Third World markets, which in turn undermines local farmers who can't compete with heavily subsidised imports, say the CAP's legion of critics. European farmers — at least the large, highly mechanised farms producing food staples — have also done very well out of the CAP: it's been said that the annual income of an EU dairy cow exceeds that of half of the world's human population.

French farmers operating large wheat, beef and dairy concerns have done particularly well. According to *Le Monde*, France received 9.24 billion euros in 2004 under the CAP scheme, or nearly one quarter of the whole EU agricultural budget.

Not surprising then President Chirac's response to the British Government in mid–2005, when it called, once again, for more reform to the CAP system: 'I am not disposed to make even the smallest concession on the Common Agricultural Policy,' he said.

With food rationing still a vivid memory for France's aging leader, Chirac believes — as with the arts and with culture — that agriculture is just too important to be left to market forces.

In France, farmers are not just mere producers of food. They are also 'custodians' of a rural culture that has lasted for centuries and which needs to be protected and supported. At least that's how farmers see their role and justify the millions of euros they receive each year in subsidies, even if they distort the world market for farm products. The end of subsidies would not only put at risk the EU's food security in the future, it would also spell the end of the countryside as the French — and tourists — know it, they argued. Bucolic vistas of green pastures and rolling hills, tidy hedgerows and old stone farmhouses, fields of brilliant yellow sunflowers and rapeseed — the picture postcard rural France we have come to know and love — would disappear, or fall into ruin overtaken by scrub and thickets.

'Parisians will have to come out to the countryside with machetes if they take away our subsidies,' was how one Loire Valley dairy farmer put it to the *International Herald Tribune*'s Thomas Fuller in July 2005.

Fuller saw this as the nub to the whole farm subsidy debate. In the United States — and in Australia for that matter — environmentalists would probably be happy to see farmland revert to wilderness. In Europe, however, attitudes to the environment are different. For Europeans, nature is neat hedgerows and pastures on which cows graze — basically all the flora and fauna that has developed around centuries of European agriculture.

'It is not only wheat that emerges from the ploughed earth,' wrote the 19th century French poet Alphonse de Lamartine, 'it is an entire civilization.'

New York Times columnist Roger Cohen wrote in 2004 that to understand France, you had to look at its villages. It was there that you would find all the tensions that were moulding the character of contemporary France. 'As seen from a neo-rural French village, it is subtle and stubborn, restless and rooted, proud and prickly, at once open to the world, and cautious about the loss of truths contained in old stones and cellars,' he wrote.

Modern and medieval France came together for us in a little village called Salles-sous-Bois in La Drôme Provençale. I'd found a house there via the Internet — not to buy but to rent.

After months of searching, we decided to give up on the idea of buying a property in rural France. There were plenty of houses for sale. But the ones we liked were always too expensive. We'd talk about taking out a mortgage. But then we'd get cold feet. Our problem, in the end, was that we couldn't commit.

'What if we end up moving back to Australia?' Michael had said after one of his bad days at Interpol. 'How would we feel about paying a mortgage on a house we'd rarely get to live in? It would be a wrench to think about our little house sitting there empty.'

So instead we opted to rent a stone cottage in the country when we needed to get away from Lyon. Years before, a couple we knew in Paris had advised us against buying a house in France, and her words had stuck in my mind.

'Why bother with buying a place in the country? They are so much hassle to maintain and then there are all the taxes to pay,' Sylvie had said. 'If I were you, I'd just rent a house in places you'd like to visit. That way you'll get to see more of France, and not get stuck in one place.'

We did, though, get stuck on Salles-sous-Bois. We regularly returned to the house we'd found there when Michael could get the time away from work — to the delight of its Swiss owners who were having trouble keeping the house tenanted. With all these foreigners buying up property, there was something of a glut of houses to rent in the French countryside in 2005.

The Salles-sous-Bois place fitted our dream of the perfect rural house. It was a big old stone house with massive beamed ceilings that had a garden as well as a south-facing terrace which captured every ray of the morning Provençal sun. An ancient stone staircase connected the garden with the terrace, which commanded spectacular views over the surrounding lavender fields and the Tricastin mountains.

From the outside, the house had a rustic look, but inside it was all Swiss contemporary. The owners had equipped the house with all the necessary modern conveniences, including a modern central heating system, induction stove tops, satellite television and Internet access to ensure the transition from city to country would be as smooth as possible.

Salles-sous-Bois is typical of what the French village has become today. There were still some farmers tending the lavender fields and olive tree plantations, but most of the village's 300 or so residents were escapees from Paris or Lyon in search of a bit of rural charm, or Dutch and German holidaymakers in search of the sun. This influx of new money meant that most of the village houses had been lovingly restored, some quirkily, such as the house up the hill from us whose fence was decorated with a row of plaster gnomes. The small Romanesque church and the *lavoir*, the covered communal area in the centre of the village that was once used for washing clothes, had also been restored.

The *lavoir* was now only really an historical curiosity for visitors. Behind the ancient stone walls of their 300-year-old homes, Salles-sous-Bois residents had the latest washing machines, dryers, flat screen TVs and computers. (I know because I used to sneak peeks into people's windows on my daily walk around the village.)

Sometimes, as we flicked from the Italian news to Al-Jazeera on the 300-channel TV service, we'd forget we were in rural Drôme. The barking dogs and the clanging of the village church bells, however, would bring us back to reality. This still was the French countryside where some traditions will never die. Each morning, the church bells would ring out across the village, to the consternation of those of us who'd rather not be roused at 7 am on a Sunday. There was no point complaining to the mayor. The traditions of angelus, we knew, would always prevail over the desires of those searching for some rural tranquillity.

Plus we were only temporary visitors. We loved coming to Salles, we often fantasised about settling down there full time. The idea was particularly appealing to Michael. 'I love the peace and quiet here,' he said. 'I'd have no trouble filling my time. I could read, write books.'

I wasn't so sure. For me, village life was starting to feel pretty isolating. I had initially been attracted to the French countryside because it seemed so accessible and alive. French villages were still beautiful places to live, but I was finding they weren't exactly the best places to make new friends.

If I'd thought the residents in my building in Lyon were cold, the few people I'd come across in the small cobbled lanes of Salles-sous-Bois seemed positively arctic. Michael and I would take a walk around the village every morning, but the only greetings we received were from the village's many dogs. The reserved Germans were never ones to exchange pleasantries with strangers. But even the indigenous residents didn't seem to talk to each other much either.

I wondered whether this was because French villages no longer had a heart, a place where people could come together and get to know each other and have a few laughs. The village shop, once the centre of camaraderie and rural life, is now a thing of the past for a majority of French villages — most of them have closed down. Studies suggested that no shop could survive economically in a French village with fewer than 400 inhabitants, and there are a lot of those in France. The last remaining Salles-sous-Bois shop had closed decades ago. The village now has no butcher, no baker, no café — you have to drive 4 kilometres down the road to a larger village for those, where there is also a weekly market and a good restaurant.

But Salles-sous-Bois, strangely, did have a pizza night. Once a week, a cheery woman with big, fat hands from a nearby village would park her pizza van in the Salles-sous-Bois square. You could put in your order at 7 pm, and half an hour later, a gigantic pizza piled high with toppings made from local produce would emerge from her built-in wood-fired oven. We liked the pizza woman, not so much for her pizzas — they were a bit doughy — but for her conversation. She'd fill us in about the weather and the current state of play with her husband's dodgy heart. She also told us the story (several times) of how she once worked as a waitress in Lyon before she was married.

'I had a ball in Lyon when I was young,' she'd say, as she kneaded her dough. 'But I always found the people to be a little cold.'

For one night of the week, Mrs Reauville's pizza truck, which did the rounds of the small villages in the area with no restaurant to speak of, was filling the chasm left by the closure of the village shop. At least it was for us. It might seem strange that a Canadian and an Australian would come all the way to France just to huddle around the hearth of a French woman's pizza van, but there Michael and I were most Wednesday nights when we were in Salles-sous-Bois, ordering pizzas, exchanging views, feeling like we were members of a local community, if only vicariously.

We even eventually met a few of our village neighbours at the truck as we waited for our pizzas to cook. As it turned out, they weren't that cold at all. A few were even as chatty and warm as the glow from Mrs Reauville's oven.

CHAPTER 8

Le Malade Imaginaire

What do you mean by his looking well in the face? He looks very bad, and it is only impertinent folks who say that he is better; he never was so ill in his life.

From *Le Malade Imaginaire* (*The Hypochondriac*)
by Molière, 1673

IT MIGHT BE GETTING harder to find a café in your average French village, but one service that is always on hand in France is a doctor. France has a higher ratio of medical practitioners than most industrialised nations. According to the Organisation for Economic Cooperation and Development (OECD), France had 3.4 doctors per 1,000 people in 2005, while Australia, for example, had 2.5, meaning you never have to wait long to see a GP.

'I can fit you in this afternoon,' said the assistant in the doctor's office I phoned for an appointment one morning. 'Dr Tocco is away but he has a summer fill-in and she can see you.'

I normally avoided GPs like the plague, unlike the French who, as Molière pointed out in *Le Malade Imaginaire*, liked nothing more than a day out at the doctor's surgery to discuss their various illnesses, real or imagined. The French make more visits to the doctor than any other Europeans. They are also up there with the Americans in their taste for pill-popping.

'We're the world's leading consumers of medicine,' an exasperated Jean-François Mattei, France's health minister in 2003, declared as he launched reforms aimed at trimming the state's burgeoning health budget. 'Three billion boxes of pills a year. It's absolutely incredible.'

I hate talking pills and I certainly wouldn't normally seek medical advice for what seemed to me to be just a common cold. But I was about to take a 22-hour flight to Australia to see my family, so I decided to make sure my runny nose and a raspy cough didn't indicate the onset of something more serious. I also wanted something to clear my sinuses during the long flight.

Our regular GP was a Frenchman who had spent the first twenty years of his life in New York, which meant he spoke English like a Brooklyn taxi driver. I was quite happy to soldier on in my tortured French in most circumstances, but when it came to medical diagnoses I much preferred to converse in my mother tongue, in case I missed something important like I'd only six months to live. Dr Tocco, with his cross-cultural, easy-going style, was a favourite among Anglo-Saxons at Interpol. He didn't overload his patients with drugs like some other French doctors.

But Dr Tocco's summer replacement didn't speak English. No matter — after all, I was only making a quick visit to get some cold medicine. There was really not much to discuss. Nevertheless, the young female doctor took her time with me, listening to my chest and peering into my ears. One thing about France: you are rarely hurried out of the doctor's surgery. She then delivered her verdict: '*Oui*, Madame Bagwell, you have a cold.'

Next she sat down at her desk and scribbled a prescription for four different kinds of medicines — potions, pills and sprays for my ears, nose, throat and chest. I was surprised she didn't offer me a suppository as well. The French are massive consumers of suppositories, which they believe are much more *efficace* than popping a mere pill or drinking cough mixture — they even use them to treat sore throats.

The doctor probably knew that we Anglophones were a little less enthusiastic about rectal remedies than her compatriots. But she did listen intently when I mentioned, as a sort of parting comment, that there were other things that were disturbing my sleep besides my cold.

Le Malade Imaginaire 183

'My grandmother has taken a turn for the worse,' I explained. 'It's the main reason I'm going home for a visit.'

I'd expected the doctor to make some comment about how hard it must be to live so far away from one's family. Instead, she took back my prescription and added another item: three months' supply of a drug called Xanax that she said would help calm my nerves. Never having heard of it before, I thanked her, thinking to myself that the pills might help me get some sleep on the plane. That's something I'd rarely managed to pull off during long flights.

After visiting the chemist on the way home, I dumped my bag of pills and sprays on the kitchen table. 'Look what the doctor ordered,' I said to Michael.

'What's this?' he said, fingering the boxes of Xanax. 'This doesn't look like something for a cough.'

'It's not. It's for my nerves,' I said. 'I'm a bundle of them apparently.' I told Michael how I'd explained to the doctor that I was feeling worried about my grandmother.

'But it's normal to feel anxious about your grandmother's health. I'm worried about her too,' Michael said.

We then checked out Xanax on the Internet. One medical website described it as a tranquilliser used for the treatment of anxiety disorders and panic attacks, and that it could lead to addiction if used for a prolonged period of time — like, say, three months or more.

'Great. Just what you need to do in France: get hooked on sedatives,' Michael said. 'You don't need a tranquilliser. You just need to go down to Australia and see your family.'

I dropped the three months' supply of Xanax in the kitchen bin.

The French are justifiably proud of their health system, and not just because it readily dispenses legal drugs.

In 2000, the World Health Organization (WHO) rated it the best in the world based on a variety of measures including access and the resulting health of the nation. Australia spent about the same proportion of its GDP on health as the French, but only managed a ranking of 32nd.

The United States, which spends a lot more than both Australia and France, came a mere 37th in the WHO list.

French hospitals are modern, sparkling and well-equipped, and waiting lists for a bed are generally short. France reportedly has the highest number of transplant units, scanners and radiation machines per head of population in the world, although in some hospitals they often stand idle. This overcapacity means that French mothers, for example, can remain in hospital after the birth of their child for as long as five days when the average antenatal stay in Australia and the United States is now around two days. I remember checking into a Paris hospital for a minor surgical procedure the second time I lived there and being given my own room, a TV, telephone and the undivided attention of several nurses.

All this gold-standard care has produced results: life expectancy in France is two years longer than the average for the Western world. Women do especially well, living to a grand old age of eighty-four on average. It didn't surprise me that the British, fed up with their long waiting lists for hospital beds, were increasingly crossing the Channel to seek medical treatment in France.

The French public health insurance system works a lot like Australia's, except in France both employers and employees fund it via 'earmarked' taxes, which are dizzyingly high. In return, the system reimburses up to 70 per cent of the fee paid up-front by patients, as well as a portion of the cost of all their prescription drugs. Cheap, supplementary private insurance, which most French households have, and which are generally funded from payroll deductions, cover the remainder of a family's health costs including the cost of prescribed medicines. If you are too poor to afford insurance, or you are unemployed, health care is free. The cost of emergency hospital care, too, is covered by the state.

Health coverage therefore is pretty much universal. But it comes at a cost. In 2004, the health budget was in debt to the tune of 14 billion euros. The government warned that it would widen to a staggering 30 billion euros by 2010 if drastic surgery wasn't carried out.

The flagging French economy and diminishing tax receipts were the cause of much of the funding shortfall. But the rest was blamed on an ageing population, and the general culture in France of over-consumption of medical services.

Experts argued that the health system indulged this over-consumption by placing no limits on the number of times patients visited the doctor (or doctors) or the amount of prescriptions they received. If you didn't like one doctor's advice, you could always shop around for another — a habit the government called *nomadisme médical*. Until changes were made in mid-2004, you could also front up to a specialist's office without a referral. Devotees of alternative medicine or *médecine douce* — as the French are, in large numbers — are also accommodated in the health system, with acupuncture and homeopathy treatment reimbursed by social security. Doctors even make house calls.

'Has the French approach to illness brought about a health system that panders to *le malade imaginaire*, or has the efficiency and popularity of the system bred a whole nation of hypochondriacs?' asked Paris doctor Fabrice Hernard in an interview published in *The Guardian* in 2003.

'Either way, it's something we should be worrying about urgently.'

Hypochondria is not a new phenomenon in France. Molière parodied the French obsession with their health in his seventeenth century satire, *Le Malade Imaginaire*, which revolves around the physician-loving Argan and his quest to marry off his daughter Angelique to a doctor. Molière himself played the role of Argan in what would, ironically, be the final performance of his life. A few hours after he walked off the Paris stage on 17 February 1673, Molière collapsed and died. Despite his declining health, the playwright liked to mock the quackery of the medical profession, although he was not above a bit of self-parody.

'If I were a doctor,' Molière has Argan proclaiming in Act III, rather presciently as it turned out, 'I would tell the ailing Molière, "die, die!"'

The French though seem to me to have more sympathy with the potion-gulping Argan than the stoic Molière.

The shelves of chemist shops in France bulge with medicines and therapies for illnesses that you won't find elsewhere. One of these very French ailments is *la crise de foie* or liver crisis, the symptoms of which are nausea, headaches and abdominal cramps. In Australia, this would likely be diagnosed as a tummy upset or constipation, the result perhaps of an over-indulgence of rich food at dinnertime. In France, things are never that simple. The French media run articles every year explaining to their readers that there is no such thing as *crise de foie*, but still the chemist shops are stacked with homeopathic remedies and herbal teas promising to flush out the tormented French liver.

The French view is why be stoic when you can take some medicine? And doctors and the pharmaceutical industry are happy to oblige.

The French spent 21 billion euros on medicines in 2003, which translates into some 2.6 billion boxes of pills and tablets, or about forty boxes per head of population. These were mostly painkillers, sleeping tablets, blood-pressure pills, tranquillisers and antidepressants.

In France, there are nearly as many chemist shops as cafés. Indeed, the country has more chemist shops than any other European country and nearly double the number in Britain, which has a similar-sized population to France. In Lyon, I rarely had to walk more than a block before I ran into a flashing green neon cross that signifies a French pharmacy.

With the public health system funding the bulk of the cost of prescription medicines, the government has tried to wean the population off its drug habit. In 2003, the French health service announced it would no longer reimburse some 20 per cent of the 4,300 prescribed medicines on its list. Dropped were drugs which the health minister said had 'little or no recognisable medical effect', such as 'bronchial lubricants' for the lungs, 'hepatitic protectors' for the liver and 'veinotonics' for circulation.

Getting the French to give up their tranquillisers and sedatives has proved more difficult. According to a study by the national health insurance fund Caisses Primaires d'Assurance-Maladie, or CPAM, in 2004, mood-altering drugs, such as antidepressants, sedatives and the like, were the second most consumed groups of drugs after analgesics in France, and their consumption was rising every year.

A survey that same year by the French Drugs and Addictions Research Institute found that almost one in five of the adult French population, including a quarter of all women, took mood-altering drugs at some time in their lives. Almost one in ten said they'd taken a sleeping pill or an antidepressant in the previous week.

The question remained, however, whether the French really needed so much sedation. According to CPAM, only 4.7 per cent of the French population were actually diagnosed with depression in 2004. On the other hand, the high consumption of antidepressants among the French population didn't seem to be doing much good either: France's suicide rate remains the fourth highest among developed countries, and nearly double that of Australia's.

Doctors blame the liberal French health system for encouraging high levels of consumption of mood-altering drugs and medicines in general.

'I get a lot of people coming to me because they think they might be getting a cold,' another Paris doctor said. 'They are not happy unless they go away with a prescription for something. If I don't give them what they want, they will go to another doctor and another until they get one.'

Others like psychiatrist Edouard Zarifian, who wrote a landmark study for the French Government in 1995 about rising legal drug use in the community, blamed lazy GPs who dispensed 80 per cent of all sleeping pills and anti-anxiety drugs in France, and the heavy-handed methods used by pharmaceutical companies to promote their goods.

'French doctors have become merchants of happiness,' Professor Zarifian was quoted in *The Guardian* newspaper as saying in 2003.

'They are unable to resist the pressures of either the patients or the big drug companies. They are the ones who really need educating.'

I've often wondered: why is it that the French are so blue, or think they are, that they pop so many sedatives?

As an expatriate who'd chosen to live in France, I couldn't work it out. Eating and drinking well is a national passion. Beauty is everywhere, in French architecture, the countryside, just in the way people promenade down the boulevards. The French also work less and live longer than most everyone else. What more could they want?

Plus, on the surface, the French always seem to be so sure of themselves, at least when they converse with foreigners. They complain about the decline of France, but rarely contemplate leaving it. I once knew an Australian journalist living in Paris who had taken up with a French woman. Tony was forever trying to convince Jeanette to accompany him on a visit to Sydney, to see where he grew up. But she always declined. 'Why would I want to go Sydney — all that way — when I live in Paris?' she explained one day.

This pride has often been interpreted by outsiders as narcissism or arrogance. But then there are those that say that arrogant behaviour is often merely a cover for insecurity and self-doubt. If the number of pills they pop is any guide, the French have both in spades.

The French, though, are well aware of these foibles in their character. National mood swings are regular topics of discussion in the French media. Psychologists offer possible explanations as to why the French could be so depressed amidst so much abundance: the regular transport strikes, rising crime, outbreaks of terrorism, even pollution and traffic jams. Persistently high levels of unemployment have also increased anxiety levels. According to some studies, the unemployed consume between 57 and 80 per cent more antidepressants than the national average.

Even those in work are feeling the stress. A French union survey in 2003 found that 70 per cent of white-collar workers felt more, rather than less, stressed since the introduction of the 35-hour week in 1998. Employees felt under pressure to cram more work into fewer hours — and then they didn't know what to do with all their spare time, or so the survey concluded. Incidents of workers being harassed and bullied by their bosses were also on the rise.

'With labour regulations in some European countries making it very difficult to fire workers, some employers are creating intolerable conditions for employees in a bid to force them to quit,' said one report.

French authorities know that stress in the workplace is on the rise because of the increasing number of employees citing it as the reason for their sick leave. I can't say whether the French workplace is any more stressful than Australia's, but I can sure say that the French do seem to take a lot of sick leave — so much so that the government has decided to launch a crackdown on fraudulent 'sick leave' absenteeism as part of its overhaul of the ballooning health care budget.

In France, sick leave is state funded, which leaves the way open for both workers and companies to abuse the system. With a doctor's certificate in hand, there appears to be no limit to how much time you can take off as sick leave in any one year. Doctors authorise how much time an employee needs off work, and the employer accepts their word, comforted by the knowledge at least that it's the government, not them, footing the sick pay bill.

The upshot is that is seems rather easy for a French worker to take extended periods of leave due to illness, even for minor ailments. At Interpol it was not unusual for an employee to furnish a doctor's certificate authorising several weeks of leave for a cold or flu. 'Bad nerves' was also a common ailment warranting any number of days off from work.

Michael had plenty experience of this in his own department. A reluctant boss, he is not one to push his staff beyond the limits. Yet his easy-going management style hadn't curbed the number of doctors' certificates coming his way authorising stress leave. There always seemed to be somebody on his team calling in sick. One week, one of his website people, a Frenchman, called in without warning to explain he had a doctor's permission to take extended leave. I asked Michael what the problem was.

'I can't say for sure,' Michael explained, bewildered. 'But a few days ago he asked me whether he could go on a particularly expensive training course outside Interpol. I said "no" because there is no money in the department's kitty for it. I told him he'd have to wait until next year.

'Today he turned up with a doctor's certificate saying he needed to take four weeks' stress leave.'

In the past, the French might have just smoked more cigarettes or opened a bottle of red wine to get over their troubles at the end of a work day. But even they have begun to accept the message that these habits are bad for the health — consumption of both are declining in France. That left prescription drugs. Psychiatrists believe legal drug use is on the rise simply because such medicines are readily available — and because expectations have changed.

'Until the middle of last century, if I couldn't sleep or was anxious I considered it part of human nature and accepted it,' Dr Philippe Nuss, a leading French psychiatrist who has written books on depression, told *The Sunday Telegraph* in Britain in 2004.

'Today we regard our bodies and our health as objects which belong to us, and we find it impossible to accept the idea of not sleeping for example. Our attitude is that we have to be well, and our doctor is there to make us well, so we will ask for something.'

But such attitudes are not limited to France. They are common across the rich world, particularly in the United States, which has an equally heavy dependency on mood-altering drugs as the French.

Nevertheless, there are those that feel that the French character is more susceptible to depression than most. One theory is that the French have become spiritually lost. In a 2003 poll, 41 per cent described themselves as atheists while 26 per cent said they had no religion. In the same poll, however, some 85 per cent also called themselves Catholic, suggesting they still weren't sure what they believed in.

Another view is that the French are simply more melancholic.

'We are the country that three centuries ago gave the world such great thinkers as Voltaire ... people who observed their inner souls and talked about it,' explained Philippe Labro, a prominent French novelist who wrote a bestselling book about his own battle with depression, in an interview on American public radio in 2004.

'Maybe we have inherited this capacity to plunge ourselves into our inner problems and maybe — maybe — not be able to get out of it.'

Or as my friend Muriel put it: 'Sheryle, there is one thing you have got to understand about the French — they are never happy.'

If French workers are in a rut, then so it seems is the whole country. France in the twenty-first century appears to be a country racked with self-doubt and despair for the future. According to French historians like Theodore Zeldin, this is nothing unusual. 'Everybody repeats that France is in crisis ... but they seem to forget that this has always been true,' says Zeldin.

Yet, in the past few years, France seems to have been in a particularly nasty funk, aggravated by everything from an ailing economy and stubbornly high jobless levels to Paris' ignominious loss of the 2012 Olympic Games to archrival London in the summer of 2005.

Philosophy professor Chantal Delsol echoed the gloomy national mood when she asked in an article in *Le Figaro* the previous summer: 'How is it that such a brilliant nation has become a mediocre power, so out of steam, so indebted, so closed in its own prejudices? To be French today is to mourn what we no longer are.'

It was all so different when we'd passed through France on holiday in 1998. The French then were on a high. Unemployment had dipped for the first time in years. The national football team had won the soccer World Cup; its rugby team the northern hemisphere championship known as the Five Nations Cup.

Michael and I were in Paris the night France won the World Cup and the mood was joyous. Thousands had descended into the streets for a night-long party. Everybody was kissing each other and waving the French flag. The reverie swept away the perennial French pessimism: in the ensuing months, some 90 per cent described themselves in surveys as being happy or mostly so.

So rare was this outbreak of happiness that *Le Monde* ran an article about it on its front page: 'As if swept away by magic, the baleful shadows which have wandered the country for so long have gone,' declared the newspaper in September 1998.

'Forgotten, the French taste for self-flagellation. Buried, the propensity to denigrate systematically. Willing moaners, the French have stopped complaining. For once.'

Indeed, by the turn of the millennium, France didn't seem to be able to put a foot wrong. It was still burdened with among the highest taxes in Europe, but tentative economic reforms introduced by the Socialist Prime Minister at the time, Lionel Jospin, were starting to bear fruit — unemployment had dropped from nearly 13 per cent to 10 per cent, productivity was soaring and the economy was growing at a fair pace. And what's more, France's prized social benefits weren't being sacrificed in the process — on the contrary, they'd been bolstered with the arrival of the government-mandated 35-hour week starting on 1 January 2000.

France was even beginning to win rare praise from abroad. 'A New France is taking shape at the dawn of the 21st century,' *Time* magazine declared in a special report in June 2000. 'The trends are clear: privatisation, decentralisation, multiculturalism, a weaker state, lower taxes and a pared-down public sector, and a more collegial European identity in place of *l'exception française* and the universal sense of mission that have heretofore defined France's place in the world.'

But then the dot-com bubble burst and the global economic boom, which had underpinned France's growth, turned to bust, stalling the much-promised jobs growth as well. With unemployment remaining stubbornly high, French spirits soon returned to their normal gloomy state, fuelled by fears that France's governing elite, increasingly seen as out-of-touch, was taking the country too far down the dreaded liberalisation path, leaving it open to the worst excesses of globalisation (rising inequality, jobs lost to countries with cheaper labour, the increasing Americanisation of French culture).

The gloom was also being fuelled by a rising crime wave in France's major cities, which far-right politicians blamed on immigrants, in particular second and third generation North African youth who tended to live in rundown housing estates clustered around Paris, Lille, Lyon and Marseille where unemployment levels of 30–40 per cent were the norm. The growing realisation that France was failing to fully integrate the immigrants it brought over from its former colonies of Algeria and Morocco as guest workers after the Second World War was unsettling to the French — concerns which were ripe for exploitation by the likes of Jean-Marie Le Pen, head of the far-right National Front political movement.

In the lead up to the 2002 presidential elections, Le Pen, a perennial presidential candidate, promised to deport illegal immigrants, build 200,000 jail cells to control crime, pull France out of the European Union, and in his words, 'give France back to the French'.

'Massive immigration has only just begun. It is the biggest problem facing France, and probably the world. We risk being submerged,' declared the man who once famously dismissed the Holocaust as a 'detail of history'.

French polls and government politicians in turn dismissed Le Pen as a racial bigot and a spent force to boot — after all, he was preaching his anti-immigration rhetoric when Australia's Pauline Hanson was still in school uniform. But such predictions proved to be spectacularly wrong. In the first round of the 2002 presidential election, Le Pen managed to beat Lionel Jospin, the incumbent Prime Minister, to win an unprecedented place in the run-off against Jacques Chirac. Chirac went on to win the second round and the presidency comfortably, but the fact that France's leading racist and Holocaust denier had come within spitting distance of the

Élysée Palace sent France, and the rest of Europe, into a state of shock.

'It was not a first round, it was a cataclysm,' wrote *Libération*, a left-leaning newspaper. 'France is being pointed at ... as a source of shame among democracies.' What was now at stake, declared Chirac after the first round of voting, was 'the future of France, of even the idea we have of our country, of its great humanist traditions, of its universal calling'.

France's lofty view of itself as a caring and just nation took a further blow the following year when the health care system — the one that was supposed to be the best in the world — failed to protect thousands of elderly people during the heatwave of 2003.

Weeks and weeks of unrelenting heat saw unprepared hospitals overwhelmed with victims: some 15,000 people died in the first two weeks of August when temperatures repeatedly rose above 40 degrees. Most of the victims were elderly women over the age of seventy-five. More than half died from preventable causes such as heat stroke and dehydration in hospitals, in retirement homes or alone in their own apartments, apparently forgotten by their holidaying families who had fled the cities for the coast.

The calamity triggered a wave of national agonising over who was to blame and what kind of society France had become.

Doctors — who themselves had taken off for summer holidays — blamed the 35-hour week for the shortage of hospital staff. Then Prime Minister Jean-Pierre Raffarin sought to deflect criticism of his government's own inept and delayed handling of the crisis by pointing the finger at ill-prepared civil servants as well as neglectful French families. The Prime Minister condemned the growing 'indifference of fellow human beings, of relatives, of neighbours, to curtains that are drawn'.

This seemed a fair enough criticism to me at the time. Many French families appeared more concerned about the health of their panting pooches (who always travelled with them) than that of elderly relatives left behind in small, stifling apartments. But some locals I spoke to felt otherwise.

The French pay dearly for cradle-to-grave health and welfare benefits and they expect top service in return. The central role of the state in French affairs, however, seemed to provide citizens with a convenient excuse to relinquish personal responsibility for society's ills when it suited. I was taking some French classes at Alliance Française in Lyon in the summer of 2003, and remember my teacher being particularly angry at President Jacques Chirac who, like most of the country's politicians that summer, had been holidaying abroad when the crisis began.

'Being the president of France is like being the father of a big family,' Claudine said. 'And what father stays away from home while the family is in crisis?'

Who would ever think of the Australian Prime Minister in such terms?

*

Temperatures eventually cooled, but not tempers. As the summer from hell drew to a close, a rash of doom-and-gloom books hit the French bookstores in the Autumn of 2003 that reflected the view among a burgeoning band of angry French intellectuals that France was in terminal decline. Leading the pack was a 135-page bestseller by historian and economist Nicolas Baverez titled *La France qui Tombe* or *France is Falling Over*.

In his book, Baverez raged against the French political leadership, the bureaucracy and French unions for conspiring to defend a state-heavy and protectionist economic model that had long passed its use-by date. Instead of implementing much needed labour reforms and opening up the economy more fully to the world, successive leaders, in particular François Mitterrand and Jacques Chirac, had pandered to populist fears about immigration and globalisation, using them as scapegoats rather than confronting France's real problems courageously.

French leaders, said Baverez, believed 'the more things change, the more must be done to change nothing'. He even dismissed the Chirac Government's opposition to the American-led invasion of Iraq in 2003 as a futile exercise in grandstanding, even if its initial position was legitimate. Throwing around 'words of power without the means of power', said Baverez, masked France's diminishing role in a divided Europe and in a world shaped by the military and economic might of the United States. (Baverez followed up his bestseller with another book on the same theme in 2006 entitled *New World, Old France*.)

'France in 2004 is a nation in doubt,' wrote Jean de Belot, the editorial director of *Le Figaro*, to sum up a series of articles the newspaper had published during the summer which canvassed similar themes.

'The [French] economy is suffocating. Big industrial groups are investing elsewhere. The best-off are fleeing, the most talented are leaving. Even the middle classes are demoralised by the taxation levels.'

At the peak of this frenzy of self-criticism, then Prime Minister Jean-Pierre Raffarin tried to bring some perspective to the debate, saying it was time to stop parroting 'a frozen theory of decline' that was resurrected 'every 20 years by people who were supposedly great intellectuals'. Indeed, as far as I could tell, the French economy, for all its weaknesses domestically, was still a major force on the international stage. France has produced a rash of world-ranking companies such as AXA, Carrefour, Renault, L'Oréal and Michelin, to name just a few. As the rage continued throughout the autumn of 2004, Air France, for example, was gobbling up its rival, the Dutch airline KLM.

Yet it was all good fodder for the editorial pages of the British media, looking on from across the English Channel that summer. The British could be a gloomy and whingeing lot themselves, but nothing seemed to cheer them up more than news that the French might be more miserable than them. If the French had hoped for some sympathy, they certainly weren't going to get it from the English.

'As with the filthy rich, no one takes the French seriously when they say they're depressed,' wrote Philip Delves Broughton in London's *Daily Telegraph*.

'If they can't find happiness with all those wines, cheeses, naughty art films and a 35-hour week, then boo-hoo.'

Such jibes though served to shake free at least one French intellectual from the self-flagellating mood that had settled over the country during the summer of 2004.

'Those French who doubt they have an identity need only listen to those who hate them to convince themselves that it exists,' was the Cartesian retort of academic Roland Hureaux, writing in *Le Figaro* in July 2004.

At the end of his war memoirs, Charles de Gaulle wrote about his country as 'old France, overburdened by history, bruised by wars and revolutions, moving endlessly from grandeur to decline and back, but regenerated, century after century by the genius of renewal'.

France and the French were certainly in the mood for a dose of that Gaullist renewal by the summer of 2005.

Grumpy French voters had already demonstrated their deepening pessimism about what an enlarged Europe could do for them by brutally rejecting the European Union's new Constitution, another humiliating slap in the face for Jacques Chirac who had championed its cause.

Chirac's popularity figures were now in freefall, but the resounding French 'no' vote in May 2005 had also sent Europe into a spin. France, after all, was a founding member of the European Union. Yet now its citizens wanted to put the brakes on the whole European unity project, fearful that it was turning into a Trojan horse for dreaded Anglo-Saxon, free market economic reforms.

To Anglo-Saxon commentators, the French, and other champions of the European social model, such as the Germans, were beginning to look like a bunch of backward-looking whingers afraid to face the challenges of a globalised future.

'Voters in "old Europe" — France, Germany, the Netherlands and Italy — seem to be saying to their leaders: Stop the world we want to get off,' wrote Thomas Friedman in *The New York Times* in 2005.

But all was not lost. There was still one thing that could help the French forget their troubles and lift morale. The 'bread and circuses' option: the Olympic Games.

'We are a little depressed in France. We need the Games,' said the French film-maker Luc Besson, just days before the International Olympic Committee (IOC) was due to announce on 6 July whether Paris had won its bid to stage the 2012 Summer Games.

Paris thought it had the Games in the bag. Having twice failed in previous bids, it now believed its time had come. It had done everything it could to dazzle the IOC with its efficiency and commitment, even getting Besson himself to direct the film that the IOC members would see during Paris's final presentation.

Hundreds of people gathered in the square in front of the Paris town hall on a drizzly July afternoon in 2005 to hear the IOC's verdict, which most believed was a foregone conclusion. *Le Figaro* was so certain of a French victory that 15 minutes before the announcement the main headline on its website read: 'Paris will organise the 2012 Olympic Games'.

But then the word 'London' rather than 'Paris' rang forth from the town hall loudspeakers, and a collective '*merde*' was heard rising from the crowd. The brass band on the stage played the theme song from a James Bond film then walked off sullenly.

'Oh great,' said Rachael, Michael's energetic British press officer, who was watching the announcement with Michael in his office. 'All of France will probably call in sick tomorrow.'

Clearly the authorities feared the same. The following morning I turned on French state radio to hear a psychologist giving advice as to how the French could cope with the news that they had lost the Games to London. Other commentators talked about how the IOC decision was really a referendum on which city was the best in the world, and Paris had to face the fact that London was now where the action was, both economically and spiritually.

The self-flagellation continued until news of the deadly suicide attacks in the London underground transport system that same morning began to filter in. When the gravity of those attacks became clear, the whining and accusations stopped.

'We are all Londoners now,' said Paris mayor, Bertrand Delanoë, who only hours before had accused the London 2012 Olympic bid team of cheating.

Indeed, the terrorist bombings on the London Tube and a bus did seem to shake the French from their torpor for a time. Stoicism replaced pessimism as the French realised that things, well, could be worse.

That theme was picked up the following week by *Le Parisien*, the city's biggest selling newspaper. In an attempt to put a *sourire* (smile) back on peoples' faces, the newspaper ran a three-part series that listed all the things the French should feel cheerful about, like its health service, its high-speed train the TGV, provincial cities like Lyon which were attracting more and more tourists, and the fact that the French had one of the highest life expectancies in the world.

'While the French are often arrogant, they also like big depressions and running themselves down ...' the paper declared.

'[But] there are reasons to hope, more numerous than one could imagine.'

That week, in fact, I did notice more people smiling and wishing me a friendly *bonjour* on the street than normal.

Or maybe the French were back on their medication.

CHAPTER 9

Cultural Exception

France makes me sick ... You may have spoken in jest about New York as the capital of culture, but in 25 years it will be just as London is now. Culture follows money.

F. Scott Fitzgerald writing from Paris to his friend
the critic Edmund Wilson, 1921

LYON HAS AROUND THIRTY museums, but my favourite is the beautiful seventeenth century fine arts museum in Place des Terreaux in the centre of town.

A former Benedictine convent, it was seized during the French Revolution and converted into a museum in the early 1800s. Less daunting in size and scope than the labyrinthine Louvre in Paris, Lyon's Musée des Beaux Arts nevertheless features all the stars of European painting down the centuries from Tintoretto to Picasso. So rich is its collection that locals have dubbed it 'the little Louvre'.

I have visited the museum several times. Its quiet, cloistered gardens are a lovely place to escape the heat of a Lyon summer. Its exhibition rooms are never crowded with hordes of camera-flashing tourists as in the Louvre and other grand museums of Paris. I have never had to elbow my way in to see iconic French paintings by the likes of Delacroix, Monet, Degas, Renoir and Matisse whose works form the core of the Lyon gallery's collection. I've had the time and space to gaze and to ponder to my heart's content.

It was strolling through the airy rooms of Lyon's fine arts museum that I came to fully appreciate how France had remained the undisputed world capital of art for a century or more.

It was here, too, that I came to understand why France isn't thought of in those terms anymore.

In the last rooms on the top floor of the gallery, which contains art from the late twentieth century, the lack of French paintings is conspicuous. It all seemed to fizzle out for the French and visual art after the Second World War. On the walls are few examples of work painted by French artists after that time — or at least work by painters whose names you'd instantly recognise. There is a Raoul Dufy picture painted in 1952 — *Le Cargo Noir* — but that is about it. The most striking modern art of recent times on show are two works by the Irish painter Francis Bacon painted in the 1980s.

Where were the French? It seemed few French painters had stepped up to take the place of the giants of modern art of the early twentieth century, such as Dufy, Chagall, Rouault and Leger, certainly not by the evidence on the walls of the Lyon art gallery. This might not have seemed so strange if it were a country other than France. Yet this was a nation whose image was inextricably intertwined with art and culture, stretching as far back as the seventeenth century when the French monarchy proclaimed itself 'Protector of the Arts' and encouraged artists and writers with state patronage.

This glorification of the arts and all things cultural had lured the finest artists and writers in the world. James Joyce, Ernest Hemingway and F. Scott Fitzgerald had all made France their adopted home for a time. So, too, had Picasso, Van Gogh, Miro, Modigliani and Max Ernst, who'd set up their easels in studios in Montmartre and Montparnasse. These painters, along with home-grown ones such as Monet and Gauguin, launched some of the major art movements of our times, including Impressionism, Cubism and Fauvism.

As Gene Kelly said in the film *An American in Paris*: 'Brother, if you can't paint in Paris, you'd better give up and marry the boss's daughter.'

Yet it all went awry after the Second World War. France was politically and financially demoralised. Those who could emigrated to places like New York, which was already developing a vibrant art scene. Even the French avant-garde artist Marcel Duchamp decamped to New York, complaining that Paris had lost its 'sense of gaiety'.

Paris though refused to acknowledge the 'radical changes' going on around it, opting instead to treat the competition from abroad with 'insouciance and disdain', according to art historian Serge Guilbaut in his book *How Did New York Steal the Idea of Modern Art?*.

Guilbaut said France was only shaken from its complacency in the mid–1960s when the country's art elite began noticing that the major French art collectors were buying up paintings in New York rather than Paris. The *coup de grâce* to French pride came in 1964 when the American artist Robert Rauschenberg won the Grand Prize at the Venice Biennale, a distinction that had almost always been previously reserved for painters from the École de Paris.

'Sleeping Beauty doesn't need Prince Charming to wake her up, but a solid kick in the butt,' wrote French arts writer Pierre Cabanne in Paris in 1967.

The decline nevertheless continued. Up and coming French artists in the 1960s were not encouraged either by collectors or the cultural establishment in France. It looked as though a lot was going on in France at the time: the modern art gallery, Centre Georges Pompidou, with its pop-art façade was opened in Paris in 1977; a new fund to buy contemporary art was set up in 1981; and the Socialist Government of François Mitterrand doubled the Ministry of Culture's share of the national budget during the 1980s. But according to *Le Monde*, these initiatives only served to mask what it described as the 'obliteration' of living French artists from the international art market.

By the turn of the new century, French artists occupied only fourth place in the world, in terms of their presence in the permanent collections of the big international cultural institutions, and in their sales at art auctions, according to a 2001 report commissioned by the French Ministry of Foreign Affairs. Whereas a century before they would have been at the very top, French artists now trailed well behind their counterparts in the United States, Germany and Britain.

'The more I was doing my research, the more I got the sense of a progressive decline, which, in the long run, if nothing is done, will lead to the disappearance of French art from the international stage,' the author of the report, sociologist Alain Quemin, told *Le Monde*.

With the Zeitgeist, went the artists. Tourists have replaced the likes of Picasso and Miro in the bars and cafés of Montmartre. 'Barely a world-class painter lives here now,' one Paris-based journalist noted recently.

No longer does the world look to Paris for exciting new art.

'Hardly anybody journeys to Paris anymore specifically to see cutting-edge art,' *Newsweek* magazine declared in 2002.

'Indeed, to the art world, Paris over the decades has degenerated into a theme park for middle-class masterpiece-browsers.'

'The power of France is the power of culture,' the Japanese architect Tadao Ando said in 2001 after he was chosen by French billionaire François Pinault to build a gleaming new museum on an island in the Seine that would eventually house the businessman's extensive collection of contemporary art. The plan was to create a museum that would rival the Tate Modern in London and the Guggenheim in Bilbao. What Ando didn't count on, however, was that other powerful force in France — bureaucracy.

'All my efforts were met with imprecise responses and vague promises,' Pinault said in May 2005, after his shock announcement that he was abandoning his grand project because of endless government red tape. Instead, he would house his collection in a palazzo he'd bought on Venice's Grand Canal, where the authorities were apparently more welcoming. Italy's gain would be France's loss.

Yet it wasn't only in the sphere of modern art where France's cultural credentials were being tested.

'Where are the major new [French] playwrights, novelists, poets or artists?' asked historian John Ardagh in his book *France in the New Century*.

France isn't the only rich country where artistic standards and cultural output have dropped. Yet Ardagh felt that France's 'cultural staleness' was more pervasive. Whether it was in philosophy, literature or the classical arts, France is no longer 'the unrivalled powerhouse of new ideas, new expression', he wrote.

'Even the cinema, though still Europe's most active, is no longer in the golden age of the *nouvelle vague*. And although television has been freed from state control, this has led it into dull commercialism, rather than down fertile creative paths as in Britain.'

You only have to watch French television to understand how far French cultural standards have slipped.

When I first arrived in Lyon, I spent a lot of time in front of the box. We still had to find a place to live, so we stayed in an apartment-hotel located near the Halle de Lyon, the city's famed covered market for the first month. While Michael was at Interpol during the day, I would flick on the small portable TV set in our room to pass the time, and because I was told it would help improve my French.

Television was also supposedly an open window to a country's popular culture, and I was keen to find out what sort of light entertainment the French enjoy. I didn't quite know what to expect from French TV (during the previous times I'd lived in France, I'd never owned a television). But I never expected to find so many game shows, reality TV programs and re-runs of (dubbed)

American cop shows long past their use-by date, such as 'Colombo' and 'NYPD Blue'.

I guess I thought there might be more period dramas, documentaries and current affairs programs — serious stuff that reflected the strong intellectual vein that was supposed to run through French society. A French version of the BBC really.

Instead, on the main commercial channel TF1, I watched shows such as '*Combien ça coûte?*' ('How much does it cost?'), '*Qui veut gagner des millions?*' ('Who wants to be a millionaire?') and '*Loft Story*' (as 'Big Brother' was renamed in France) — all the same sorts of TV shows that you'll find almost anywhere in the world. Still, watching TV was a great way to learn French.

I cheered when a young, spotty lad named Grégory became the first *garcon* in France's short reality TV history to win the final of 'Star Academy 4', France's monumentally popular take on the Pop Idol franchise. Grégory took home more than one million euros in prize money as well as a recording contract. But first, we had to sit through a painful rendition of 'New York, New York', sung in English by the host and his celebrity guests.

I was also glued to the *télé-réalité* hit of 2004 — '*La Ferme Célébrités*' — which marooned a bunch of C-list French celebrities on a Provençal farm with neither running water nor electricity. The guests included a Caribbean-born transvestite who tottered around the mud in stiletto heels and a choreographer who donned rubber gloves to herd sheep.

When the show was first broadcast, it broke French records for reality TV, pulling in 8.5 million viewers or 46 per cent of the audience. *The Economist* magazine, looking across the Channel from Britain, put the show's extraordinary success down to the fact that it depicted city folk struggling to come to terms with rural life.

'Farming has long had a peculiar grip on the French imagination, blending nostalgia with genuine traditions,' *The Economist* concluded. 'Today, though, only 3.5 per cent of the population is engaged in agriculture ... [the guests'] metropolitan disconnect from rural life strikes a chord with viewers.'

My conclusions after having watched this stuff, however, are that the French, like the rest of the world, just love to watch trashy TV. Abroad, they might be seen as haughty, sophisticated and connoisseurs of fine art and wine. But at home they love nothing more than to put aside their Derrida and Foucault in favour of watching a bunch of celebrities trying to deliver a kid goat, or tax inspectors staking out the houses of the filthy rich.

Serious issues do get a run on French TV. Most nights you can find a talk show, which might bring together politicians, writers, actors and even members of the studio audience to discuss pressing issues of the day, such as why the French love junk TV.

A short attention span and minimal French vocabulary is all you need for the French quiz show. But you need the endurance of a desert rat for the talk show.

This is TV at its most lugubrious: it isn't the 30-minute, once-over-easy kind of debate with lots of graphics that you get these days on Anglo-Saxon TV. In France, the discussion could go on for hours, reflecting the French love of debate. Once, I turned on a talk show on health care reform at around 7.30 pm, switched it off to cook and eat dinner, and then came back to the telly to find the discussion still going strong at 11 pm.

The French seem very nonchalant about their lack of new world-beating artists — when you've already produced the likes of Monet, Gauguin, Renoir and the rest, I suppose you can afford to take a break. But one thing they were hot under the collar about in 2004 was the apparent disappearance of the French intellectual from public life.

'Why don't intellectuals of the left and right occupy a more prominent place in the public arena?' asked an article in *Le Figaro*'s literary supplement in 2004. This was an important question to ask in France, for nowhere in Europe had the so-called 'engaged intellectual' been more prominent or accepted as a political player.

It all began with writer Emile Zola and his inflammatory pamphlet *J'Accuse*. Written in 1898, Zola denounced an army conspiracy against a Jewish captain named Alfred Dreyfus who had been sent to the infamous Devil's Island in French Guyana for crimes he didn't commit.

Zola's denunciation of anti-Semitism set an example that encouraged French intellectuals of all political and religious persuasions to take a stand and push a cause. They wrote seminal books, attacked the political elite and held court in smoky Left Bank cafés. In the years immediately following the Second World War, they included such towering figures as André Malraux, Raymond Aron, Jean-Paul Sartre, and his existentialist comrade and author of *The Second Sex*, Simone de Beauvoir.

But the end of the Cold War snuffed out the ideological warfare that had so sustained the intellectual debate in France. Newspapers such as *Le Monde* and *Libération* that used to serve as vehicles for the engaged intellectual were now losing circulation. French university campuses can still be hotbeds of left-wing protest — as recently as March 2006, students staged massive sit-ins and blockades in protest over proposed government labour laws aimed at reducing youth unemployment. But that was at the public universities — it was all quiet on the campuses of the highly selective, elite colleges and grand schools that turn out well-trained graduates recruited by the big banks and globalising French corporations where profit-generating skills rather than old-fashioned intellectualism is more highly prized.

The government, too, no longer saw the need to court intellectuals, at least as fervently as it used to. Indeed, the two groups seemed to be at loggerheads for most of the time. Intellectuals accused the centre-right government of Jacques Chirac of waging 'war' on them by cutting scientific and other research budgets, and launching reforms to the generous system of state benefits that went to artists and performers.

'All the sectors of learning, research, thinking, all the producers of knowledge and public debate, are today the target of a massive attack by an anti-intellectual government,' the editors of the French music and culture magazine, *Les Inrockuptibles*, declared in February 2004.

The magazine asked readers to sign an on-line petition against this 'war on intelligence' and within a few months it had collected 80,000 signatures. Those who'd signed included the deconstructionist philosopher Jacques Derrida, the hero of the May 1968 student and worker revolt Daniel Cohn-Bendit and the former Socialist Prime Minister Michel Rocard. The mainstream French media then took up the cause, publicising the petition through numerous articles and supportive opinion pieces.

All of this activity and comment however just proved to me that the intellectual hadn't gone missing in France. In fact, it appeared they had simply moved on to television. Only in France could I turn on the TV to find a former politician describe himself as a philosopher — as the ex-education minister Luc Ferry did on a program I was watching where he had been asked to review a crop of new books. If Paul Keating said he'd left politics to become a philosopher, I suspect he'd be laughed out of Australia, labelled a Chardonnay Socialist or a perfumed pointy-head.

In France, cultural and intellectual life might be on the decline, but it still seems to be more active than in Australia or the United States, where intellectuals tend to be mocked or just ignored. The French still prefer to live in a world of ideas, even if those ideas no longer change the world.

'There's a story we tell in Britain,' a Paris-based correspondent for a London newspaper once told a French magazine. 'Two politicians, one French, the other English, try to resolve a problem. The Briton proposes a solution and the Frenchman responds: "Ok, that might work in practice, but will it work in theory?"'

These days, France still treats its remaining intellectuals as national treasures. It even invented the genre of the celebrity intellectual. Chief exponent was the fabulously rich and camera-friendly thinker Bernard-Henry Levy, who is probably best known to Anglos for his controversial book about the murder of *Wall Street Journal* reporter Daniel Pearl by Islamic extremists in Pakistan in 2002.

With his trademark floppy dark hair and open-neck white shirt, BHL, as he is simply known here, has been the darling of television chat shows for the past three decades.

I once tried to contact Levy at his grand apartment on the Left Bank of Paris that he shared with his beautiful actress wife — he also owns a palace in Marrakech — but he didn't return my calls.

Pity. One of the questions I had wanted to ask him was why he thought the French watched so much junk TV.

I was walking home one sunny June afternoon through Lyon's main thoroughfare when I noticed that roving bands of musicians had taken over the streets. I'd already spent a few minutes listening to a police band playing American show tunes to a crowd of shoppers gathered outside the main department store, but as I headed towards my apartment I could hear music emanating from all quarters. At the next corner was a group of North African rappers, warming up their rhyming French slang, and as I got closer to home, three teenagers were setting up a drum-kit and amplifiers for their guitars on the pedestrian mall.

'What's going on?' I asked one of the teenagers, thinking that the local council must have eased restrictions on busking. 'It's the *fête de la musique* of course,' he replied, looking at me as if I had just landed from Mars.

Of course, the Festival of Music. On 21 June each year, amateur and professional musicians alike take to the streets in nearly every village and town across France to celebrate music of all kinds and just generally have a good time. The street festival is a particularly French pastime: thousands are held across France every year, usually in the summer months, to celebrate some aspect or another of the country's rich artistic and cultural heritage. There are festivals of poetry, gardens, food, the French language and even one celebrating the Internet. Some are internationally renowned, for example, the theatre festival in Avignon, founded by the actor and director Jean Vilar in 1947, and the film festival at Cannes each May. But the majority, such as the Festival of Music, are popular events aimed at the ordinary French person in the street, and are generally free. All are heavily subsidised by local, regional and national government.

The sheer number of festivals and their diversity is another reason why I have trouble buying the argument that French culture is dead or dying. There might be fewer well-known individual artists burrowing away in their ateliers producing great works to international acclaim. But there is certainly a lot happening at the community level among groups of actors, dancers, musicians, writers and the like who see their role primarily as bringing the arts to the general public.

These local festivals are also a great place to catch up with some leading foreign names. In a two-week period in July 2005, for example, Lyon residents had the opportunity to see Indian instrumentalist Ravi Shankar, Canadian jazz pianist Oscar Peterson, American rhythm and blues man B.B. King and Cuban singer Ibrahim Ferrer of *Buena Vista Social Club* fame. The performers were spread out between two separate music festivals running at the same time in and near Lyon. And this was in a city with a population about one-sixth the size of Sydney's. Nevertheless, their shows were all sell-outs. Foreign performers, particularly American jazz musicians, love to play in France not only because of the number of festivals at their disposal, but because of their appreciative audiences.

And for that they could thank the support of the French state, without which festivals and cultural activities would likely not exist. The central role of the state in arts probably explains why private arts sponsorship has never really taken off in France.

Historians claim it all began in the seventeenth century with King Louis XIV, the builder of the glittering Palace of Versailles and the man credited with inventing the whole idea of high fashion, *haute cuisine* and luxury goods — sectors that have been associated with France ever since. The Sun King's ambition was to make France the global leader in all things stylish, and he dispensed much state aid to make that happen.

State patronage of the arts ebbed and flowed after that — there was a lot to distract the state in the ensuing years in the form of civil wars and revolutions. It was put firmly back on the agenda in the 1950s when the French leader at the time, Charles de Gaulle, appointed the novelist André Malraux to the post of arts minister. Malraux pledged to make France 'the world's foremost cultural nation' and set about opening new museums and scrubbing clean the façades of the old ones. He also launched a network of arts centres or *maisons de la culture* in the provinces that were designed, as John Ardagh wrote, 'to destroy the notion of culture as a bourgeois preserve and draw a new social class into theatres and galleries'.

This decentralisation away from Paris continued under the presidency of François Mitterrand, himself a highly cultured man who saw the arts as inextricably linked to national and global prestige. Despite the recession, Mitterrand nearly doubled the Ministry of Culture's share of the national budget, an amount unmatched in modern times. 'The Socialist enterprise,' Mitterrand asserted, 'is first of all a cultural project.'

His arts minister was the flamboyant Jack Lang, who had more of a common touch than Malraux. Despite his Bohemian good looks and designer suits, Lang maintained an egalitarian attitude to the arts: he would as likely fund a school for circus performers as an opera company. It was Lang who encouraged arts festivals in the regions and launched the yearly Festival of Music. For his efforts, he became the most high-profile and popular minister during the Mitterrand era. He still pops up everywhere in France. Some commentators have said he might even run for the presidency in 2007.

Mitterrand, on the other hand, was determined to leave his mark on history in a grander, more concrete way.

He launched an unprecedented building spree in the 1980s and over the ensuing decade presided over a redrawing of the Paris cityscape that rivalled that of the previous century's Baron Haussmann, who had widened medieval streets into grand boulevards. The most radical of Mitterrand's grand projects was the construction of a 21-metre-high glass pyramid in the central courtyard of the Palais du Louvre, probably the world's most famous museum. The idea was to provide an eye-catching entrance to the Louvre's new grand reception area under the courtyard, which in turn would give visitors an easier and more central access to the Louvre's dizzying maze of galleries. At the time, it outraged Parisians despite the fact that they rarely visited the Louvre themselves — that was for tourists. Many walked around Paris at the time wearing buttons that said 'Why the Pyramid?'.

'You rub your eyes, you think you're dreaming,' wrote one *Le Monde* commentator at the time. 'It seems that you've gone back to the era of castles for sale and Hollywood copies of the temple of Solomon, of Alexander, of Cleopatra ... It doesn't seem justified to treat the courtyard of the Louvre like a Disneyland annex or a rebirth of the defunct Luna Park.' *Le Figaro* published a survey showing that 90 per cent of Parisians opposed the pyramid.

You still hear Parisians talking about how much they hate the pyramid. But it has since proved to be a big hit with tourists who use it in their thousands every day.

Other Mitterrand projects though have yet to be redeemed. There was a general consensus among architectural critics and opera-goers alike that the Opéra Bastille, which Mitterrand commissioned for the 200-year anniversary of Bastille Day in July 1989, was ugly and soulless and hardly a worthy replacement for the gleaming neo-Baroque style Paris Opéra, built a century before. Equally derided was the collection of windswept, high-rise towers that made up the last major monument of the Mitterrand era, the controversial Bibliotheque Nationale or the François Mitterrand library. 'French folly' was one of the milder epithets given to the building when it was opened in 1996. Almost four hundred prominent French and foreign personalities signed a petition protesting that the architecture was 'monumentally bad'.

Yet at least these grand, contemporary projects signified to the world that Paris was still a city where architecture mattered, just like Baron Haussmann's sweeping modernisation of the Paris cityscape did in the 1860s. The results might not always be good, but as *The New York Times* architecture critic, Nicolai Ouroussoff, wrote in 2005, Mitterrand nevertheless understood 'that no great city can remain creatively vital by wallowing in the past'.

With Hollywood the dominant force in the global film industry, it is easy to forget that the pioneers of cinematography in the late 1800s were the French.

In fact, it was only a short métro ride from our Lyon apartment to the extraordinary Art Deco mansion that was the former home of the Lumière brothers, the inventors of the cinematographic projector. They were also the fellows who came up with the idea of putting sprocket holes in film so it could run through a camera and projector.

The mansion was now a museum and featured a magnificent archive of photos and films created by Auguste and Louis Lumière, including a copy of the film considered to be the first real moving picture, scenes of workers leaving the Lumière family's film factory in Lyon in 1895.

Prolific inventors, the Lumière brothers, however, weren't much in the way of entrepreneurs. They declined to on-sell their invention, stating that 'the cinema is an invention without any future'. Their part, thus, in the history of film was exceedingly brief. So too was Lyon's role as the film capital of the world.

That lost opportunity might help explain France's obsession with Hollywood competition, and its continuing battle to defend and protect the French film industry from what they see as the creeping incursion of the English language and American culture.

To the continuing consternation of the Americans, France pours public money into its cinema in amounts that other national film industries can only dream about. In 2003, the state subsidised French film to the tune of around 475 million euros, raised from a range of taxes on the entertainment industry including an 11 per cent levy on movie tickets. As American films tend to account for the majority of French box office takings, this means that Hollywood is indirectly subsidising the French film industry. Indeed, the state often pays French producers advances on box office earnings so they don't have to wait for profits (if any) before making their next movie.

Aside from attacking the economics of the subsidies handed out by the French Government, free-marketers complain that they also encourage banality and elitism in film-making, rather than creativity and good storytelling.

'It's my observation that countries like France and Canada, which have been largely dependent on [government subsidies], have created a non-inclusive sort of cinema,' the respected American film commentator Peter Bart said in 2000.

'Their movies do not travel. Other countries have lost interest in their product. The most effective results occur when film-makers draw more and more of their financing from private sources as well.'

Yet there is little doubt among film critics that when subsidies were first introduced by André Malraux in the 1950s, they did help nurture a new generation of groundbreaking French film-makers whose work did travel well — such as films by François Truffaut, Alain Resnais and Jean-Luc Godard. This *nouvelle vague* of French film-making has long since waned. But at least the French film industry has managed to survive the onslaught of the Hollywood blockbuster, certainly better than its counterparts in Europe.

In 2004, France churned out 203 feature films — much more than in any other European country. There were several clunkers among them, perhaps enough to satisfy those critics who argued that the French subsidised films they didn't watch themselves. Only about 36 per cent of the 193 million cinema tickets sold in France in 2004 were for French films — although in previous years that percentage has been as high as 50 per cent.

Nevertheless, some of the longest queues outside Lyon cinema houses in 2004 were for domestically made productions. The top box office earner that year was Christophe Barratier's *The Chorus*, a low-budget feature about an inspirational music teacher at a boarding school for delinquent kids in 1949 France. It managed to outperform *Shrek 2* and other big-budget film imports, a cinematic feat in any language.

The French point to such success stories as proof that protecting and subsidising the arts pays dividends, and not only because it keeps Hollywood at bay. It means that from time to time cinemagoers have to listen to a film spoken in French even if fewer and fewer foreigners are learning the language. Indeed, keeping the French language alive remains a primary goal of state patronage of the arts.

Yet films aren't the only beneficiaries of state aid. It also subsidises the production of televised versions of French novels, high-brow drama which sits incongruously beside the quiz and reality programs on French TV. Since 1996, the state has also demanded that at least 40 per cent of popular music played on French radio be in the French language.

Although the Americans complain that quotas and subsidies for the arts constitute an unfair trade practice, the measures have wide public support in France. Not even the current president, Jacques Chirac, who is not considered to be a major champion of culture himself — his favourite performer is said to be John Wayne — has dared to suggest that the system be dismantled. In 2004, the United Nations described France's 'cultural exception' policies as a 'successful example of public support for cultural industries'. So far, even the World Trade Organization has accepted the French defence that culture is too important to be left to market forces, ensuring that arts and entertainment products remain excluded from international trade negotiations.

Yet the culture wars between the United States and France continue to rage. Emblematic was the very Gallic debate over the relative 'Frenchness' of that other cinematic blockbuster of 2004, Jean-Pierre Jenet's film *A Very Long Engagement*. In 2001 Jenet had a worldwide hit with his film *Amelie* and cast the elfin star of that movie, Audrey Tautou, in this, his follow-up film. A World War I love story, *A Very Long Engagement* had a budget of 45.8 million euros, making it the third most expensive film in the history of French cinema at that time.

But was it French enough to deserve government subsidies? It would be hard to find a more quintessentially French film: set in France, *A Very Long Engagement* was filmed in France, spoken in French and employed hundreds of French actors and technicians. But two associations of independent French film producers claimed it wasn't wholly French because the film's production company was 34 per cent owned by Warner France, a subsidiary of the Hollywood giant. They took their complaint to court.

'The company behind this film is a Trojan horse for Hollywood,' complained Marc-Olivier Sebbag of the independent producers' union, Le Syndicat des Producteurs Indépendants (SPI). 'To be blunt, French subsidies should not be funding US majors.'

In the end, the anti-Hollywood activists won the day, and government support was withdrawn. It was the second time Jenet had felt the wrath of France's cultural elites: previously, *Amelie* had been attacked for presenting what they claimed was an antiseptic view of life in France to global audiences.

No doubt Jenet cried all the way to the bank. But over in the US, American conservatives like to frame such attacks on Hollywood as part of a broader plot, orchestrated by the hated Jacques Chirac and his neo-Gaullists cronies, to curb the global influence of the United States.

Indeed, when it comes to the arts and entertainment, the protectionist measures have ensured that at least within

France's own borders, the American dominance of popular culture isn't entirely pervasive. You can see French films at the cinema if you chose to, watch French-made drama (and game shows) on TV and listen to French music on the radio. Not all of it is good and a lot of it is derivative. But at least it is made in France — like French rap and hip-hop music. This style of music, pioneered by ethnic singers mostly of North African origin who adapted the American genre and called it their own, is big business in France — helped in part by French content rules on radio which gave stars like MC Solaar access to a wider audience. As a result, France now has the biggest hip-hop market outside of America.

Yet French content rules are really only a leaky finger in the dyke against English-language popular music that has, and continues to, flood over France. Despite the protectionist measures, much of the music played on French radio is still very much Anglo-Saxon in origin. Even the new wave of French rock bands say they prefer to record in English. As F. Scott Fitzgerald said, culture always follows the money.

This fact of life still outrages the French artistic elite, but as far as I can tell, it doesn't seem to bother the legions of young French fans of American and British contemporary music. They don't wring their hands or express much angst about the fact that the music they love has English lyrics — at least not judging by the numbers who listen to American hip-hop music on headphones in my local record store, a branch of the big entertainment and book chain FNAC. These days, most French youth are clamouring to learn English. The post-Berlin Wall generation isn't hung up about nationalism or preserving cultural identity.

Perhaps they also accept that while France has contributed more than its fair share to Western culture, one thing it hasn't been able to master is popular music.

No matter how long I live in France, I'll never warm to French rock music. There is just something about the French language that doesn't fit with the sound. It works with romantic, poetic ballads like '*Ne me quitte pas*' ('Don't leave me'), but not with the likes of 50 Cent's 'What Up Gangsta' or 'I Can't Get No Satisfaction'.

'Johnny Hallyday is no Mick Jagger, no matter how much he rolls those hips,' I said to Michael one evening as we watched France's most famous old leather-clad rocker sing a pop song on a French TV show.

Artists still come to Montmartre in Paris to paint. They set up their easels at Place du Tertre for the benefit of the hordes of tourists who are drawn daily to the neighbourhood that Toulouse-Lautrec and Renoir often depicted in their paintings.

'Can I do your portrait?' a well-dressed man with an East European accent asked me during one visit. He worked in crayons. 'It will only take 15 minutes. I'll charge you 50 euros.'

Montmartre attracts its share of more serious, accomplished painters, too — like Sydney-born Ralph Heimans who now calls Paris home. Ralph is no pavement painter — on the contrary, he paints large portraits on commission for wealthy banks, lawyers and large corporations. His most recent portrait is of fellow Australian Princess Mary of Denmark. Ralph paints portraits in modern contexts, but in the old chiaroscuro style of the Dutch Masters, such as Vermeer and Rembrandt. His work has appeared in exhibitions around the world; one of his paintings hangs in the National Gallery of Canberra. When I first met Ralph in Paris in 2004, he'd recently sold a portrait of the 2003 French World Cup Rugby team to the Electricity Foundation of France for 25,000 euros.

Ralph could live anywhere, but he said he'd chosen Paris to pursue his painting career because it gave him inspiration. He reckoned Paris still had far more cachet for an artist — and even marketability — than Sydney, or even London. It might have long ago lost its pre-eminence in the art world, but there was still an atmosphere of romance about the place. And then there was the soft, muted light of a Paris night — the same light that inspired the Impressionists. Besides, if he needed to visit clients in London, where most of them were based, he only needed to board the Eurostar.

'I've grown up, living here, and so has my art,' Ralph told me in 2004. 'In seven years living in Paris, I have achieved much more than I ever would have in seven years in Australia.

'I feel like I'm living life more fully. Maybe that's because everything is more of a challenge here.'

Who knows whether Ralph, still relatively unknown in the art world, will achieve international acclaim for his painting. But at least he has time on his side.

'Even for Picasso, it took him ten to fifteen years to develop a profile,' Ralph's art dealer in Paris, Stephane Jacob, told me. 'Ralph is still a young artist.'

Perhaps by then the Zeitgeist, which never rested too long in one place, might have drifted back to Paris.

CHAPTER 10

Sex, Gender and *La Petite Différence*

One becomes aware in France, after having lived in America, that sex pervades the air. It's all around you, like a fluid.

Author Henry Miller in an interview recorded in 1961

THE AUSTRALIAN VOICE AT the other end of the line was breathless.

'I got your answering machine yesterday. It was just wonderful,' he said.

'Wonderful? What do you mean?' I asked, a little puzzled.

'The French ... when you spoke French. I think that

Sex, Gender and La Petite Différence

language is the sexiest in the world. I could listen to it all day.'

I was talking to my Sydney accountant, a normally rather sober man. Until recently, he lived with his mother. Yet here he was swooning over a few words of Australian-accented French that I'd recorded as a greeting on my Lyon answering machine. Lucky I wasn't a native French speaker, I thought — it might have thrown him for days.

His rapturous response to my French recorded message got me thinking: how *have* the French managed to corner the market on sexiness?

Was it just the soft, pursed-lip sound of their language? Or did it merely evoke for foreigners images of France and the French passed down through the ages: of a country and people more sexy and sexually permissive than anywhere else bar Scandinavia?

Certainly if their films and literature are any guide, the French are having more sex, and in more exotic ways, than the rest of us.

They aren't hung-up about issues like nudity in their advertising, which to my chaste Anglo-Saxon eyes seemed to border on soft porn at times. French men don't flinch from their reputation as serial adulterers, even when such infidelities are committed by the nation's leaders. The women don't mind because they take lovers too.

Sexual overtures in the workplace don't send employees scurrying to sexual discrimination tribunals. On the contrary, flirting is considered normal behaviour in a country where the sexes are said to enjoy 'sweeter' relations than anywhere else.

'There will never be a war of the sexes in France,' was the way Sylviane Agacinski, philosopher and wife of the former French Socialist Prime Minister Lionel Jospin, once put it.

Yet as an observer of French society, I often wondered whether France was truly the paradise for the sexually liberated that it has been made out to be. Do the French really enjoy better sexual and social relations than we do in so-called puritanical Anglo-Saxon countries where the sexes seem (to the French) to be constantly at loggerheads? Or was it a myth, cleverly exploited by the giant French cosmetic and luxury goods companies that have capitalised on the rest of the world's feelings of sexual inadequacy (compared to the French)?

French women have told me that they feel they are men's equals — 'equal but different' they'd emphasise — in the bedroom and in the workplace. Yet while the former might be true, they certainly don't earn the same salaries and they are pretty much absent from the upper levels of French business and politics, at least compared to women in other European countries.

France has produced some of the most notorious erotic novels of the twentieth century — for example, *The Story of 'O'*, a sadomasochistic fantasy of female submission, and

Emmanuelle, a confessional rollick through the sexual adventures of a French diplomat's wife. Other books written by foreigners like Nabokov's *Lolita* and Henry Miller's *Tropic of Cancer* found their first publishers in Paris.

Without surveillance cameras in people's bedrooms, it is impossible to say whether the French actually engage in more sexual activity than other nationalities. Surveys have tried to look under the sheets. But they are usually deceptive guides — as social researchers like to joke, they always double reported levels of sexual activity and halve those of alcohol consumption. Still, the surveys make intriguing reading.

In 2004, for example, the condom maker Durex asked people in a global poll posted on the Web how many times they made love in a year. The French said they did it on average 137 times, which put them at the top of the list. Second place went to the Greeks (133). Way down in the poll were Australians who only managed 103 times a year. The least sexually active were the Japanese at 79 times a year.

On the other hand, a survey conducted around the same time by a New York marketing agency suggested the British might actually be the more promiscuous ones. Nearly 60 per cent of Britons surveyed felt it was normal for a person in his or her thirties to have more than ten lovers during their single years, compared to 30 per cent of French.

I asked my friend Muriel whether she thought the French had more sex than anyone else. No prude herself, she nevertheless believed her compatriots were more talk than action.

'French women have this reputation for being "easy" but I can assure you it isn't true,' she said.

'When I was living in London, I found British girls to be much more "liberated" than us French girls ...'

She added with a laugh: 'You know, in France we talk about sex all the time. But that's all we do — talk.'

I had gone to Muriel's apartment specifically to ask her about French attitudes to sex, love and romance, given I had no experience of it myself, being happily married to Michael and never having taken a French lover.

Muriel, though, thought it was funny that I was seeking her views on these matters, given, as she put it, sex and romance had been rather missing from her life of late. At forty-seven, Muriel had never married but she'd had a number of lovers of various nationalities over the years. An attractive woman who dressed smartly, drove a snazzy sports car and who mixed easily with her work colleagues, she nevertheless found it increasingly difficult to meet men her own age (or older) for anything more serious than friendship. The men she liked preferred much younger women.

'French women have the same relationship problems as anyone else,' Muriel complained. 'It's just not that easy to meet men anymore.' She said a lot of women in France were resorting to the Internet to meet potential partners. In fact, some 800,000 French men and women used the Web regularly to find dates, according to an online survey published in the French magazine *L'Express* in July 2004.

This didn't fit the universal image of France as the world capital of romantic love and unfettered desire. There was so much kissing happening on park benches in Lyon that I didn't think the French needed the help of technology to form relationships. Such was the French man's well-honed eye for inner beauty that the age of the object of his desire was also supposed to matter little. As French author Mireille Guiliano pointed out in her bestseller *French Women Don't Get Fat*, French and Italian men 'naturally' consider older women desirable, even sexy, and are often caught 'turning around to look at one entering a restaurant'.

'The French rightly acknowledge there is a particular mystique to *une femme d'un certain âge*, an expression with layers of meaning including respect but also worldliness and hints of seduction', she wrote.

Maybe. If the women they were eyeing looked like Catherine Deneuve or Charlotte Rampling perhaps. I know quite a few attractive, well-dressed — and yes, slim — French women 'of a certain age' in Lyon who live alone and yearn to be noticed by the opposite sex in a restaurant, let alone swept off their feet in a wild affair. Just like women I know in Australia for that matter.

And the contradictions don't stop there. In 2005, the French media was awash with articles about how marriage was back in fashion and how the young were overwhelmingly in favour of fidelity and commitment.

According to a survey published in *Le Figaro* to mark St Valentine's Day, some 90 per cent of French men and women between the ages of fifteen and thirty-five thought it was possible to remain faithful to one person their entire life. Nearly eight out of ten French people thought they could love just one person throughout their lives. The same number said they definitely planned to marry one day, if they hadn't already done so.

'Their vision of the institution [of marriage] contrasts strongly with that of the May 1968 generation,' noted French sociologist Olivier Galland in the accompanying article. 'For young people today, marriage is no longer an intolerable constraint but a way of formalising, with a symbolic ceremony, a relationship that they imagine will be lasting.'

However, that image of the French as incurable romantics, faithful to their one true love, didn't match the findings of an investigation by *L'Express* which suggested that *infidelity* was actually on the rise. Just a month after the magazine ran a report about the apparent surge in support for family values across France, it published the findings of a new survey in which some 39 per cent of married men and 24 per cent of married women admitted to cheating on their partners. For women, this was three times more than in the 1970s.

'A paradox?' asked *L'Express* in July 2004. 'It seems we

dream of exclusivity, but we are excited by a sexuality fresh and vagabond. We navigate between the two hypocrisies: the everything-possible and the everything-forbidden.'

Of course, cheating on your partner is not only a French pastime — ask the Clintons. But I'd always thought the French were supposed to be more relaxed about infidelity than the rest of us. The classical writer François de la Rochfoucauld summed up the French attitude to extra-marital affairs more than 300 years ago thus: 'When love becomes laboured, we welcome an act of infidelity towards ourselves to free us from fidelity.'

Yet it would seem French women were becoming rather less tolerant of their husband's mistresses than in previous eras. According to sociologists quoted in the *L'Express* report, some 40 per cent of French marriages end in divorce, with adultery cited as the leading cause. And in 88 per cent of the cases, it is the woman who asks for the divorce. As a female friend in Lyon said, being cheated on by your partner hurts whatever your nationality.

Indeed, many commentators have suggested that French 'naughtiness' excites foreigners more than it actually does the French themselves. As Theodore Zeldin, an historian and leading English social commentator on French society points out, *The Story of 'O'* sold about 800,000 copies in France, compared to more than four million in the United States. 'The French may write erotic books, but they are not quite satisfied by them,' he wrote in his book *The French*.

Historian John Ardagh holds a similar view. In his book *France in the New Century*, Ardagh described the long-standing view of France as the land of 'unfettered *amour*' as one of the 'silliest of foreigners' clichés'.

Ardagh said the mistake foreigners made was to confuse French public tolerance 'which has always sanctioned such conspicuous activities as Montmartre night life or Left Bank free-living Bohemia' with how ordinary French people lived their own lives, which was much more constrained by rules and religion.

'If you were outside [French] society, on your own, then the guardians of morality would ignore you; and so Paris was a favoured refuge for those wanting freedom and privacy', he said. 'But if you belonged within one of society's rigid compartments, then you had to obey its often hypocritical rules.'

In fact, until 1975, adultery was an offence under the strict *Napoleanic Code* of 1804, with unfaithful husbands being charged a fine while an adulterous woman could be sentenced up to two years in jail.

Regardless of whether the French really sleep around or remain chaste, one area where the French do differ from us Anglos is in their discretion towards the private lives of public figures.

The bedroom romps of aging politicians rarely make it

onto the front pages of the French press, unlike in Britain and the United States where such 'scandals' are the bread and butter of the tabloids. As far as the French media is concerned, what people do behind closed doors is their business, even if the adulterer is the president of the French Republic. The public seem to concur.

I had first-hand experience of this particular French tolerance during our second sojourn in Paris in 1991.

Michael and I were at a jazz club in the Montmartre district where the Australian trumpet player James Morrison was performing. After a couple of sets, I noticed some activity in the back of the room, and watched as a distinguished-looking elderly gentleman was shown to an elevated table at the rear with a prime view of the stage. He was accompanied by a young girl no more than seventeen years of age. She had the same dark hair and oval face as her much older companion. Later, I walked past the table on my way to the toilets, and realised that the man was none other than François Mitterrand, the president of France at the time. The only clues that the jazz lover was a very important person were the two men, whom I presumed were bodyguards, seated discreetly near the table talking into their cufflinks.

But who was the young girl? I scoured the newspapers the next day for some snippet of news about the president's surprise Left Bank outing, but found nothing.

It was a few years later that I figured out that the girl with Mitterrand that night was probably his daughter

Mazarine — not the progeny of the then president and his wife, Danielle, but that of Mitterrand and his long-term mistress, Anne Pingeot. Although journalists had apparently long known about the liaison and the child, they had kept it out of their newspapers — until the gossip magazine *Paris Match* broke the taboo in 1994 with the publication of a photo of Mitterrand with his hand on Mazarine's shoulder as they were leaving a Paris restaurant together. By then, Mazarine was nearly twenty years old. The French public only got a glimpse of Mazarine's mother and Mitterrand's long-term lover in 1996 when she was pictured alongside Danielle at Mitterrand's funeral.

Although the story got wide coverage after that, the revelations that François Mitterrand had led a double life for more than two decades didn't provoke the sort of condemnation in France that would have likely ensued in Britain or the United States had Margaret Thatcher or Ronald Reagan been found to have strayed from their marriages. Mitterrand's comments at a press conference after the *Paris Match* story appeared seemed to sum up the French public's attitude to the affair at the time.

'Yes,' Mitterrand said, 'I have a natural daughter. *Et alors?*' Which roughly translated means: 'And so what?'

Indeed, the revelation that the aging Mitterrand had an attractive albeit illegitimate daughter whom he apparently loved dearly, phoned daily and even took on as a presidential adviser in the last years of his life had probably given his reputation in France a boost at the time. At the end of his political career, Mitterrand was not a popular figure with the public. But their dismay at his political management of the country did not stretch to the complicated management of his private life. Some 55 per cent of people polled at the time said they didn't disapprove of Mitterrand's dalliance with Madame Pingeot — although to be fair, they were less impressed with the revelation that the state had been paying for the charming digs on the Left Bank where Mitterrand had kept his mistress and daughter from public view all those years.

'Yes, I remember people weren't too pleased about that aspect,' said my French teacher when I asked her one day about the Mitterrand affair. 'But the relationship itself didn't bother people ... Everyone knew by then anyway that Danielle Mitterrand also had a lover.'

Contrast that attitude with the uproar in the United States over former President Clinton's relationship with a young White House intern named Monica Lewinsky — an affair which nearly destroyed his second presidency but not, it appeared, his marriage to his wife, Hillary. For the French, it was yet more evidence of the gaping chasm between the two cultures, and their standards of morality.

'A lot of noise about a small thing,' was how my teacher summed up the Clinton furore. That view was reflected in French opinion polls. Only 8 per cent of those surveyed by *Le Point* magazine in September 1998, at the height of Clinton's troubles, thought Clinton should consider resigning over the affair, while a massive 88 per cent said they felt the American media had gone too far in its treatment of the affair. An overwhelming majority — some 85 per cent of those polled — also replied 'no' to the question: should a politician be taken to court when he lies about his private life?

The attitude in much of Europe to Monicagate was summed up by a local journalist at the time thus: 'Clinton lied, nobody died.'

Yet the French forgot that the American press used to turn a blind eye to the private lives of their leaders. The affairs of John F. Kennedy were never reported while he was alive.

Times had changed, and so had attitudes, rightly or wrongly, in the Anglo-Saxon media to the private activities of politicians occupying high office. As a journalist, I wasn't that bothered myself that Clinton had been caught with his pants down (again). But I was concerned that an American president had been caught playing around with a young woman who'd occupied a role at the lowest rung in the power hierarchy of Washington. He then made things worse by lying about it. What did this say about the man occupying the highest office in the land, I openly wondered in a column I wrote at the time in Australia. I realised after I moved to France that this is not a question the French media usually put to their own leaders.

On the contrary, the French media's ability to ignore the private lives of their leaders means they never have to lie about them in the first place. This is either refreshing or boring, depending on your predilections, for an Anglo reader of the French press who is used to more revelatory fare. The French make no apologies for this: French journalists argue that they simply have a different view of news than the scandal sheets of the Anglo-Saxon press — the fact that people have sex with other people who are not their spouses is simply not newsworthy enough to warrant their attention.

Some commentators argue though that the French media's reticence about investigating the private lives of their politicians has more to do with stringent French privacy laws than the media's 'gentlemanly' national scruples. For example, it is unlawful to photograph an individual in France without his or her consent even if the photograph is not for publication. (Gossip magazines, such as *Paris Match* and *Ici Paris*, usually focus their telephoto lenses on celebrities and members of minor European Royal families who either give their consent, or never bother to sue.)

Others believe it is more to do with the 'cliquish' relationship between the French media and the political elite. In his 2003 book *Nos Délits d'Initiés* (*Our Inside Trades*), writer Guy Birenbaum attacked the French media for its arrogance in the way it condescended towards its readers and audiences. The attitude of the French media was 'we sort out what is good for you and what you need to know', he told the BBC.

'It's been like this for years and there is no reason why it should change,' Birenbaum added.

Yet under pressure from falling circulation, the French media are changing their tune somewhat, as evidenced when a press adviser to the then Prime Minister Jean-Pierre Raffarin was caught soliciting a prostitute in the Bois de Boulogne in Paris, who later turned out to be an under-aged immigrant. The man lost his job. He was also charged with an offence and fined 2500 euros. The story got wide — although not sensational — coverage in the French media. Nevertheless, it was one of the few times that I've seen a public figure in France penalised publicly for his private behaviour.

There have been other taboo-breaking milestones. Mazarine Pingeot lifted the lid on her '19 years in the shadows' in a tell-all memoir which was published to much media attention in 2004. Titled *Bouche Cousue* (*Sealed Lips*), the book told the story of her secret life as the love-child of President Mitterrand, a man she was not allowed to call her father in public until she was twenty years old. She spoke affectionately about 'Papa' whom she clearly loved and admired. But she also revealed her loneliness as a young girl with few friends who was forced to deny her true identity while Papa strutted the political stage like a monarch.

'My mother and I, we learnt to live differently from other people,' Pingeot said in interviews.

Pingeot had kept quiet about her double life until long

after her father's death. French screen star Isabelle Adjani wasn't quite so willing to stay mum about what she saw as the sexual double standards of French men — and that of her philandering boyfriend, the noted musician Jean Michel Jarre, in particular.

Breaking the ultimate French taboo and causing a firestorm of debate in the process, Adjani went public in July 2004 about Jarre's affair with another French actress, Anne Parillaud. Admitting that she was acting 'absolutely unFrench' by dumping on Jarre in the media — she described him in a *Paris Match* interview as 'an emotional serial killer' — she was nevertheless unrepentant.

'If you ask Anglo-Saxons what is the cultural criterion that sets the French apart, they'll answer: "Every man has a mistress in this country",' an angry Adjani told *L'Express*.

'The equation for them is simple: French = baguette + wine + mistress.'

Adjani said she didn't approve of what she called American 'sexual Puritanism' but she thought the French obsession with tolerance and privacy in matters sexual was equally hypocritical.

'The American hypocrisy is that everything is serious,' she said. 'The French hypocrisy is that nothing is serious.'

'Henry VIII, the Duke of Windsor — even Prince Charles — they all eventually married their mistresses.

'They didn't keep them in the shadows like the French. The English were always more courageous than us.'

I was having a discussion about French feminism with writer Madeleine Morati-Schmitt in the lounge room of her spacious apartment overlooking the Rhône River. A retired scientist now in her seventies, Madeleine had written a book called *Troisième Millénaire: la femme?* (*The Third Millennium: and women?*) which detailed the evolution of women's rights and power in France in various spheres down the centuries, from love, the family and religion to work and politics.

Madeleine was the first woman I'd met in Lyon who hadn't resiled from calling herself a feminist — a label that I'd come to learn wasn't all that popular in France, even though the French had invented it. (The eighteenth century French Utopian Socialist Charles Fourier was credited with inventing the term *feminisme*.)

'To be ashamed to call yourself a feminist, that's really going too far,' she told me. 'It's really quite stupid, and in terms of women's rights, quite retrograde.'

Other women I've met, though, thought otherwise. Janine, one of my many French teachers who'd also become a good friend, told me that the word 'feminist' in France has such a bad connotation that she'd never call herself one, even though she supported the principle of equal rights for women. Muriel, too, was all for equality, but not for feminism.

'When I think of a "feminist" I think of a woman who doesn't take care of herself and who doesn't wear make-up, or shave her legs,' said Muriel, echoing the view of some younger women I knew.

'In France, we think that women can be sexy and beautiful and intelligent all at the same time. It's not necessary to look like a man to be taken seriously.'

The stereotype of feminists as hairy-legged man-haters doesn't only flourish in France — I've heard the same sort of thing in Sydney. But the word seems to carry a particularly negative stigma in France. To be described as a feminist in France is 'nearly an insult', Madeleine agreed. If the French think of the feminist movement at all, they see it as a throwback to another era which refused to accept that the battle for women's equality had been won, she said. Worse, feminists were seen as women who deliberately suppressed their femininity and denied their seductive power — which in France is a very un-French thing for women to do.

I knew what she meant. I had just picked up a copy of the left-wing newspaper *Libération* which carried the following headline: 'The French woman: active, seductive and fertile'.

In one of those sweeping generalisations that newspapers are apt to make, the *Libération* article published in July 2005 claimed that French women juggled work and family responsibilities more productively than most other women in Europe, and furthermore they didn't have to sacrifice their 'seductive' charms in the process.

Explaining why French women were able to have on average 1.9 babies (among the highest birth rates in Europe) and make great strides into the workforce, a male sociologist by the name of François de Singly told the newspaper that 'the French woman, when she becomes a mother, wants to hold on to her educational and professional capital, but also her seductive capital. She believes she can juggle all her potentialities.'

Welcome to France: the land of George Sand and Simone de Beauvoir and lingerie shops on nearly every street corner. Where bras might be removed but are never burned.

'Cliché or not, this has been the land of *la petite différence*, not of suffragettes, nor Anglo-Saxon-style women's clubs,' declared John Ardagh approvingly in *France in the New Century*.

'French women today expect equality of rights and career prospects, equal personal freedom (sexual and otherwise), and equality in marriage. But they do not want to become the same as men; nor do they hate or shun men, like some militants. They want it both ways — to be flirted with and told they are beautiful, but also to lead an emancipated life. And why not?'

Ardagh failed to mention, however, that a militant feminism did flourish in France, at about the same time that it burst on the scene in the United States, Britain and Australia. The French women's liberation movement was born out of the student and worker unrest that rocked France in May 1968, when women realised they were 'expected to do the typing and make the coffee while the decision-making would be left to the men' as one French feminist writer put it. French feminists decided to organise separately and they campaigned on several fronts, most notably for the right to free contraception and legal abortions.

In August 1970, a group of women made front page news when they tried to lay a wreath at the Tomb of the Unknown Soldier at the Arc de Triomphe in honour of the unknown soldier's wife. The following year *Le Monde* and the magazine *Nouvel Observateur* published a feminist manifesto in which more than 300 women, some well-known in France at the time, declared that they had had an abortion, an admission that put them at risk of arrest. In fact, one of the last women to be guillotined in France was an abortionist who was sentenced to death under the Catholic Vichy regime in 1943.

There have been pockets of feminist direct action since, led by groups such as *Les Chiennes de Garde* (literally Guard Bitches), which regularly took a paint brush to outdoor advertising on Paris streets they found degrading to women (and still do), and *Ni Putes Ni Soumises* (Neither Whores Nor Doormats), a popular organisation which fights for the rights of abused Muslim women in France. Indeed, there are some

1700 women's groups in France campaigning on various issues including poverty, exclusion and domestic violence.

But it was also true that the French women's movement had taken a very public detour in the late 1970s and '80s into what Madeleine Morati-Schmitt called a more 'intellectual struggle' and away from the sort of direct action campaigns that characterised the women's movement in Anglo-Saxon countries.

Led by writers such as Julia Kristeva, Hélène Cixous and Luce Irigaray, the so-called philosopher-feminists crowded out the political campaigners who wanted change on the ground in terms of women's legal rights, and didn't want to sit around and talk about women in ethereal terms and as 'sacred mothers' as they did. As a result, splits in the French women's movement ensued.

'Even in Paris (where the biggest feminist bookstore of the seventies is now a maternity clothing store), the movement was as good as dead, replaced by a designer collection of literary and psychoanalytical theorists ... who spoke (and wrote) an entrancing and often entirely mystifying language of their own,' Jane Kramer wrote in the *New Yorker* in 2002.

'They were interested in the "female voice" and in dreams and in the permutations of eroticism ... They were not at all interested in plotting feminist campaigns.'

Madeleine told me in our interview that she believed direct action had undergone a 'renaissance of sorts' in

France with the arrival on the scene of pro-action groups such as *Ni Putes Ni Soumises*. But she admitted that in the end, militant feminism was never a popular choice for French women. Women tended to agree with the view put forward by Kresteva and others that, at the end of the day, relations between the sexes were 'sweeter' in France than anywhere else in Europe, and certainly sweeter than they were in the United States, even if women were still expected by their husbands to make the dinner and pick up the kids after school.

'Men just weren't that nasty towards women in France,' was how Madeleine put it.

Yet they weren't that eager to share their power either. Despite their motto of *liberté, égalité, fraternité*, the French revolutionaries expressly refused to give women the right to vote and be elected to public office. French women had to wait until 1944 to win those rights — some forty-two years after Australian women achieved them. They had to wait another twenty years to be able to work, or open a bank account without the permission of their husbands. By 1981, when the Socialists took power, it was still illegal for a married woman to sell any of her own property without her husband's consent. It was only under the Socialists that marriage and divorce laws were fully updated to guarantee equal rights.

Meanwhile, while French women have marched into the workplace at a steady pace thanks to supportive government childcare policies — four in five French women aged from twenty-four to forty-nine reportedly have at least a part-time job — very few women have risen to the top jobs. According to Madeleine Morati-Schmitt's book, only 1 per cent of senior executives in private companies in France were women in 2003. When they worked, women received a salary that was often nearly 30 per cent less than what their male colleagues received, even when they were in the same job, and had the same qualifications. In 2005, the average net salary for men was around 1,943 euros ($A3,117) per month, compared to 1,561 euros ($A2,504) for women.

As Corinne Maier remarked in her 2004 bestseller about French corporate life, *Bonjour Paresse*, equality in the French workplace remains 'a far-off dream'.

Far-off too is gender parity in French politics. France has often been criticised for being among the least advanced of European countries in terms of opening the political scene to women. In 2002, only about one in ten elected posts were filled by women, compared to one in four in Australia.

On the other hand, as I write, a woman, Michèle Alliot-Marie, holds the difficult portfolio of defence minister in the Chirac Government, a role few woman have been accorded in other Western governments. Divorced, childless and in a long-term de facto relationship with another legislator, Alliot-Marie has even been touted as a future prime minister of France, and possibly even president.

Sex, Gender and La Petite Différence 259

When I put that possibility to a former journalism colleague who now works in the Chirac Government, he scoffed, adding that France isn't 'ready' for a female president. That view, however, isn't shared by the French women I talked to in Lyon. 'Of course the French would vote for a woman president,' said Madeleine. 'We've had a woman prime minister, why not a woman as president?'

Indeed, Edith Cresson broke the glass ceiling in a dramatic way by becoming France's first and only female prime minister in 1991. She was appointed to the post by François Mitterrand who during his presidency tried to open up more government positions to women, especially outside their traditional portfolios. At the time, though, Cresson's elevation was hailed not as a victory for women's rights, but rather one for 'the generation of women who have succeeded without having had to resort to forever battling a confrontational kind of feminism,' said Cresson's ministerial colleague Élisabeth Guigou.

In fact, it turned out to be a victory for neither. Cresson was in the Prime Minister's gilded offices courtesy of Mitterrand, and when her ratings plummeted, he dumped her.

In truth she wasn't very good at the job. Cresson is remembered today more for her gaffes than for her political and economic acumen — as Prime Minister she claimed one in four British men were homosexuals and that the Japanese were 'ant-like'.

But her short tenure did mark a change of sorts. When Cresson was ridiculed for her poor performance, French women politicians responded that equity would only be achieved when there were as many incompetent women in French politics as there were incompetent men.

'From condescending indifference and contempt to open hostility, we have been able to measure the gap between public principles and reality in the behaviour of the political class,' wrote ten prominent women politicians from both sides of the political sphere in 1996, in a manifesto demanding that the concept of political parity be enshrined in the French Constitution. Four years later, the Socialists brought in a ground-breaking law requiring all political parties to present equal numbers of female and male candidates at elections.

The 2000 *parité* law was met with widespread public and political support, which was surprising given France's traditional opposition to quotas and affirmative action policies. The law, though, has yet to radically change the gender make-up of French politics. In 2005, women held only 73 of the 577 seats in the French National Assembly or Parliament. But at least that was double the numbers that were there in 1995.

There have been other milestones. In 2004, feminists celebrated the thirtieth anniversary of a law legalising abortion, legislation which only won passage through the then very male and Catholic-dominated French Parliament because of the crusading efforts of the popular women's rights campaigner and legislator Simone Veil. A survivor of the Auschwitz and Bergen-Belsen concentration camps, Veil was health minister in the Conservative Government of Valery Giscard d'Estaing at the time. Her association with the abortion campaign has helped entrench a law that in other countries, such as the United States and Australia, is increasingly being challenged by the Religious Right. In France, women today can obtain the so-called abortion pill or RU486 on prescription from their doctors.

Yet anomalies remain, as they always do in France. As a woman, I've felt perfectly at ease here. French men flirt with me regularly, even in the local supermarket, but it is a playful *badinage* that rarely descends into the sort of degrading wolf whistles and leers on the street that pass as flirtation in some other countries.

But a troubling machismo still lingers throughout French society. It is, at its roots, still a Latin culture with strong Catholic traditions that identifies the man as chief breadwinner and the home as a women's domain even if most French women now work outside the home. For example, a 2000 survey by the French National Institute of Statistics and Economic Studies found that when it came to 'hard core' domestic tasks, such as cooking, cleaning, washing-up and taking care of the children, French women still did 80 per cent of the work.

For me, the biggest problem was how to hold on to my identity. I hadn't changed my name to Michael's when we married in 1990, which causes me all sorts of problems in France. On all my personal documents, from my driver's licence to my bank statements, I am identified by my birth name of Bagwell. Yet in France, letters from government departments and the like are addressed to me in Michael's name of Rose, despite my insistence otherwise. Even on my health card, an essential item in France, I am identified as Madame Rose despite the fact I'd made my application for health benefits as Ms Bagwell.

Indignant, I rang the health department when my card arrived to tell them I wanted it changed.

'Well, I suppose it's possible to issue you a new card, but it will take some time,' said the weary voice at the other end of the phone.

'How long?' I asked.

'It could take six months,' she replied.

I opted, out of necessity, to avoid further bureaucratic entanglement and keep my original card. Which causes great confusion when I front up at the doctor's office, as I still make my appointments in my own name, a habit I've found hard to break after forty years.

But that's France. Though I can't seem to control the name that appears on my health card, I can at least control my own body. I could use my health card to get an abortion if I wanted, and the costs would be reimbursed by the state.

*

I often read, or am told, how mature France is compared to the uptight United States when it comes to relations between the sexes. Inequalities might still exist in the French workplace and in politics, but in the social sphere men and women are pretty much equal. The French game of flirtation is played and enjoyed by both sides, which explains, claim some, why sexual harassment complaints are rare in France.

'In Paris, I'd often get compliments about the way I dressed, I'd be smiled at and I'd be flirted with at times. In London, though, I feel like I don't exist as a woman,' Chantal, a young French banker working in London, complained in an interview with a British newspaper that was then reprinted in *Le Monde* in 1998.

It wasn't that British men were homosexual, as Edith Cresson had famously remarked, said Chantal. Her work colleagues were simply 'asexual'. 'I earn a lot of money here, but I feel bad,' she added, referring to her personal life. Only weekends back in Paris lifted her spirits.

Chantal would no doubt agree with John Ardagh and many others who believe that France has managed to find the 'ideal balance' between old-fashioned female subservience and 'the American-Nordic downgrading of the prized *la petite différence*'.

Yet not everyone I've met thought that the French had got this balance right. Ralph, the Sydney-born portrait artist I'd met in Paris, was having similar problems as Chantal in adapting to the strange customs of an alien culture, but in France.

Ralph had grown up in Sydney where he said patronising the barmaid would probably ensure you were never served a beer at that pub again. Not so in Paris, where becoming a master of the subtle put-down was the key to getting things done. You either learned the useful Parisian art of *s'engueuler* (telling people off) or you employed that other mainstay of French social interaction: flirting.

He quickly learnt that simply being nice and polite to the bureaucrat, the bank teller — and even to his new French girlfriend — rarely got him anywhere.

'It took me a long time to work out that niceness is not a virtue here. In fact, it's seen as a weakness,' Ralph told me. 'It sounds extreme but it's really the case. If you're really nice and sugary and sweet to people, it's almost like you have no spine or backbone. You are deemed to be a sucker and therefore vulnerable.'

Ralph found the same to be true in his new personal relationships. In Australia, he felt his relationships with women were pretty much based on equality and mutual respect. Back in Sydney, he said he was often scolded by his former girlfriend for not being nice enough. In Paris, he soon found himself under attack for being too considerate.

'Why are you so nice all the time — to me, to everyone?' complained his girlfriend, whom he'd met soon after moving to Paris. 'It won't work here, you'll get squashed.'

She, too, seemed to be equating Ralph's sensitive and gentle personality with weakness. Like most French women, she was a strong and independent woman who took no nonsense from the bank teller, the shopkeeper or the bureaucrat. Yet at home, it seemed to Ralph at least, she wanted someone else to make the decisions, to be the tough guy, to be the domineering presence. To an Australian male born well after the dawning of the women's liberation era, this old-fashioned gender role-playing was hard to fathom.

So was French women's seemingly endless tolerance for even the crudest compliment. It seemed to Ralph that if you didn't try to seduce a woman at least once a day in Paris, you were considered strange.

But what he found more shocking was the advice he received from men his own age to his problems with his girlfriend. 'You have to show her who wears the pants,' a young Parisian male acquaintance told him at a party one night. 'If necessary, you might have to slap her around a little.'

Were they pulling his leg? he wondered. Ralph certainly had no intention of turning into Neanderthal Man. But as his relationship with his girlfriend headed for the rocks, he did try to act 'more French' in a last ditch attempt to make it work: 'I thought, OK, I won't call her when I said I would. I'll be unpleasant from time to time. And I'll occasionally boss her around.'

To his astonishment, Ralph found that the relationship immediately began to improve. But he couldn't keep up the act. 'As soon as I started to be myself again, the relationship failed,' he said.

Ralph has since met another Parisian woman with whom he has developed a close relationship. He hasn't had to play the same macho games. 'Her attitudes towards relationships are similar to mine,' he said.

Yet Ralph said he still occasionally missed the 'straightforwardness' of relationships back in Sydney.

Conclusion? Maybe relations between the sexes in France are sweeter after all. But to paraphrase Bill Clinton, it might also depend on what you mean by the word 'sweet'.

CHAPTER 11

France and the World

The French constitute the most brilliant and the most dangerous nation in Europe and the best qualified in turn to become an object of admiration, hatred, pity or terror but never indifference.

Alexis de Tocqueville, 19th century French political thinker and author

WHEN I HAD TOLD people we were packing up our bags and moving to France, it tended to elicit one of two responses.

The first was a kind of envy: people had visions of me wiling away my day in cafés, having my hands kissed by hordes of flirtatious French men or having absurd encounters with baguette-wielding locals in the bucolic French countryside à la *A Year in Provence*.

The second response was a kind of a sarcastic sneer, from people who invariably viewed the French in less admiring terms, particularly when it came to their often maverick political strutting on the world stage.

Having moved to Lyon just as the US-led invasion of Iraq was getting underway in early 2003, Michael and I copped more of the sneers, and less of the envy bit.

France, of course, had opted not to follow America into Iraq for a second time around, and was urging a diplomatic solution in the United Nations instead. This had won it plaudits from several countries, but not with a lot of people I knew. In fact, at the height of the Iraqi conflict, mentioning the word 'France' in Anglo-Saxon circles tended to elicit a string of invective in which hypocrites, wimps and chauvinists were the milder form.

And that was from people I knew who were opposed to the war.

'What are those French up to?' one Sydney journalist friend asked me when the US-led coalition rolled into Iraq in March 2003. 'Probably trying to curry favour with Saddam so they can sell Iraq more arms.' (The scandal surrounding the Australian Wheat Board's $300 million in alleged kickbacks to the Saddam regime had not yet surfaced.)

I reminded my friend that France was still a democracy, and that the Chirac Government was actually reflecting the wishes of the French public, who overwhelmingly opposed the American invasion and were actually urging their leadership to use France's UN Security Council veto to prevent it. The French were also viscerally anti-American, which made them natural members of any Coalition of the Un-Willing anyway. Left-wing sections of the French media liked to stereotype the United States as a global bully intent on world domination. Only France had the guts to stand up to America, went the line. 'We are the only country in Europe that has not simply become yet another star on the American flag,' was how one official at the Élysée presidential palace put it.

Yet few people I knew outside of France thought the French were really peaceniks, were doing the world a favour, or deserved any morsel of the moral high ground at all. In fact, I didn't know very many people who had essentially nice things to say about the French. (Or at least the French male — French women were still universally viewed as sexy and chic.)

'Those frogs,' said one of my former neighbours in Sydney. 'They are really up themselves.' And this from someone who took holidays in France and who admired its culture and cuisine. 'Love France, hate the French,' seemed to sum up the general attitude.

I should plead guilty here to harboring similar thoughts at times, especially when I first came to France. When my first Parisian landlady turned out to be not very pleasant, I presumed she was genetically programmed that way, like all

Parisians. It didn't take me very long, however, to meet Parisians, and French people in general, who didn't fit the snobbish stereotype; they were charming, friendly and helpful, and not the least bit arrogant.

I have had some dreadful encounters with French waiters and shop assistants, but no more probably than in New York, Sydney or London. As *Washington Post* book reviewer Judith Warner once put it, good and decent people do exist in France, if you have the eyes to see them.

Yet seeing is rarely believing. French obstinacy towards American foreign policy was an opportunity for several American commentators to profit from their Francophobia. As the Iraq conflict unfolded, book shelves in the US were groaning under the weight of a rash of anti-French tomes bearing titles such as *Our Oldest Enemy*; *Vile France: Fear, Duplicity, Cowardice and Cheese*; and *The Arrogance of the French: Why They Can't Stand us — and Why the Feeling is Mutual*.

The starting point of these books was the oft-repeated jibe that casts the French as 'cheese-eating surrender monkeys' — first uttered by Bart Simpson well before the Iraq invasion, and then resurrected by the conservative American website National Review Online. Another one was the pithy *New York Post* headline: 'Axis of Weasels'.

These, of course, were references to France's capitulation to the invading Nazis in June 1940, which the French then made worse by failing to show enough gratitude to the

Americans when they eventually liberated them. 'The only value the French could have in a coalition of the willing would be to teach the Iraqis how to surrender,' repeated the columnist Miranda Devine in *The Sydney Morning Herald* in February 2003, quoting the words of a former American Green Beret in *The Washington Times*.

Yet while France might not have resisted the Nazis as much as it had boasted, they had hardly been the only country in Europe to find themselves overrun by German tanks — think Poland, the Netherlands, Belgium and Luxembourg, for example. And what about Germany itself? It also opposed the US-led invasion of Iraq in 2003, but it didn't suffer the same sort of taunts about its wartime history.

All this made me realise that the attacks on France and the French sprung from somewhere much deeper than current affairs or history: they were more the product of deep-seated and nebulous notions of national character that tended to label the French — and Europeans in general — as weak and effeminate, and Anglo-Saxons — and Americans in particular — as strong and macho.

Writing in *The New York Review of Books* in February 2003, author and historian Timothy Garton Ash thought that a study should be written on 'the sexual imagery' of these stereotypes.

'If anti-American Europeans see "the Americans" as bullying cowboys, anti-European Americans see "the

Europeans" as limp-wristed pansies,' he wrote. 'The American is a virile, heterosexual male; the European is female, impotent and castrated. Militarily, Europeans can't get it up.'

Or as *The Washington Post*'s David Montgomery put it a month later: 'So much of America's self-image — egalitarian, plain-speaking, practical, macho — defines itself best against a perfectly opposite foil: supercilious, obscure, effete — qualities Americans conveniently bundle and label French.

'Never mind that both these summations of national character are stereotypes based on dubious kernels of truth. This is the murky world where culture-bashing occurs.'

In other words, when Dominique de Villepin, France's haughty foreign minister at the time of the Iraq invasion, stood up in the United Nations and lectured Washington and its allies about the need to give weapons inspectors in Iraq more time, most people didn't immediately think about France's war record.

They were probably thinking about the rude retort they'd received from a Paris waiter on their recent vacation, and how much it pissed them off.

The media, of course, could hurl abuse at France because at the end of the day there was no real French lobby in Anglo-Saxon countries to offend, at least not of the size of, say, the Italian or Vietnamese communities. Millions of Europeans had immigrated to the United States and Australia, but very few French had been among them. That made them sitting ducks.

This didn't mean the insults didn't hurt. One morning back in February 2003, I was having a coffee with some other language students at my French school when one of the teachers overheard our conversation about the conflict in Iraq. By this stage, the outbreak of French-bashing in the American media was getting wide coverage in France, particularly the jibes which labelled the French as cowards.

'It's an insult to all the *ancient combatants* still alive and the millions who died in the last two world wars,' said Sylvie, a young teacher at the school, seeming close to tears. 'And Americans call us arrogant.'

Most people I met at that time, though, were pretty blasé about France's run-in with the Americans. The French had a remarkably resilient self-image, even if they regularly put themselves on the psychiatrist's couch. Being a target of America — conservative America at least — only underlined for the French how different they were from Americans, who after all still visited France in greater numbers than the French visited America.

'The idea that we are different from others, and that others envy us, is important to French identity, going all the way back to Asterix and his village-defying world,' was how Claude Fischler, a French sociologist, once put it. (Asterix, the famous French comic book character, lived in a fictional village in 50 BC, which was celebrated as the only part of ancient Gaul that hadn't been conquered by the Romans.)

On the other hand, their indifference might also have been due to the fact that the more colourful jibes from abroad tended to lose much of their venom when translated into French. In *Le Monde*, for example, 'cheese-eating surrender monkeys' became '*singes capitulards mangeurs de fromage*', while in *Libération*, 'axis of weasels' was translated as '*l'axe des sournois*' which kind of meant an axis of the underhanded. Not quite so pithy really.

Besides, the French gave as good as they got. 'Les Guignols', a popular satire show on French TV that used puppets to send up current events, had a field day with American president George W. Bush. His puppet was a sort of idiot child who liked to play with cowboy dolls, small rockets and nuclear devices and who said only a few words like 'yeah', 'America' and 'papa'. Alleged Bushisms, such as 'The problem with the French is that they don't have a word for entrepreneur', were also regularly recycled, to much ridicule, on French websites and in the media.

France was often labelled — and by the French themselves — as the most anti-American country in Europe. Most people I knew, though, were more anti-Bush and his crusading foreign policy, than anti-America and Americans per se.

Philippe, an old journalist friend who went on to work for the French defence minister, thought the French actually weren't anti-American at all; they were just 'anti' the idea of one 'hyperpower' telling the rest of the world what to do. 'The French would prefer a multi-polar world,' explained Philippe. A world, of course, where France would take its rightful place as a major force for liberty and justice alongside America.

French polls tended to suggest that the French thought highly of Americans, even if they couldn't stand their politics. That 'love America, hate the American government' mantra, however, was put under pressure when the results of the 2004 US presidential election suggested that a majority of Americans did support George W. Bush and his foreign and domestic policies after all.

In France, it took some time for that message to sink in. Three months after the defeat in the November 2004 US presidential election of John Kerry — whom the French liked a lot because he spoke French and had relatives in France — biographies of the Democratic candidate were still being sold in Lyon's main bookstore. This made France perhaps the only place in the world where books about Kerry were still being prominently displayed. It was as if the French couldn't believe that George W. Bush had won re-election.

The Kerry books took their place alongside translations of anti-Bush tomes by the likes of Michael Moore and Paul Krugman and others which always found a large audience in France. As did conspiracy theory books, such as one which argued that the events of September 11 were a sham devised by the Bush Administration to justify its military expansionism abroad. *L'Effroyable Imposture* (*The Appalling Sham*) by journalist Thierry Meyssan sold 100,000 copies in its first week when it was published in 2002.

Like most other people living in France, I got my news not from the staid French press, but from the more lively morning radio. It was here that the anti-Bush rhetoric tended to morph into a general scatter-gun critique of American society, which the French generally thought was inferior to theirs.

Not a day went by during the height of the French–US deep freeze over Iraq when I didn't hear some French politician or intellectual criticising the United States for its perceived failings: its inequality, its gun crime, its support of the death penalty, its lack of universal health care, its conservative moral values pushed by an ascendant Right, its determination to impose its culture on the rest of the world. 'Traveling to parts of America is like traveling to the Third World,' said one.

The commentators blamed the policies of US Administrations for America's woes. But even from a cursory glance at the literature chronicling US–French relations over the centuries, I could see that French antipathy towards the United States went way beyond current affairs, back to the very beginnings of America itself when France first recognised the seeds of a nationalism and global presence that would eventually rival and surpass its own.

'America is completely English,' complained the French foreign minister Talleyrand after visiting America in the 1790s. France had been a strong supporter of the American Revolution, but Talleyrand saw that the newly independent America would inevitably forge a closer bond not with France, but with its old enemy Britain, with whom it shared a common language and traditions.

'The word "anti-Americanism" entered the French language in the late 1940s, when opposite sides of the political spectrum — Left Bank, communist intellectuals and General de Gaulle and his followers — focussed on the need to counter the domineering presence of the US,' French academic and Princeton scholar Sophie Meunier wrote in a paper for the European Studies Newsletter in January 2005.

'The Vietnam War further reinforced the image of the US as an imperialistic, expansionist, out-of-control superpower representing a threat to world order. By the end of the Cold War, French rhetoric had accumulated a variety of anti-American arguments, ready to be dug up should the opportunity arise.'

These days, with the French economy stagnant and jobless queues still long, there were even more opportunities for the political elite in France to promote negative images of America, argued well-known French critic Jean-François Revel.

'Here we see how the Americans are useful to us: to console us for our own failings, serving the myth that they do worse than we do, and that what goes badly with us is their fault,' Revel concluded in his 2003 book *Anti-Americanism*.

'America is the scapegoat made to bear all the sins of the world.'

I asked Muriel over dinner one evening what she thought about the love–hate relationship between France and America.

'France and the United States will always be at each other's throats because they both see themselves as leaders of the world,' she said simply. 'America in terms of military might and France in terms of food and wine and culture.'

I didn't bother to tell her that lots of people no longer viewed France as a global leader in these areas, but it didn't matter. I knew what she meant: both countries shared remarkably similar self-images. As *The Economist* concluded at the height of the US–French rift over the Iraq invasion, both the United States and France believed they invented the rights of man, had a unique calling to spread liberty around the world, and possessed a 'variety of other attributes that made them both utterly and admirably exceptional'.

It was another form of sibling rivalry, where one of the siblings was now indisputably more powerful than the other and thus more capable to impose its will, its values, and its language on the rest of the world.

But at least the French could console themselves with the knowledge that the rest of the world still admired their beautiful women, their fashion, their food and wine, and their culture of the long holiday.

As soon as the rhetoric over the Iraq conflict died down, friends began to tell us once again how much they envied our decision to set up a home in France.

If the low-water mark in US–French relations was Iraq, Australia's French moment had come nearly a decade before, when France announced it would resume nuclear testing in the South Pacific.

The decision landed like a bomb in Australia. Protesters set up a 'peace camp' outside the French Consulate in Sydney. French champagne and other Gallic exports were boycotted. T-shirts depicting Chirac as Napoleon over the words 'Liberty, Equality, Stupidity' appeared on the streets, as did graffiti such as 'Stop the Frogs!'. *The Sydney Morning Herald* ran an article with the headline 'Why the French are bastards'.

'It is hard to escape the conclusion that Jacques Chirac and his service chiefs are merely hankering for a whiff of the old Gaullist *gloire,* displayed with such murderous arrogance in the sinking of the *Rainbow Warrior* in Auckland Harbour 10 years ago,' commented Mike Carlton in *The Sydney Morning Herald* in 1995.

Relations softened after France called a halt to nuclear testing the following year. Yet a lingering resentment towards all things French remained among many Australians. This would occasionally flare up into full-blown nastiness when prickly Austro-Franco spats from the past — like the one over the use of French regional names such as Champagne and Burgundy on Australian wine labels — were recycled by the Australian media. And then there was France's stand on Iraq.

'The events of June 6 serve as a reminder of the fact that, over the past century, French governments have spoken loudly but carried a small stick,' wrote Gerard Henderson in *The Age* in a column in 2004 on the occasion of the sixtieth anniversary of the D-Day landings at Normandy in north-west France. 'Here's hoping that D-Day kick-starts some modesty on the part of the French political class. But don't bet on it.'

Yet while Australians might regularly rage against 'those arrogant frogs', I've never found that anger turned back on me. The French might harbour a deep resentment towards Americans, and they constantly make jokes about the British, particularly about their food. But Australians? They seem to love us.

Few people I've met since moving to France remember the *Rainbow Warrior* incident, or France's role in it. Many who did were equally outraged by France's neo-colonialist arrogance in the South Pacific: indeed, France's anti-globalisation hero José Bové travelled to French Polynesia in 1995 to protest nuclear testing and was even invited on board Greenpeace's new *Rainbow Warrior* ship. But as the French have huge nuclear power stations in their own backyards, many never quite understood the fuss about nuclear testing. The French, on the whole, are not Greenies.

When it came to military conflicts, older French were more likely to recall the heroism of Australian and New Zealand diggers fighting to liberate Europe in places like the Somme during the First World War, than wag a finger at Australia's participation in the American invasion of Iraq. That's probably because most French had no idea Australia followed the United States into Iraq. Media coverage of Australia is as poor in France as it is in other parts of the world.

To most French, Australia is an exotic place far away, ringed by sandy beaches and filled with strange animals, a sports-mad population and lots and lots of empty space. 'Australia, the kingdom of the surfers, is attracting more and more young French visitors,' *Le Monde* declared in an article under the headline 'Australia: The New Eldorado' in 2002. 'They leave in search of the great outdoors, fresh air and to discover another way of life that they find *très cool*.'

Occasionally the local media did shine the spotlight on Australia's 'Aboriginal problem' and its off-key treatment of asylum seekers, which challenged the 'fair-go' stereotype. But mostly the French saw Australia as a trouble-free country unburdened by a history of war on its soil, or by bad times in general. I'd lost count of the number of times locals had told me how much they wanted to visit Australia.

'*C'est mon rêve!* (It is my dream!)' was the usual response when I told them where I came from. Only when they found out how long the flight was from Paris — 'Twenty-one hours? It's not possible!' — did they seem to be put off.

The French I knew seemed to admire Australia's reputation for larrikinism, mateship and above all, for having a good time. In France, the only Western country with a legislated 35-hour work week, the citizenry shared Australian's devotion to leisure time and holidays. Rugby-mad, they also admired Australia's sporting prowess — Paris even had six Australians working on its bid for the 2012 Olympic Games. (Alas, it didn't make a difference.)

It probably helped though that while we Australians spoke English, we weren't actually British.

I came to understand just how complicated France's relationship with Britain is during the 2003 Rugby World Cup. Michael and I watched the grand final between Australia and England on a big TV screen put up for the occasion at the Ayers Rock pub in Lyon — one of two Aussie-themed bars in the city that liked to play Midnight Oil at 100 decibels. (Aussies were the new Irish.)

We were outnumbered by visiting Brits, who in turn were outnumbered by the French. Britain might be a fellow member of the European Union, yet all the locals were barracking for the Australian team in the grand final.

'I would have much preferred the Australians to win,' said the young Lyonnais sitting next to me, when the Australians lost. Since the Battle of Waterloo, the French have never liked it when the British win at things.

These days, there are a splattering of Australian-themed bars and cafés across France, run by enterprising Australians — and French Australophiles — hoping to cash in on France's affection for Australia. Apart from the Ayers Rock pub, there is Café Oz in Paris, and the Two Up Australian Café in Marseille. There is even an Australian 'bush tucker' restaurant called Le Boomerang in the Bugey hills not far from Lyon, run by ex-Adelaide engineer Brent Perkins and his French wife Rose-Marie. The Perkins's cuisine is hardly *haute:* just Aussie-style barbecues and Pavlovas and crates of Jacob's Creek, served up each weekend to curious French day-trippers.

'The main attraction is our Australianness,' explained Brent, who keeps a kangaroo in his backyard. 'People just seem to want to find out more about Australia.'

The Perkins', however, are a rare breed. From my days as a business reporter, I knew that that the majority of Australian entrepreneurs still balked at the idea of investing, or finding markets for their products in France, or continental Europe in general. Unlike the French, who enjoyed a $3 billion trade surplus with Australia thanks to healthy sales of French perfumes, hand bags, insurance and pharmaceuticals.

Australians cited the language and trade barriers as reasons for their reluctance to set up shop in France. Yet today more and more French speak English. And while beef, wheat and dairy farmers still face restrictions on what they can sell into the European Union, all other areas of trade are pretty much wide open, as Australian wine makers have found out. Trying to buy a bottle of Australian wine in Lyon is no longer like looking for a needle in a haystack — they now sit alongside Californian and Chilean wines in the foreign sections of the supermarket shelves.

Yet if Australians look to do business at all in continental Europe, it is still usually from the 'safer' shores of the United Kingdom.

I think they might be missing out on a huge opportunity. If the French drive kilometres out of their way to sample Brent Perkins's bush barbecues, then it might do well for Australian entrepreneurs to take another look.

Although the French strike a pose of indifference to American jibes, they are still amazingly preoccupied with how foreigners view them.

Recently, at least two books critical of the French and written by foreigners have become bestsellers in France.

One is called *Sacrés Français!* (*Bloody French*), in which

American journalist Ted Stanger, writing in French, takes pot-shots at French anti-Americanism, French love of leisure and the sort of French hypocrisy that could make a national hero out of a guy who trashed a McDonald's restaurant when everyone knew the French ate at McDonald's more frequently than most other Europeans.

The second is a 'novel' written in English by a Paris-based British writer which has the witty title *A Year in the Merde*. The story revolves around the misadventures of a twenty-seven year old Londoner who comes to Paris to work for a French company and encounters all the stereotypical Gallic foibles: sex-mad Parisiennes, arrogant waiters, corrupt bosses and the French love of suppositories.

A laddish send-up that didn't put the French in the best of lights, *A Year in the Merde* nevertheless became a bestseller in France in its French translation. No one was more surprised than the author.

'I didn't write it for the French but it's French people who have bought most of the copies that I've sold,' Stephen Clarke told the *Times of London*. 'They have this capacity to laugh at themselves that we didn't imagine they had.'

This French obsession with their own image may be more narcissism than insecurity. But whatever it is, the French I know are at least curious about how they are perceived by foreigners.

'Do you really think we are arrogant and aloof?' my warm and self-effacing French teacher asked me one day.

'Well, yes and no,' I replied, trying to be diplomatic. 'I did seem to run into a lot of rude waiters and shop assistants when I first came to Paris years ago. But I can't say I do that much anymore.'

And it was true. Michael and I rarely had run-ins with rude French waiters these days. Maybe we had just become more accustomed to the gritty way all French people seem to interact. Or maybe the Lyonnais are simply more polite than Parisians. When we go to a restaurant, we no longer sit for ages before a menu appears, or are forced to wave our arms to get the attention of the waiter, who then studiously ignores you.

'Are you enjoying your meal?' the young waiter at a recently opened restaurant near our apartment asked us not once, but three times during our meal. At the end of the evening, he then wished us a heart-felt 'bon weekend' as he held open the door so we could all stagger merrily into the night.

'What a nice waiter,' we remarked, as if it were an oxymoron.

There were, of course, still occasional lapses. A few months earlier, we had taken some visiting Australian friends to our neighbourhood *bouchon* — run by the indomitable Marie-Danielle — who then watched amazed as she castigated the two men sitting next to us for putting salt on their food.

'You could at least taste it first,' she hissed.

Another night, at one of Paul Bocuse's many bistros around Lyon, a young man who'd been serving us with a smile all evening, quickly got his back up when one of our group complained that her moussaka had been a little dry.

'I don't think you know how moussaka is supposed to taste,' he snapped.

Once upon a time, such encounters were deemed typically French, but now they were few and far between, and when they did occur, they tended to enrage the French as much as us Anglos. (Our moussaka-eater was French who gave the waiter a piece of her mind: 'Of course I know what moussaka tastes like, you chump.')

The message seemed to be slowly but steadily filtering down to the French restaurant floor, in these more straitened economic times, that if you are nice to customers, they might come back a second time and they might even leave you a tip. Even the government had gotten into the act, launching investigations into areas of the French service industry that foreigners complained could do with a niceness makeover.

One place singled out for attention was Paris's main airport, Charles de Gaulle-Roissy, which a government report said too often presented a 'negative' image of France to new arrivals.

Visitors often complained of surly and unhelpful staff: immigration officers who never smiled, baggage handlers who were slow and taxi drivers who didn't speak English. 'A welcome without a smile and without warmth is like a cold shower for a traveller who is expecting to be enchanted by a romantic city', the 2004 report concluded.

The tourism minister added: 'Our aim is to let tourists know that France is trying to improve its welcome and that the French have to do better.'

In a population that views service industry jobs as a sort of bondage, no one, not least the government, expected the French to start greeting visitors with a cheery 'Have a Nice Day!' But the message being spread by Paris officials — particularly in the run-up to the city's bid for the 2012 Olympic Games — was that tourists should no longer be viewed as a nuisance, especially when fewer of them, including Americans, were choosing France as a travel destination in the wake of the rift with the United States over Iraq and the rising euro.

Not so long ago, three-star Michelin restaurants in Paris used to practise an informal quota system to limit the numbers of American customers at any one sitting. If you had an American accent or American name, chances were if you telephoned to ask for a reservation that day, you would be turned away.

Yet if a French person phoned, suddenly a table would miraculously become available. When the practice was exposed in the media, restaurants justified their discrimination by arguing that they wanted to ensure a reasonable balance of French and American patrons. The real reason, however, was that Parisians didn't want to be surrounded by loud-talking

Americans who they felt didn't appreciate the art of fine French dining like the French.

Then came terrorism, the Iraqi invasion and a strong euro, and many Americans decided to take their vacations elsewhere. France's top restaurants suddenly found themselves with empty tables, and Maitre d's began clamouring for any foreign business they could get. Business got so bad at the luxury end of the market that the French Government called on New York film director Woody Allen to help it out.

'I don't want to have to refer to my French-fried potatoes as "freedom fries",' 67-year-old Allen pleaded in a promotional video called 'Let's Fall in Love Again' aimed at luring Americans back to France.

'And I don't want to have to freedom-kiss my wife when what I really want to do is French-kiss her.'

I don't know whether the video worked: visions of an aging Woody Allen French-kissing his child bride were a turn-off for me. Yet a year after the Iraq invasion, there were signs that Americans were prepared to let bygones be bygones: they'd stopped pouring their French champagne down the sink and vacationers were returning to France in pre-Iraq war numbers.

It would probably take a lot more than a video, though, to convince foreigners that France had become nice and polite. The pervasive image abroad of French people being all cold and unhelpful still persists. The Japanese even have a name for it: Paris Syndrome.

Coined by a Paris-based Japanese psychiatrist, the syndrome is a type of depression that hits mainly young Japanese women who came to live in the French capital but found their fantasy didn't match the rough reality of Paris life. Dr Ota explained to *Libération* that sufferers were coming to her with complaints such as: 'They [Parisians] laugh at my French'; 'They don't like me'; 'I feel stupid in front of them'. A quarter of Paris Syndrome cases ended up in hospital before being repatriated to Japan.

'Shy Japanese feel that the French, when they are impatient, are being hostile towards them,' explained Dr Ota. 'The Japanese think it's vulgar to speak too much — it becomes a sort of violence when they try and make themselves understood. French humour can also provoke serious feelings of persecution among the Japanese.'

Of course, most tourists who feel victimised by the French just finish their holiday and go home.

I, for one, would be disappointed if the French became like everyone else in tourist areas, putting on a sugary politeness simply so they could extract more of your money. I kind of admire the French (sometimes) for their perverse resistance to the globalising force of the 'have a nice day' commerce-driven culture.

Anyway, it was all part of the French experience. Tourists expect the French to be rude to them: I've actually observed Parisian waiters playing up to the part. It gives us Anglos something to talk about when we get back home.

CHAPTER 12

Race, Riots and the Headscarf

In the deprived suburbs, a kind of soft terror rules. When too many young people see nothing ahead but unemployment after they leave school, they end up rebelling.

Jacques Chirac, speaking in 1995, just a few months before winning the French presidency

IT TOOK ABOUT 20 MINUTES to drive from our apartment in central Lyon to Venissieux, a suburb of grey high-rise housing estates, or *cités*, near the petrochemical plants on the city's south-eastern outskirts. Yet for most Lyonnais, it might as well have been another country.

Venissieux is typical of the more deprived suburbs that seem to proliferate on the outskirts of many of France's major cities and towns. It is home to some 55,000 residents, more than half of whom are first and second generation Arab and black African immigrants from France's former colonies — countries such as Algeria, Morocco, Tunisia and Mali.

They first came to France in the 1960s and 70s when jobs were plentiful and manual labourers were in demand. At Venissieux, the immigrants filled positions in the local plants and other surrounding factories. But when the jobs vanished, Venissieux descended into a spiral of poverty and isolation.

Suburbs like Venissieux have become black spots on the French landscape — although the French middle classes hardly notice what goes on in these faraway suburbs because few of them ever venture there.

But in late October 2005, the accidental death of two teenagers fleeing police one night in a rundown neighbourhood north-east of Paris sparked two weeks of full-scale rioting that eventually spread to scores of cities and towns across the country. This could not be so easily ignored.

Before passions eased and cold weather forced the teenagers indoors, more than 9,000 cars had been set alight across France. Buses, too, had been firebombed and neighbourhood schools and shops destroyed not just in the far suburbs of Paris, but on the outskirts of other French cities such as Toulouse, St Etienne and Lyon. It was the worst social turmoil in France since the student-led riots of 1968, but although property was destroyed, there was only one death as a direct result of the rioting. That is something to be said for France: it has no gun culture, at least not on the streets.

The clashes were still largely limited to the outlying housing estates — indeed, if you were visiting Paris as a tourist at the time of the October 2005 riots you wouldn't have noticed anything. Until, of course, you switched on your hotel TV to CNN. The foreign media coverage made it seem like the whole of France was in flames. I received several calls and emails from family and friends in Australia wondering if I was OK. A colleague of Michael's at Interpol, an Iraqi, was phoned one night by a concerned family member in Baghdad who'd been watching coverage of the French riots on CNN. 'They're in Baghdad and they are worried about me living in quiet old Lyon?' he said.

Yet while the foreign media may have exaggerated the extent of the unrest in France that autumn, the root causes of the rioting were real enough — poverty, unemployment and widespread discrimination. Until the riots of autumn 2005, the French Government had seemed to be in a state of denial about the problems plaguing the immigrant community. Now they were forced to confront the issue. No longer could the French ignore the underclass seething in the suburbs. No longer could they avoid the question: why was this great country, which preached the values of liberty, equality and fraternity to the rest of the world, seemingly unable to integrate and grant dignity to its own large ethnic minorities?

Venissieux isn't the sort of place you'll find mentioned in Lyon tourist brochures. Still, some two months before the October riots exploded onto our TV sets, Michael and I decided to take a run down to see Lyon's very own Islamic garden suburb for ourselves — besides being known for its large Muslim population, Venissieux was also recognised for its landscaped parks, having won a national competition for the best 'Flowered Cities of France' three years running. Yet some of Michael's colleagues seemed astonished that we would want to visit.

'Why do you want to go to Venissieux?' asked one policeman. 'It's where kids set fire to cars. Your wallet will be stolen right from under your nose.'

The morning we visited, however, Michael and I found a suburb more in flower than in flames. It was the first weekend after the long summer break, and the sprawling market at Les Minguettes housing estate — one of Venissieux's poorest and supposedly most troublesome *cités* — was bustling with shoppers of all hues stocking up with food and groceries for the coming week. Families on a budget came to Les Minguettes because the bulk produce was incredibly cheap. We had come because we were told you could find things that were generally absent from traditional French markets, like multi-kilo bags of couscous, fresh figs and bananas, and hard-to-find Asian vegetables like bok choy.

Les Minguettes market also supplied other needs. At the entrance, an elderly man was selling gilded copies of the Koran, right beside another selling the Bible in Arabic. Further on, a young French woman was hawking pastel-coloured Islamic headscarves. She wore no head-covering herself, but that didn't seem to bother her veiled clientele who were clamouring for her cheap, synthetic scarves. A few men, meanwhile, were being drawn to another stall laden with multi-coloured prayer mats, some of which, conveniently, had compasses sewn in at one end. Not that the residents of Les Minguettes needed directions to point them to Mecca: the satellite dishes perched on the balconies of their apartments in the tower blocks overhead were already facing that direction, to pick up the Arab television programs that they preferred to watch over those from France.

Indeed, Les Minguettes market was a place where you could hear both Arabic and French in equal amounts, often intermingled in the same sentence. Amidst the shouting of stallholders and the crying of babies was an atmosphere of camaraderie and community, no doubt forged through shared experiences.

'Here,' said a young mother in a voluminous veil and robe, who'd picked up the five-cent euro coin I'd dropped while paying for my tomatoes. 'You never know when you might need it.'

It was hard to reconcile this bustling Saturday morning market scene with the stories of urban mayhem that had occasionally appeared in the French press. In the adjacent landscaped park, old men on benches were taking in the midday sun. The streets were swept clean of rubbish.

But according to civic leaders, crimes like car theft and drug trafficking had become endemic in the area, where one in three working-age adults were unemployed. A working-class industrial suburb with a proud heritage — in the old town centre there was still a meeting hall for former World War II resistance fighters — the tower blocks of Venissieux had become a place that even poor white families had now shunned. In the past two decades, Venissieux had lost 20,000 residents.

'The whites left and we were stuck in the ghetto,' a Venissieux community leader commented to a foreign journalist in 2004. 'You're born, you live and you die in Les Minguettes.'

The seeds of the 2005 riots were widespread discrimination and economic deprivation. But there were other contributing factors; the breakdown of traditional parental authority in some immigrant homes and the French tendency to segregate its poor and underprivileged in bleak, publicly-owned housing estates that further isolated them from the other France, the one of elegant, tree-lined boulevards and historic city centres.

I also thought the French police were part of the problem. Overwhelmingly white and incredibly rude and cocky, I would often see them stop young men in the streets of Lyon and demand their identity papers for no other reason, it seemed to me, than that their faces were brown or black. I often wondered how long it would be before these angry young men fought back. The answer came soon enough when a group of about fifty youths clashed with police in 'Blade Runner' style riot gear brandishing tear gas grenades in Place Bellecour, Lyon's central square which is just a few hundred metres from our apartment. It was about two weeks after the first rioting flared up outside of Paris. The Lyon police quickly 'calmed' the situation with truncheons and tear gas and about ten kids were arrested. No cars were torched nor people injured. But it made news around the world as the first 'riot' in the centre of a French city.

All too quickly, the riots of 2005 were linked with religion. 'Like a Middle Eastern *intifada*, the violence [in France] is stripping away whatever comfortable assumptions existed about the authorities' ability to cope,' *Newsweek* magazine reported. But this was not simply a religious war between the Christian and Muslim way of life. These teenagers were calling for jobs, not *jihad*. As *The Economist* commented: 'This was the angry rebellion of a beardless, Nike-wearing teenage underclass.'

Nevertheless, it was difficult to ignore the fact that a majority of the rioters were French-born Arab and African Muslims, communities France was having more difficulty integrating than previous waves of immigrants. While sociologists played down the religious factor in the French riots, others openly wondered how long it would be before radical Islamist groups sought to exploit the economic and social deprivation in France's poor suburbs for their own ends, or whether they were already doing so.

Fears that the *cités* might become fertile recruitment grounds for Muslim extremists had been around for some time, ever since France suffered a series of Islamic terrorist attacks back in 1995, the first Western European country to do so.

Zacarias Moussaoui, the so-called 20th man in the September 11, 2001 attacks and who was still on trial in the United States in early 2006 and facing the death penalty, grew up in Narbonne in southern France, an area of intense anti-immigration sentiment. Moussaoui, his family said, showed no interest in Islam until he turned up one day in Chechnya, fighting on the side of Muslim separatists against the Russians. Paris sociologist Farhad Khosrokhavar described men like Moussaoui as 'the new martyrs' — alienated young working-class Arabs from France who felt neither French nor Arab.

'Islam is the only plausible identity they can endorse,' Khosrokhavar told veteran American investigative journalist

Seymour Hersh for his book *Chain of Command*. 'To accept their identity as French might mean accepting the inferiority they feel in their daily life as a second-rate citizen. The inevitable result is hatred for France and, by extension, for the West.'

Alienated citizens, ethnic tensions, ghetto suburbs ... it wasn't meant to be like this. France, never shy to articulate what it stands for as a country, has always rejected the multicultural model of other countries, what it calls *communautarisme,* because it believes that policy encourages apartheid-like segregation and the establishment of exclusive communities that undermine social cohesion.

'France did not proclaim itself as a multicultural state,' wrote Rod Kedward, in his epic 2005 study of France titled *La Vie en Bleu.* 'Diversity was encouraged; difference that implied incompatibility was not.'

Indeed, since the days of the French Revolution, France's leaders have preached a policy of assimilation and integration: racial and religious differences would be tolerated so long as immigrants signed on to the dominant culture and became French, first and foremost. The sacred principle of the French Republic was that all French citizens were equal and indistinguishable in the eyes of the state, regardless of where their families hailed from originally.

In keeping with this philosophy, it is illegal for the state to collect statistics based on ethnicity, religion or language — as far as the state is concerned, once you are French, you are nothing else.

This has its upsides: never again could the French state use data against its citizens to discriminate on the basis of race and religion — as the Vichy regime had done against the Jewish community and other minorities during the Second World War. But the downside is that the French these days are kept pretty much in the dark about the extent and needs of its burgeoning immigrant community — for example, no one really knows for certain how many French citizens are of Arab or African origin; how well they perform at school and university compared to white native French; or what percentage of the prison population they comprise. This lack of reliable data has allowed anti-immigration political parties such as Jean-Marie Le Pen's far-right *Front National* to exaggerate immigrant numbers and inflate the social problems blamed on them.

France's sacrosanct model of equality also means the state is forbidden to discriminate in favour of its ethnic and religious minorities. There are no government programs or special treatment for these communities specifically that might help them secure jobs or places in universities, as exist for disadvantaged minorities in other countries. When the centre-right politician and 2007 presidential hopeful Nicolas Sarkozy suggested that affirmative action was now required to aid French Arabs and Africans, he was slapped down by both the current leader President Jacques Chirac and opposition left-wing politicians for propagating 'un-French' ideas.

As Chirac explained in a speech in 2003, affirmative action and Anglo-Saxon style multiculturalism goes against the founding principles of the French Republic where 'all the children of France, whatever their background, whatever their origin, whatever their beliefs, are daughters and sons of the Republic'.

'Splitting society into communities cannot be the choice of France,' Chirac added.

'It would be contrary to our history, traditions and culture. It would be contrary to our humanist principles, our faith in social advancement solely on the strength of ability and merit, and to our commitment to equality and fraternity among all French people.'

That is, at least, the grand theory behind the French Republic. In practice, however, things are very different for the children of France with immigrant backgrounds, especially those whose families hail from Arab or African Muslim countries.

Rather than being accepted by their French compatriots as fellow citizens, members of one big happy, fraternal Gallic family, French Arabs and blacks regularly complain of racial discrimination, isolation and harassment, particularly at the hands of the police. Tensions over this state of affairs boiled over as far back as October 1983, when tens of thousands of

French Muslims marched from Venissieux to the Paris offices of then President François Mitterrand to demand the equal rights and integration that the Republic had promised them.

Dubbed the 'March of the *Beurs*' — the name for French-born children of North African Arabs — it won the troubled Lyon suburb national publicity. Socialist politicians in charge at the time lined up to promise the marchers and the ethnic communities they represented that things would change.

However, more than twenty years after that national event, the gap between the Republican ideal and the reality on the ground seemed to me as stark as ever.

France is home to Europe's largest Muslim community outside Turkey: an estimated five to six million people of Islamic faith, or with a Muslim cultural or ethnic background, making up nearly 10 per cent of the population.

Yet, to date, no French Muslim, brown or black, has sat in the gilded chamber of the 577-member French National Assembly or Parliament. One or two politicians of North African heritage hold minor posts in the French Government, among them Azouz Begag, the well-known French sociologist and writer of Algerian descent, who was appointed Minister for Equal Opportunity in the government of Prime Minister Dominique de Villepin in June 2005. And much fuss was made in 2004 when an Algerian-born Frenchman was named *préfet* or governor of the department of Jura in eastern France, the first immigrant from a Maghrebi (North African) country to attain such a post. But that is about the extent of French Arab or African representation in French politics.

In other areas of public life, ethnic faces are also scant. The French soccer superstar Zinedine Zidane, also born of Algerian parents, is a national hero, cited regularly in polls as the country's most admired citizen. But beyond the fields of sport and popular music, France's ethnic communities have few role models.

Unlike in Britain, the United States and Australia, you rarely see someone of visibly ethnic origin reading the news on TV, or holding down positions of authority. As the Paris think-tank Institut Montaigne noted in a report in 2004, blacks and Arabs were 'invisible or nearly invisible' in the world of politics, in the judiciary, on television, in senior management, and certainly under-represented in the public sector and in posts which are in contact with the public, including the police force. The only French Arabs or Africans most people — and foreigners like me — come across are those who run the local corner shop or clean their offices and houses.

'The young kids are rioting today because they have no role models,' Soumia Malinbaum, one of a handful of second-generation French Algerians who had succeeded in business, told the *International Herald Tribune* during the 2005 riots. 'It's a scandal.'

Young people from a Maghrebi or African background, particularly young men, complained of being blocked at every turn when they sought jobs or promotions. The Institut Montaigne said that even with a university degree or equivalent qualification, French Arabs and Africans were more likely to be without a job. 'Their rate of unemployment, which borders on 30 per cent, is more than three times higher than that for the bulk of the population,' the Institut noted.

In May 2004, the French employment agency Adia, with the help of French sociologist Jean-François Amadieu, sought to test how widespread discrimination was in the workplace by sending out some 1,800 fictitious résumés to 250 employers who were advertising for senior salespeople and managers.

Almost 30 per cent of male applicants and 26 per cent of women applicants with French-sounding names received positive responses. However, when the same résumés were topped with Arab-sounding names, the positive response rate dropped to 5 per cent. Only handicapped applicants fared worse, receiving just 2 per cent positive responses.

Twenty-six year old Farid Quesnel-Djedid, born in France of Algerian parents, found out how much of a handicap his name was when he applied to a prestigious business school in Paris a few years back. The school rejected his application, telling him his grades weren't good enough. The following year, Farid applied again but this time under the name Xavier. He was accepted.

Now employed at a Paris travel agency, Farid still goes by the name of Xavier to avoid discrimination.

'If I call and say "It's Farid on the line" I won't get the account,' he explained to a journalist in 2004.

Farid said quite a few of his friends had now changed their names: there were no more Mohammeds and Bashirs, just François' and Frédérics.

For those born on French soil to immigrant parents, that was what assimilation French-style meant today.

Does France deliberately discriminate against its Muslim community? There is no simple answer to this. As others before me have observed, it can be hard sometimes to figure out the French — particularly when it concerns policies aimed at their ethnic communities.

On one hand, France is opposed to American-style affirmative action policies and quotas that might help boost the representation of ethnic minorities in the workplace or politics. Yet in 2000, the French Government introduced a law requiring all political parties to present an equal number of female and male candidates at elections. These were not quotas, I was told, because women made up half the population so the law was just reflecting that.

Similarly, the French wax lyrical about their commitment to secularism. In 1905, a law was introduced separating Church from state in the public sphere. Hailed by

Republicans as a victory over the all-powerful Catholic Church, it was meant to guarantee French citizens not only the freedom to practise any religion they chose, but the freedom to practise none at all.

Among the French, the 1905 law is a point of pride that further marks them out from that other big secular Republic across the Atlantic — the United States — which seemed to French eyes to be tilting towards a theocracy under its Bible-thumping president George W. Bush.

As far as the French are concerned, religion is a private matter, and has no place in the public arena. That is why you will never hear a French president intone the words 'So help me God' on his inauguration day, as is custom in the United States. And why there was so much debate in France following the death of Pope John Paul II in 2005 as to whether it was appropriate to fly flags at half-mast on public buildings. (Many town halls chose not to.)

It also explained why the French Government could not compromise and allow Muslim girls to wear the Islamic headscarf to school. Or so I was continually told.

Under a new law reaffirming French secularism that would come into force at the start of the September 2004 school year, students would no longer be allowed to wear 'conspicuous' religious symbols of any kind in state secondary schools. This included large Christian crosses and Jewish skullcaps. No one, though, was in any doubt that the new law was primarily aimed at the Islamic headscarf, whose growing popularity was raising concerns in France about a shift within the French Muslim community towards religious fundamentalism. Under the new law, Muslim girls who persisted in wearing the *hijab* would face expulsion from school.

Yet, as far as I could tell, religion, at least the Catholic version — the dominant religion in France — was still very much part of the French education system. The whole state school calendar seemed to be based around Christian holidays, and under pressure from the Catholic Church, school kids are still even allowed a day off in the middle of the week, ostensibly to pursue their religious education (although few used their free Wednesdays for that purpose these days).

However, if Muslim kids said they needed to take off days during Ramadan, the Muslim month of fasting and celebration, or wanted to eat halal food in their school canteens — or Jewish kids kosher food for that matter — they were told that this was unacceptable because it contravened the sacred Republican principle of secularism.

Nevertheless, the government's decision to bring in a new law that specifically enforced secularism on school pupils had wide support in France, even if it potentially contravened another of the country's basic rights — the right to a free education. The religious symbols' ban was backed by all major political parties including sections of the Communist Left. In polls, some 80 per cent of French said they supported it as well.

In fact, virtually every French person I knew, regardless of whether they were on the Right or Left, were of the working or professional classes, seemed to think it was a good idea.

When I ventured that I thought the law was racist and an unnecessary encroachment on people's fundamental freedom to wear whatever they chose — and worse, risked pushing Muslim girls into private Islamic schools where French equality and secularist ideals would never reach them — I was usually shouted down as a misguided Anglo-Saxon multiculturalist who didn't understand French society or its history.

'This is not a racist law or anti-women,' Sylvie, one of my French teachers at Alliance Française insisted, when I raised the issue during a classroom debate.

'I always hear the same argument from my Anglo-Saxon friends. You just don't understand how important *laïcité* (secularism) is to us French.'

It was true. I didn't really know anything about France's religious history. I'd always thought of France as a predominantly Roman Catholic country, full of churches and religious holidays, where children were often named after the Saint connected to their birth date. It remains so, although it has to be said that religion plays a much-diminished role these days in the lives of the ethnic French. (In surveys, 40 per cent of young people said they had no religion.)

Yet I soon came to realise that France is also, paradoxically, a militantly anti-religious country, zealously devoted to upholding the principles of secularism. Anti-church sentiments run deep in French history: they were forged during and after the bloody French Revolution when the anti-clerical Jacobins waged a war against religion. A truce was only struck in 1905 when a new law came into force that formally separated the Catholic Church from the state. The guiding principle of France's secularist Republic was that all citizens had equal rights before the law, regardless of their racial origins, class or religion.

In a country that was historically a patchwork of different ethnic groups and languages, the Republican revolutionaries of the eighteenth century wanted to build a single French identity — a unitary state — through a policy of integration and assimilation that invoked the central principles of *liberté, égalité, fraternité*.

The revolutionaries' goals were more political than humanist, but it did result in France becoming the first country in Europe to offer citizenship on the basis of residency rather than religion or bloodlines (as Germany practised until 2000, for example). For the French, the concept of assimilation has a much more positive connotation than it does for, say, Australians who associate it with a loss of cultural identity. As far as the French are concerned, immigrants who settle in France are not giving up their identity, but gaining a new, rather privileged one — that of being a French citizen, and with it, all the rights and obligations passed down through history that that entails.

One of the main obligations, as the French see it, is that Muslim citizens of France should practise 'a French form of Islam', as Nicolas Sarkozy once put it, which seemed to mean they should practise their religion in private, or at least not in an overt manner, like wearing the Islamic headscarf in schools. Blending into French society is an obligation not just for Muslims, but for all those who come to live in France.

But it was clear that many French, including my French teacher Sylvie, had some special concerns about Islam: in particular, the way religious conservatives interpreted the role of women in Muslim society.

As a believer in equal rights for all, Sylvie said she found it difficult to respect a religion that didn't treat women as equals. To Sylvie and many other French women and men I knew, the *hijab* was a symbol of a systematic degradation of women, as well as a glimpse of how Islamic fundamentalism was beginning to seep into French society.

She cited reports in the French press of how conservative Muslims were trying to change the cultural fabric of French society: clerics were demanding that public swimming pools be segregated; Muslim students were walking out of classes on Darwinism or the Holocaust; Muslim men were refusing to allow women in their families to be examined by male doctors.

'I see this law as helping to protect Muslim girls from the pressure of overbearing fathers and brothers who might be ordering them to wear the veil against their will,' she said.

Indeed, the need to provide children of all denominations with a 'neutral' space in which to learn and study was one of the main justifications for the religious symbols' ban in schools, according to the 2003 independent commission investigating the issue.

'[Since 1989], and especially in the last two years to three years, it has become clear that in schools where some Muslim girls do wear the headscarf and others do not, there is strong pressure on the latter to "conform",' said immigration expert Patrick Veil, who also sat on the commission.

'This daily pressure takes different forms, from insults to violence. In the view of the [mostly male] aggressors, these girls are "bad Muslims", "whores", who should follow the example of their sisters who respect the Koranic prescriptions.'

According to another member of the commission, Professor Gilles Kepel, the French Government had no choice but to ban the headscarf in schools. If it did not, 'then you will have schools like you have in the United States where the kids of the rich white middle class go to private schools and the public school system is left for the poor and the blacks,' he told the American network NBC.

I had to admit that there were many Muslim women in France, having rejected the wearing of the veil in their lives, who'd applauded the government's ban, even if it was recognised by many as a shrewd political manoeuvre by President Jacques Chirac to undercut support for the far-right leader Jean-Marie Le Pen.

A passionate supporter of the headscarf ban in schools was *Ni Putes Ni Soumises* (Neither Whores Nor Doormats), a group that campaigned for equal rights for Muslim women, who they claimed were frequent targets of abuse and violence in immigrant neighbourhoods. It saw the headscarf ban as part of a larger fight against rising Islamic extremism in the suburbs, and a defence of secularism and French Republican values which the group believed better protected female equality.

'Let's remember that first and foremost [the veil] is a tool of oppression, of alienation, of discrimination, an instrument of power that men have over women: it's not an accident that it's not men who wear the veil,' wrote the group's founder Fadela Amara, a French Muslim town councillor of Algerian descent, in a 2004 book explaining the philosophy of *Ni Putes Ni Soumises*.

'We must tell young people again that you can be a Muslim today without wearing the veil. I am a practising Muslim and I've never worn the veil. Nor did my mother. Nor did my grandmother before her.'

I had sympathy with those sentiments. At times, I even found myself defending the headscarf ban with my Anglo friends who tended to see everything the French did as wrong and hypocritical. 'There are many French Muslims who actually support the new law,' I'd point out. Nevertheless, in my heart, I was still unsure whether the government's heavy-handed ban on religious symbols in state schools was the best way for France to encourage a more modern, moderate form of Islam in France.

But at least it hadn't seemed to have led to a major rupture between France and its Muslim community as some had feared.

In the beginning, the law did split French Muslims, with the more devout calling the ban an affront to Islam and an attack on religious freedom. Hundreds of women — many of whom had replaced their headscarves with the French flag — took to the streets in France in peaceful marches demanding that their rights be respected too.

Politicians in the United States and Britain, accustomed to having the finger pointed at them by France for their 'colonialist' attitudes towards the Arab world, were quick to describe the ban as a retrograde step for human rights. A United Nations' report released in September 2005 argued that the ban had humiliated Muslim girls and caused further problems for women who wore headscarves in their daily lives.

'The stigmatisation of the so-called Islamic headscarf has triggered a wave of religious intolerance when women wear it outside school, at university or at their workplace,' claimed Asma Jahangir, the United Nations' special rapporteur on freedom of religion or belief.

Nevertheless, in schools themselves, the ban didn't cause major splits and there have been no ongoing mass protests.

French officials said that only a dozen girls defied the ban when school re-opened in September 2005, compared to 639 when the 2004 school year began with the new law in place. Considering that around 1,500 schoolgirls were wearing Islamic headscarves before the law was introduced, French authorities believed that things had gone relatively smoothly. Aside from a minor upset when some students in a suburban Paris school demanded that a Christmas tree be removed from a classroom because it, too, was a religious symbol (request denied), the atmosphere has remained relatively calm.

For this outcome, credit must go to the leadership of the French Muslim community who urged children to obey the law. When insurgents kidnapped two French journalists in Iraq and demanded that France repeal the headscarf law or the captives would be killed, French Muslims closed ranks behind the *tricolour*, declaring themselves French before all other things.

Religious leaders told the journalists' captors in no uncertain terms to stay out of France's affairs.

'Today we have to worry about the fate of the two hostages,' Mohammed Bechari, vice president of the French Council for the Muslim Religion, told reporters before heading to Baghdad as part of a French delegation to win the hostages' release in September 2004.

'The political battle — a purely French one — for religious freedom will resume later on.'

CHAPTER 13

What it Means to be French and a Muslim

How many times have I gone into Paris and have been shouted at 'Go Home!'. Home is here. But it doesn't feel like home ...

Hocine, a 23-year old French Muslim of Algerian descent, speaking to journalists during the Paris riots, November 2005

'NOBODY CAN TELL ME it's not racism,' said thirty-year-old Ahmed. 'I'm absolutely convinced 100 per cent — 200 per cent — that it's racism.'

I'd come to the home of Ahmed and his wife Sara to talk about the Islamic headscarf ban and what it was like to be a practising Muslim in France. I'd talked to my French teacher and my friends, watched the French television news and read the French papers and the opinions of legions of French intellectuals. But now I wanted to talk to someone for whom race and religion were more than just a dinner party conversation. Ahmed and Sara struggled with these issues every day of their lives.

Ahmed was born in a town to the south of Lyon, to Tunisian parents who'd immigrated to France in 1970 to seek a better life for their children. Ahmed's father had arrived at the tail end of what had become known as '*les Trente Glorieuses*', the thirty 'glorious' years of economic expansion which had made France the fourth largest industrial power in the world. According to Ahmed, those were the days when French bosses went from house to house 'knocking on doors asking for workers'. Those days, however, were long gone.

Ahmed was born five years after his parents moved to France. A shepherd in Tunisia, Ahmed's father easily found a job as road worker when he first arrived, but by the early 1980s, he had been retrenched. He hadn't been able to get another job since. This made his father all the more determined that all his children — he had five daughters and three sons — went on to higher education. All did. One of Ahmed's sisters was a nurse, while another became a journalist — she was about to start a new job as a reporter on the private TV channel M6, one of the few people with a Maghrebian background to have attained a reasonably high profile job on French TV. After Ahmed failed his university exams to become a doctor, he'd switched to computer studies. He was now a Microsoft-certified systems engineer.

I'd sought out Ahmed, to whom I'd been introduced once by a friend, because he seemed to be doing well in his parents' adopted country. He held down a good job in a multinational organisation, and was well-liked by his work colleagues. He lived in a comfortable apartment in a suburb just north of Lyon with Sara, his 'native' French wife, and their three young children. Ahmed was also a devout Muslim: he prayed five times a day and wore a beard.

Sara, too, was devout. She had converted to Islam when she was seventeen years old, after her best friend had done so. This was not an entirely rare occurrence in France — by some estimates, approximately 30,000 native French had converted to the Islamic faith in the last few decades.

'I was brought up a Catholic, but my parents weren't practising,' Sara explained. 'My best friend converted before me. At the start, I couldn't understand why she did it. I started to read books about Islam to understand more, just to inform myself. Then little by little, I got interested in the religion, then really quite a lot.' It was then that Sara became a practising Muslim: she prayed daily, and began to wear the veil outside of her home.

At first, it was hard for her parents to come to terms with her conversion because all they knew about Muslims came from the television.

'It wasn't that they were racist, although there is a lot of racism in France,' she said.

'But my parents, they were seeing all these negative things on the TV — "Muslim men hit their wives"; "women are slaves to their husbands". To them, I was also renouncing my origins for something else.

'After three years, though, they realised I was very attached to the religion; it wasn't just a passing fad … and when I met Ahmed, they knew I hadn't converted just for him. I did it years before we met. I did it for me, not for him.'

Sara said she now had a close relationship with her parents. Her father — her mother had died the previous year — was a frequent visitor to the family home. Others though had not been so accepting. On the street, in shops and on the bus, she often had to put up with insults and jibes from her fellow French for wearing the Muslim headscarf.

'It's not just a question of schools, the French believe you can practise your religion, but only if you do it at home, out of sight,' said Sara.

'They expect Muslims to do the same: do what you want at home, but when you go outside you have to be like everybody else. This is their idea of integration. But it's a false melting pot because everyone is not the same. Everyone should be allowed to have their own beliefs.'

Needless to say, the new law banning the Muslim headscarf and veil in schools had angered Ahmed and Sara.

'When someone says "I'm a feminist", I reply that I, too, am a feminist,' she explained. 'In France, it's easy to say you are a feminist — but where were the feminists when my neighbour was being hit by her husband who was French, which I witnessed when I was young? Who offered to help this poor woman then?

'People only seem to bring up feminism when they see people like me wearing a veil, which I've have chosen to do under no pressure from anyone else, but out of conviction for my faith.'

Added Ahmed: 'People always ask me: "Why did you make your wife wear a veil?" Yet it was her decision entirely. Sara would even like to wear the veil that covers her face, leaving only an opening for the eyes. I don't mind. But I had to tell her: "It's already difficult for us in France. It will be even harder if you do that." If one day we end up living in a Muslim country, then she can do what she wants.'

Indeed, Ahmed said he was now considering packing up his family and leaving France for a Middle Eastern country where he could practise his religion freely, or even moving back to Britain where he'd spent a year after graduation.

'When I was in England I discovered that you could pray at university. I was shocked: Here in France it's forbidden; you can't practise your religion on campus,' said Ahmed.

'In Britain, Muslims are much more organised, more visible. The British accept you for what you are. They don't care if you wear a beard. In France, the French want you to look French. They expect you to assimilate.'

According to Ahmed, it was doubly difficult for Arabs who were practising Muslims to get ahead in France. He claimed French companies regularly discriminated against Muslims who wore beards, and it was almost impossible for women wearing the headscarf to get jobs that dealt with the public.

France has laws against racial and religious discrimination in the workplace. But that hadn't stopped it. Ahmed told the story of his best friend, also trained as a computer systems engineer, who was told in an email after one job interview that even though his qualifications were impeccable, they couldn't hire him 'because of the way he looked'. 'They said his beard might upset people,' said Ahmed. His friend had been unemployed for the past ten years: he was only thirty.

'The only reason I'm working is because I found a job with an international organisation,' said Ahmed, who'd also picked up English when he lived abroad. 'I've never managed to get a job with a French company, not even a summer job.'

Ahmed predicted that relations between the communities would worsen following the headscarf ban, which he believed would eventually be extended to the French workplace. Sara thought the law had already encouraged racists, who had kept their views hidden in the past, to speak out more freely.

'How can you speak about freedom when you force

someone to abandon her religion to go to school?' asked Ahmed.

'This is a law against diversity. Yet if you remove diversity from society you end up with a *société bâtard* — a mongrel society.

'Diversity is the key to everything. Yet in France, they don't believe in the world village; they are still taking about a France that is for the French only.'

Listening to Ahmed and Sara's account of racial discrimination in France was deeply troubling. As an expatriate living in privileged conditions, I rarely saw the downside of this beautiful country. I knew few people of North or West African descent, except those who had been despatched by their national police forces to Interpol. And despite my occasional visit to Venissieux, I rarely ventured into Lyon's farther suburbs. Not that you had to travel into the suburbs to be reminded of the trials of France's immigrant community these days.

Aside from the Paris riots, some of the most shocking images of 2005 were the spate of fires which broke out in dilapidated apartment buildings housing legal and illegal African immigrants in the very heart of Paris. The blazes killed a total of forty-eight people in a four-month period, many of whom were children. One fire was in a budget hotel where the government had put up immigrants waiting for their residence papers and working permits. It was located just around the corner from a glamorous Parisian department store.

Like many Western countries, France was struggling to accommodate a rising tide of impoverished illegal immigrants washing up on its shores, from Africa, and from Eastern Europe as well. At the same time, according to the testimonies of people like Ahmed and Sara, it was also failing to meet the expectations of those immigrants who'd been living in France legally for a generation or more, and who'd been told repeatedly that the French Republican ideal of liberty, equality and fraternity also extended to them.

This was causing all kinds of divisions and fault lines in French society. Aside from a surge in civil unrest and vandalism in housing estates outside Paris, Lyon and Marseille, racial attacks and anti-Semitic violence were also on the rise.

According to the French Human Rights Commission, the number of reported hate crimes in France in 2004 jumped to their highest level since the non-governmental organisation began compiling statistics. A report from the group in March 2005 found far-right extremists were increasingly setting upon Muslims in city streets and firebombing mosques, while disaffected Muslims were taking out their anger on Jewish targets — France had not only the largest Muslim community in Europe; it also had the largest population of Jews in Europe (an estimated 700,000).

The Human Rights Commission claimed the increase in the number of reported attacks against the Jewish community in France had coincided with a rise in tensions in the Middle East following the start of the second *intifada* in 2000. It blamed people from 'an Arab-Muslim background' for the majority of the incidents, which included arson against synagogues and schools and the desecration of Jewish cemeteries. In a speech in July 2004, the then Israeli Prime Minister Ariel Sharon urged French Jews to immigrate to Israel immediately to escape what he saw as 'the wildest anti-Semitism' in Europe.

The criticism stung a country still haunted by the memory of the Vichy Government's complicity in the deportation of some 75,000 French Jews to Nazi death camps during the Second World War. The Chirac Government responded with an immediate crackdown involving increased police surveillance and arrests, and in the first half of 2005, reported incidents of anti-Semitic violence had dropped markedly. Yet even Jewish leaders thought the anger being directed towards their community had its roots closer to home than the Middle East.

'These [Muslim] groups have focussed much of their anti-French hatred against the Jews who live alongside them in some of France's poorest suburbs,' Menaham Gourary, the European director of the Jewish Agency which helped Jews move to Israel, told *The Guardian* in 2004.

'This is the problem which France has never addressed.'

Indeed, French political leaders have preferred to put their faith in a policy of gradual integration. Given time, said these optimists, immigrants from places like Algeria, Morocco, Tunisia, Senegal and Mali would be absorbed into French society and accepted by the French, just as Portuguese and Italian immigrants were before them.

Think-tanks such as the Institut Montaigne thought the politicians, however, were fooling themselves.

'The tradition in France is that we wait for the situation to improve itself spontaneously, in two or three generations, like it did for immigrants of recent times,' it said. 'Yet time has passed and nothing has improved for immigrants of Arab descent.'

Did this mean that France was a more fundamentally xenophobic country than others? Ahmed and Sara clearly thought sections of the population were, as were government policies such as the ban on religious symbols in state schools. But they were quick to point out they knew many French people who were not.

The problem with the French, they said, is that they are not very good at accepting cultures different to their own.

The *Front National* leader Jean-Marie Le Pen, who campaigned for the expulsion of North African immigrants, put this most starkly in an interview in 2002: 'There is an Islamic population in France, most of which comes from the North African countries. Though some may have French citizenship, they don't have the French cultural background or sociological structure. They operate according to a different logic than most of the population here. Their values are different from those of the Judeo-Christian world.'

Yet there were other reasons, too, for France's problematic relationship with immigrants from North Africa, aside from cultural differences.

According to some observers, the tensions were a legacy of France's colonial past. The bitterly fought Algerian War of Independence in the 1950s and 60s, when Frenchmen and Algerians killed each other with fanatical brutality, still haunted relations between the two communities, often spilling over into negative attitudes towards North African immigrants in general.

Journalists Jean-Benoît Nadeau and Julie Barlow, in their 2003 book *Sixty Million Frenchmen Can't Be Wrong*, claimed the Algerian War produced a 'powerful resentment' among those who had embraced the cause of a French-Algeria, whether they were the many thousands of French who were born and grew up in Algeria (known as *pieds-noirs*) or old stock French from the mainland. A prominent member of this latter group was Jean-Marie Le Pen.

'Born and brought up in Brittany, Le Pen belongs to the class of Frenchman who seek revenge for France's humiliations,' said Nadeau and Barlow.

'The foreign press often accuses Le Pen of being a Nazi, but nothing could be further from the truth: Le Pen's beef is

Algeria and Indochina. The fact that Le Pen captured 19 per cent of the vote in the second round of the 2002 presidential elections — his highest score ever — shows how resentment about Algeria is still lingering in France 37 years after the end of the war.'

Nevertheless, it would be wrong to paint an entirely bleak picture of a mean and divided France in constant conflict with its immigrant community.

Although the state has not effectively addressed the social and political isolation felt by Muslims of Arab and African descent or done enough to fight discrimination, it had at least mitigated the despair in the housing estates with expensive welfare programs, ensuring a minimum standard of living that only a generous French social model could provide — free health care, good schools and heavily subsidised public housing.

Even as rioting youth went on the rampage in suburbs like Clichy-sous-Bois outside of Paris during the autumn of 2005, government wrecking balls were there tearing down the concrete tower blocks of the neighbourhood to replace them with more liveable, mixed-income public housing, part of a multi-million euro urban renewal project. In the meantime, money continued to pour into the neighbourhoods to create as pleasant an environment as possible, with green lawns and parks breaking up the monotony of the grey towers in housing estates such as in Venissieux. Concrete ghettoes yes, but at least they had flower beds.

And while the older generation has had a hard time accepting and adapting to the changes swirling around them, younger people have been embracing the vibrancy of North and sub-Saharan African culture for years — particularly its music, its artists and its writers, and even its language. On the streets of Lyon and Marseille, you can hear kids of all colours speaking a street French called verlan, a form of French argot popularised by the children of Arab immigrants which reverses the syllables of a word ('*keuf*' for example was verlan for '*flic*' or the police in French). These kids are also more likely to be listening to French rap music, which exploded out of the *cités* in the 1980s, and which quickly moved from the margins of French culture to the mainstream. Black and Arab singers such as MC Solaar, Khaled and Cheb Mami have gone on to become international stars.

Meanwhile, a few educational institutions have been quietly looking at ways to boost the numbers of children from immigrant families in their enrolment, despite an official policy which frowns upon quotas and affirmative action. Since 2000, the elite university Institut d'Etudes Politiques in Paris, better known as Sciences Po, for example, has run a special admissions track in high schools in poor neighbourhoods across France to help Arab and black children gain places at the university. Some TV networks, too, have made discreet moves to include more ethnic faces in its rosters of mostly white TV presenters: the state-run network France Televisions broke new ground when it hired a black woman, originally from the French overseas department of Martinique, to read the main evening news program on its France–3 channel in 2005.

And every French football fan understands that the chances of their national soccer team winning international competitions would be slim without the contribution of first and second generation Arab and African players such as Zinedine Zidane. The French team that won the soccer World Cup in 1998, to much national euphoria, was exceptional in Europe at the time for the mixed origins of its players: they came from Algeria, Guadeloupe, Senegal and even New Caledonia. These players and others coming through the ranks have become role models for thousands of young French kids, Arab, black and white alike.

Amidst the anger and fury in 2005, there remained hope among many people I knew that race relations could improve in France with determination and goodwill. As even Ahmed and Sara acknowledged, there are good people in France trying to change things, but more needs to be done.

As Ahmed explained it to me: 'I love France. It's the place which has given me an education. It is the place where my friends and family live. It has a special place in my heart. It would be very sad if I had to leave my country because of the actions of some people ... we just want people to be kind to us.'

To me, the challenge to ensure that Ahmed and people like him are not lost to France forever is simple enough: France has to accept the cultural diversity in its midst and embrace it, just as Australia is learning to do in the wake of its own ethnic clashes on Cronulla Beach in New South Wales in December 2005. (Most Australians I know think Australia became a much more interesting place after the arrival of significant numbers of immigrants in the decades following the Second World War.)

Rather than merely acknowledging that millions of French citizens have foreign roots, France needs to declare that immigration can actually change and enrich its culture and society for the better. There is no point boasting that the state is colour blind, when the society in which people live clearly isn't. The state has to start a positive dialogue about immigration with its citizens, including its ethnic and religious minorities, so that the stage is not left to far-right politicians like Le Pen who exploit the population's fears and ignorance.

In return, France's immigrants and their children need to respect the basic tenets of the proud Republic within which they live, one that affords women and men equal rights and the freedom to live their lives the way they chose.

Having said that, they might find it easier to sign on to the Republican ideal if they could find a job, rise to the boardroom and take their place in government and the parliament.

As the Italian author Alain Elkann once said, the path to a peaceful Europe can only lie in a better understanding of cultural diversity.

'More and more we're becoming a multi-ethnic, multi-religious continent, and we have to learn to share and to live together in an open-minded community,' said the writer of a trilogy of books on religion.

In other words, nations can either resist immigration, or they can adapt and exploit its potential. It is a challenge hardly limited to France.

CHAPTER 14

Dogs, Turnips and Other Joys of France

The more I see of man, the more I love my dog.

French 17th century philosopher Pascal

MY FAVOURITE MORNING ACTIVITY in Lyon is to take a long walk around the *Presqu'île*, the peninsula that slices through the core of the city. I usually end up at Le Spleen café, my regular haunt, where I can down a couple of *noisettes* — the local term for an espresso with a dash of milk — for just a euro or two while I try to decipher the local papers.

Before I settle in at Le Spleen, I like to stroll along the cobbled-stoned banks of the Saône, the river that runs at the foot of our long street. The tranquil Saône meanders like a country stream compared to its big sister, the mightier, more industrious Rhône, which runs on the eastern side of the peninsula. Even though the Rhône is closer to our apartment, I always head to the Saône.

Along its quieter, willow-shaded banks, sheltered from the busy street above, I might find a few homeless men chatting and sharing their first drink of the day, or a young couple grabbing a quiet moment before heading their separate ways to work. If it is nearing summer, several holiday boats are likely to be already moored there, flying flags from Britain and from other northern European countries where the sun is always weaker than here.

Mostly though, my companions on these walks are local dog-owners giving their normally apartment-bound mutts a much-needed morning stretch. And inevitably, their daily routine includes leaving behind some doggy souvenirs on the pavements. This, after all, is France — delightful one minute, infuriating the next.

The city places waste bins with a supply of plastic bags along the banks of the Saône for the use of dog owners, but to no avail. The mess tends to stay where the dogs have left it, transforming the ancient cobblestones into not-so-charming traps for hapless, dogless ramblers like me.

France and the French have changed a lot since I first went to live in Paris. There is snack food now in the supermarkets, a McDonald's restaurant at nearly every métro stop in the bigger cities and enough Starbucks outlets on

Dogs, Turnips and Other Joys of France

the Left Bank of Paris to make those hallowed café-dwellers Jean-Paul Sartre and Ernest Hemingway roll over in their graves. Now even fat people can be found on French streets, and they aren't all American tourists.

But one Anglo-Saxon habit that the French haven't adopted is an abhorrence towards *déjections canines* — as the French politely call their dogs' droppings. I'm not the first foreigner to complain about the piles of dog business on the streets and country lanes of France, and I'm not likely to be the last. I'm sure the French are sick of hearing about it. But the reason we keep coming back to the subject is because it is just too hard to avoid. We are simply surrounded by the smelly stuff.

Think of France and you almost always immediately think of fine wine, good food and glorious scenery. But in fact, the first thing my overseas friends mention when they visit us is the dog mess on Lyon's streets — and in particular the streets in our neighbourhood, the 2nd arrondissement, which has a reputation for being the city's worst when it comes to dog poo. Walking along the pavement outside our nineteenth-century apartment block is a daily exercise of leaps and side steps.

'I'd love to look up at the lovely buildings,' one friend visiting from London commented, 'but I just can't afford to take my eyes off the ground.'

This particular day, we counted ten steaming mounds of dog poo on the pavement between the front door of our apartment and the next corner, a distance of about 20 metres. Not surprisingly, France has the largest pet population in Europe — more even than pet-obsessed Britain. According to the (booming) French pet food industry, France has about ten million dogs and eight million cats. Some 53 per cent of households have at least one pet (including birds and goldfish).

I don't know whether the French treat their animals better than the British. But they certainly treat them well; taking them on holiday, buying them gourmet pet food and dressing them in knitted jackets during winter. In fact, a dog crèche complete with a canine gymnasium has now opened in Paris for owners who can't bear to leave their precious pooch home alone when they're at work or away — and it charges by the hour.

It's been said that for many French living in tiny apartments, dogs have become substitutes for children, spouses — even lovers. Indeed, sitting at Le Spleen one day, I felt like a voyeur as I watched a young woman at the next table coo, kiss and fondle her little Chihuahua between sips of coffee. She had clearly signed on to the dictum apparently first uttered by the seventeenth century French philosopher Pascal: 'The more I see of man, the more I love my dog.'

I often wonder whether the French prefer dogs to children. When I was living Paris in 1988, I witnessed a waiter castigating a young mother for discreetly breastfeeding her newborn baby at the table.

'Would Madame like a seat in the back where it is more private?' the waiter sniffed. As the young mother gathered her belongings, the waiter turned to the next table, where another diner was giving her Scottish terrier a drink of water from her ashtray. Nothing was said.

A few years later, Michael and I were eating a light lunch in a village café in the Loire. Just as we were tucking into our chef salads, we noticed at our shoulder the owner's cocker spaniel peeping over the top of our leather booth. He was clearly hoping to scrounge a morsel or two. Without giving it much thought, Michael gently brushed the pooch away — we were not in the habit of feeding dogs at our table.

This, however, was not a good move. The light tap from Michael's hand had sent the cocker spaniel tumbling backwards into the adjacent booth where it landed on its scrawny bottom. It was unhurt, but the unexpected rebuff had clearly put it off-guard, and the mutt gave out a plaintive yelp.

Well, we may as well have spat on the French flag. The locals at the bar, behind which stood the formerly jovial *patron,* stopped talking and drinking and glared at us menacingly. We quickly got the message it was time for us to leave.

These days, we try to be more tolerant of the country's love affair with the dog even if it upsets our Anglo-Saxon hygiene-obsessed sensibilities.

I no longer make a scene when I find myself seated next to a mutt in a restaurant — sometimes French dogs are far better behaved than some children, I've found. Nor do I do a double take when I notice a poodle peeking from the hold-all of a woman sitting next to me on a domestic flight — after all, the pooch is zipped up in a special doggie bag supplied by Air France. (Yes, it's true: Air France and other European airlines, such as KLM and Lufthansa, let you carry your dog or cat right onto the plane, so long as it is small and in a container.)

Michael and I knew a Parisian banker who ran a bed and breakfast in a château near Valence, just south of Lyon, in his spare time, and who used to travel with his French bulldog on the TGV fast train all the time. Nestor was a great dog, a real character, but he had a habit of grunting like a pig at times, and he didn't always smell that good. I don't know whether I would have wanted to share a two-hour journey with him in close quarters.

There aren't very many places where you won't find dogs in France; bakeries and butcher shops included. France has laws against bringing animals into shops where food is sold, but I've never seen them enforced, at least not in our neighbourhood. And it doesn't stop there. The four-star Trianon Palace in Versailles has even launched a $US400 a night Heavenly Pets package deal for dogs and their owners. For that, you get a deluxe double bedroom with breakfast for you and your dog.

But catering to a dog's every need is one thing, allowing them to do their business in public places is another.

According to city figures, Lyon is home to approximately 140,000 dogs who leave behind 40 tonnes of excrement each year — only Paris with some 300,000 mutts has a larger dog mess problem. Much of that excrement ends up on the bottom of your shoes, bicycle wheels, pram wheels, and the paws of other dogs. In Paris, at least 600 people are said to break a limb each year, from slipping on dog droppings or trying to remove the mess from their shoes.

The French are concerned about this state of affairs — in a 2005 survey carried out by the Paris municipality, some 74 per cent of residents blamed dog droppings as the leading cause of the city's griminess. But they don't seem that inclined to do their civic duty and pick the stuff up. I once castigated a dog owner for allowing his German shepherd to do his worst on the pavement in front of me. He retorted that it was the state's job to clean it up, not his — 'That's what I pay my taxes for,' he said.

Such attitudes are typical of the French. 'In terms of anti-social behaviour, of recognising that certain kinds of freedom amount to irresponsibility — whether it's going through red lights or striking for the least reason — we have a serious problem in France,' said André Midol, Paris's foremost anti-dog dirt campaigner, in an interview with a British journalist in 1997.

'There is not a sense that you find in other countries that individuals owe some kind of duty to society to make daily life tolerable. There is a sense, instead, that it's up to the state to look after things.'

But things are changing. Once upon a time the French state did accept the burden: in Paris, the city used to dispatch a team of *moto-crottes* — vacuum-equipped green motorcycles with uniformed riders — to suck up the dog poo. But Socialist Mayor Bernard Delanoë ended that program in 2004 citing the high costs. It would now be up to Parisians to pick up after their dogs, the mayor said. If they didn't, they would face stiff fines.

A few months after we arrived in Lyon, the city, too, announced a new get-tough campaign on dog droppings, which were said to be costing the city nearly 600,000 euros ($A960,000) to clean up each year. From November 2003, municipal police were to fine dog owners 38 euros ($A60) for every dropping they left behind on the city's pavements.

Lyon's mayor, Gerard Collomb, warned he would raise the fine to as high as 450 euros ($A721) if owners continued to allow their dogs to foul the streets. To press the point, the city scattered 10,000 red plastic dog turds across the city centre, emblazoned with the message: 'Is police intervention the only solution?' (The *fausses crottes* soon disappeared from the streets, picked up by amused Lyonnais who kept them as souvenirs.)

Two years on, I had yet to spot the mayor's new dog squad on the beat, nor had I noticed any decline in the volume of dog mess on Lyon's streets. The police complained they were too busy with other crime to worry about dog owners. Meanwhile, Lyon's citizens, who seemed to have an uncanny knack of avoiding dog poo, unlike me, continued to take the mess in their stride, so to speak.

'Hey, you'll have good luck all day now,' one passer-by joked recently, after I put my foot into yet another pile of dog doings on the banks of the Saône.

It seemed dogs would have the upper paw in France for some time yet.

I am more partial to cats anyway, and for a long time, I tried to convince Michael that what we needed in France was a French cat.

'But you have an allergy to animals. They make you sneeze,' he reminded me.

'I know, but that was back in Australia. Maybe a French cat will be different.'

I'd spotted some pretty interesting cats at the local market. There was a dog market every Sunday at Place Carnot, right next door to the weekly open-air food market — well, it is France after all. Usually, there are one or two cat breeders among the dog sellers, and one day Michael and I came across a woman who had a few Persians and a lovely grey-blue

Chartreux for sale. We were taken with the Chartreux, which had a perfectly round face and luxuriant fur.

'May I hold her?' I asked the breeder.

'It's a he — but yes, go ahead,' she said. 'He likes to be held.'

It was then that the cat gave out a little noise. It wasn't so much a purr, but a miaow spoken, I was absolutely sure of it, with a French accent. It made a different sound altogether from an English cat. Could it be that the Chartreux spoke French? It had never occurred to me before that animals might speak — or respond to — a language other than English. How typically Anglo-Saxon of me.

I suddenly realised that all around me in the market, the dogs and cats were responding to their masters' orders in French.

'*Viens ici*' (come here), '*couchez*' (lie down), the breeders were commanding. And the animals obeyed. Clearly if I took on a French dog or cat that had already been trained, I would have to speak to it in French.

Well, there was another good reason to own a French cat, I thought, as I gave the woman back her Chartreux. I could practise my French in the privacy of my own home, and not get any backchat about my poor grammar. Unfortunately, by this stage, I had started to sneeze uncontrollably. I would just have to find a French cat with non-allergenic fur.

Dogs, Turnips and Other Joys of France

I certainly could do with some extra help. Ever since I'd set foot in France some fifteen years previously, learning French had been a vexing subject for me. I reasoned that this was because I'd come to the language late: like most Australians, I didn't feel compelled to take foreign languages at high school, although I had taken a year of Latin. By the time I made my first visit to Paris, I was already thirty and my brain seemed too crammed with one language to make room for another.

I also didn't seem to have what some call an 'ear' for languages. At a party in Lyon soon after we arrived, I'd met a young musician from Northern England who spoke French with the accent of a native. As a matter of fact, on first meeting I thought she was French. She claimed to have picked up the language from scratch in three months.

'I play the violin,' she explained. 'So I just plugged into the music of the language.'

I, on the other hand, seem to miss the beat completely. It didn't help that up until we'd moved to Lyon, I'd only ever stayed in France for a year at a go. One year wasn't long enough to really perfect a language, at least not for an aging student like me. Each time I approached the edge of fluency, it was time to leave. Years then separated my next visit. By the time we had returned to France for a third time, it had been nearly ten years since I'd spoken any French at all. I felt like I had to start all over again.

But I was determined to get on top of the language this time around, if for no other reason than to justify the vast amounts of money I'd spent so far trying to learn it. I would no longer worry about how I sounded. That probably had something to do with age.

In Paris in 1988, I hardly opened my mouth for fear of ridicule. Journalists prided themselves on their clarity and incisiveness. I had neither in French, so I thought it best to remain silent and let my finger do the talking wherever possible — pointing was always a great communication device.

But no longer. I was too old to care. I would speak French whenever I had the opportunity even when I saw people's faces twist up at the way I was torturing their lovely language. Initially, the main problem for me was getting the opportunity. Despite being surrounded by the language, the majority of our friends in Lyon are English-speakers — even Muriel, who'd learnt English as a teenage exchange student in Britain, preferred to speak English with me.

Yet when I did speak French, I still hadn't completely exorcised my fear of sounding ridiculous. I have to admit that language remains the one sore point in my continuing love affair with France — that, and my French food-induced weight gain. Every time I struggled with a word or phrase, the same question popped up in my head: what am I doing here? And why am I struggling to speak a language that I could never hope to speak as well as my own?

Of course, it was to communicate with the people around me and to profit from the experience of living in

Dogs, Turnips and Other Joys of France

France. But there is more to speaking than just being understood. There are all the other bits that make language so interesting and fulfilling: the small talk — that necessary tool of the journalist when an interview lags — the ironic phrases, the nuances, the *double entendre*. How I missed playing around in a language.

Some two years after we'd moved to Lyon, I was making great strides in the language. I was translating French news copy into English at EuroNews. And I could watch the French TV news without having to constantly flip through a dictionary at the same time. I even felt confident enough to accept an invitation from my Swedish friend Camilla, who spoke excellent French, to accompany her to a play being staged by a local theatre troupe. It was an ensemble piece, containing some extracts from Molière, so I wasn't sure whether I would get much out of it. But I was surprised by how much I was able to follow. 'You seemed to laugh at all the right bits,' Camilla said later. 'I could tell you were getting it.'

But it was all still hard work. Especially when I was trying to conducts interviews for stories over the phone. I can read the French newspapers well enough, but posing sensible questions on complicated issues in a telephone interview is another story. Usually I'd spend hours preparing for an interview that would probably only take 15 minutes, writing down every question painstakingly in French and anticipating the answers so I would know what to say next.

I'd inevitably record the whole conversation too: speaking and writing at the same time in French is not a skill I've managed to master.

This doesn't make for very lively and revealing exchanges. Nevertheless, I found the French, on the whole, to be very patient. I don't subscribe to the view that the French are particularly rude to foreigners who make a mess of their language. Perhaps it is because I was living in Lyon where the locals seem less harried than in Paris. In Lyon, I'm always being told how much people love my accent in French and how they wish they could speak English as well as I speak French. They lie, of course. But I appreciate their kindness.

The French, though, can still be a touch arrogant about their native tongue.

'English is a much easier language to learn than French,' is something I've often heard from French friends in Lyon who speak a smattering of English. This was not so much an expression of sympathy regarding my battle with French, as a subtle message that French is inherently richer, more complex and thus more superior to English.

This belief in the intrinsic superiority of the French language goes back a long time.

'Of all the languages, the French language is the only one that has an element of probity attached to its genius,' wrote the eighteenth century French essayist Antoine de Rivarol.

'Defined, social, and reasonable, it is not only the language of the French, but the language of humanity.'

Unfortunately for Monsieur de Rivarol, more of humanity now prefer to speak English these days. Until the early twentieth century, French and English were neck and neck as the global languages of choice. But no longer. According to language experts, a mere 128 million people around the world speak French today, putting it in ninth place in the language league table, while English is the second most popular language in the world with 508 million speakers.

That is only about half those who are thought to speak Mandarin Chinese, the language world cup holder. But English is far more widely spoken than Chinese, the vast majority of whose speakers live in China.

Even the French are learning English in greater numbers. Some 90 per cent of high school graduates in France, and 65 per cent of those under the age of thirty speak some English, according to the government. In a 2005 survey of twenty-six large French companies, sixteen said English was now their official working language, among them Renault, Aventis and Danone. Even in those companies where French remains the official language, French executives tend to speak English more often during their working day than their native tongue, according to the survey.

'Today, to not speak English is the same as not knowing how to read or write 50 years ago,' said one of the French executives in the survey, published in *Le Figaro*.

This must really annoy the government, which has done much to defend and protect the French language from marauding English. It has imposed a 40 per cent quota of French-language songs on radio. It has also insisted that all advertising that carries English words or phrases at least include the French equivalent in a footnote. Thus in France, the Nike motto 'Just Do It!' is always marked by an asterisk that refers to the French translation: '*Allez-y!*'

It is the task of each government ministry to root out foreign words creeping into the language and forward them to the Ministry of Culture's General Commissariat of Terminology and Neology, which will then come up with an equivalent French word to replace it. This it does in consultation with the Académie française, the institution set up in 1635 to protect and defend the French language and which has the final say on what constitutes proper French.

These days, the Académie has its work cut out for it. With the continual invention of new technology, new words, usually in English, are flooding in, requiring a French equivalent. Sometimes the Académie's adjudications are accepted by the general public; sometimes they aren't. For example, words such as '*ordinateur*' for 'computer' and '*courriel*' for 'email' have passed into mainstream usage, although '*causette*' for 'chat' as in Internet chat-room has not. I've also never heard anyone say '*toile d'araignée mondiale*' (literally, global spider web), which is the Académie's translation for the World Wide Web.

Dogs, Turnips and Other Joys of France

Indeed, in everyday speech the French tend to use quite a lot of English-inspired words that probably make the Académie française cringe. In conversations and in magazines, the French talk about having '*un lifting*' (face-lift) to '*changé de look*'. They would say they'd found '*un super-job*' in '*public relations*' or '*marketing*'. In conversation, '*businessman*' is beginning to replace '*un homme d'affaires*'; a new club might be described as '*cool*' or '*un must*' rather than '*branché*' (itself a modern French word). People go '*jogging*' rather than '*la course à pied*', or '*surfing*' rather than '*la glisse*'. Often, the French put their own spin on English words — for example, in French, a 'walkie-talkie' has become a '*talkie-walkie*', while 'shampoo' has become '*shampooing*'.

The authorities have tried to fight back. A few years ago, a campaign was mounted to prevent former French president Valéry Giscard d'Estaing from being elected to the Académie française. His crime? He had spoken English to foreign journalists in public during his presidential election campaign three decades previously — a big no-no in France. President Jacques Chirac, for example, speaks excellent English but you'll never hear him utter it in public. The campaign against Giscard d'Estaing nevertheless failed to capture the public's imagination and he was duly elected.

But the battles continue. Disturbed by the power of the English-speaking global television news channels during the

Iraq invasion, President Jacques Chirac announced that France would establish a rival international network — a CNN à la *française* — that would put forward a French world view. The French and Germans are also funding a project to develop a more 'Euro-centric' search engine to compete with Google and Yahoo! Search that would favour French and German information over English.

Most French, though, seem to accept as inevitable the encroachment of *anglicismes* in their language, particularly via popular culture and business where English dominates. Keeping such words out is an uphill struggle. As one French newspaper noted: 'You cannot stop the ocean with your hands.'

Yet at least the French can console themselves with the knowledge that the flow has also gone the other way. French words have been enriching the English language for centuries — like 'tennis', for example, which I'd only just learned came not from the English but from the French word '*tenez*' which means 'to receive or take'.

On the street, French loses much of its Académie française formality anyway — you hear not only a splattering of English words, but a whole variety of slang and argot, including verlan, which is popular among French Arab youth in the suburbs of Paris.

On the other hand, all this openness and flexibility doesn't make French any easier to learn. I don't care what the linguists say, French *is* harder to learn than English.

Although I now feel much more confident in the language, I still make some horrendous mistakes.

'*Je suis navet,*' I said to a colleague recently. I was trying to apologise to her for some mistake I'd made. But from the laughter my words prompted, I knew I hadn't succeeded.

'You've left out a rather important consonant,' she explained, as she wiped away her tears.

It turned out that instead of saying 'sorry' ('*Je suis navrée*') I'd said something that sounded like: 'I'm a turnip.'

If you drive into the market town of Nyons in the heart of the Drôme Provençale region of southern France, you'll be reminded that there used to be many more languages in France than French.

Below the town sign is the word '*Nioun*' — Nyons translated in the local patois of Provençal. It is one of a couple of dozen regional languages and dialects that still exist in France, albeit marginally. According to *Le Monde*, some 27,387 public school students were studying a regional language in 2003 — languages like Basque, Alsatian, Corsican or Breton. A small number compared to the 4.2 million French high school students who were studying English the same year — but an indication, at least, of the current resurgence in regional languages and cultural identity in France which the centralising French state had once tried to stamp out in the name of a unitary republic.

It was a reminder, too, of how difficult it is to pigeonhole the French. To foreigners, they are proudly nationalistic. But if you ask an individual where they come from, they will talk rapturously about their region or *pays* before they talk about their nationality, or what it means to be French.

Pays literally means 'country' in French, but inside France, it also refers to an area that is distinct but which is not necessarily delineated on any map by a legal border or an administrative boundary. Thus, people will say their *pays* is Beaujolais, Provence or the Auvergne, for example — areas of France that still have a powerful hold over their psyche even if they haven't lived there for decades. Even though Muriel has lived in Lyon for sixteen years, has travelled widely and describes herself as an Anglophile, her conversation is always peppered with references to her *pays* of Savoie, where she grew up, and the little village near Annecy where her mother still lives. For her, that is home.

Travelling through some of these areas, I have come to understand why the French are so keen to preserve their rural heritage and traditions. When I first came to France, I saw no point venturing beyond Paris — for me, that grand, beautiful, sensual city *was* France. Most Parisians felt the same way.

But then I discovered the châteaux of the Loire Valley, the seaside towns of the Mediterranean, the rolling green hills of the Dordogne, the spectacular mountains of the Chartreuse region, the flat fields of northern Provence. Few people might speak the old languages in these places anymore, but they still retain their diversity and uniqueness — virtually every region or *pays* in France boasts its own cuisine, its own wine, its own particular history and geography.

One of our favourite car drives in France is a 25-kilometre stretch of meandering back road between Salles-sous-Bois, the little village in Drôme Provençal that we'd escape to whenever we had the chance, and Nyons which was known for its vibrant weekly Provençal market.

The drive to Nyons took us through medieval villages, Côtes du Rhône vineyards and fields of Drôme's famous lavender. Closer to Nyons, the lavender and vineyards gave way to olive groves. The Mediterranean was still several hundred kilometres away to the south, but the warm climate of Nyons and its sheltered position in the Eygues valley had enabled it to become a major centre for olive production in France. Indeed, it is amazing how quickly the climate can change in this country. One January weekend, we left a snow-covered Lyon to find the sun shining in Salles, the cold Mistral wind having swept the blue sky clear of clouds.

Driving through this picture-postcard landscape, it is easy to forget the other side of France, the one we Francophiles (and most French) would prefer not to acknowledge. This is the less palatable France, the one where dog owners let their animals foul the beautiful country lanes, where nuclear reactors often spoil the stupendous views, and where rural poverty and racial prejudice are as much a feature of the French countryside as the châteaux and the vineyards.

After three years living in Lyon, I have to admit that I am still baffled by France. As other puzzled foreigners have observed over the years, there seems to be at least two countries here trying their best to ignore each other.

There is the old, beautiful France, the France that foreigners admire, with its respect for traditions and history, its pride in its culture and language and its commitment to state support and intervention.

This is the France of top-quality hospitals at any price, museums in every town, well-maintained roads, very fast trains, a 35-hour work week and long summer holidays. It is also the France that harbours a solid anti-capitalist tradition, demonises America and every aspect of globalisation, tolerates a large and strike-happy public sector, and claims the right to be — or at least to sound — 'different' in world affairs.

The other France is modern, entrepreneurial, competitive and unafraid of risk. This is the France that has become one of the most efficient and productive economies in the world, which has embraced globalisation and the privatisation of state assets, and had created world-class companies, leaders and thinkers.

This France doesn't baulk at constructing modern, glass pyramids alongside historical iconic buildings, enjoys

American movies without being threatened by them, speaks English without believing it undermines the culture and language, and believes that more flexibility needs to be injected into the French economic and social model, so that more and better jobs can flow to all its citizens, new immigrants included.

On the other hand, this is also a France that builds ugly supermarket malls and housing estates at the edge of country towns, abandons traditions like the long restaurant lunch for the fast service of McDonald's and Starbucks, and is showing the ominous signs of emerging obesity among its younger citizens.

At the end of the day, France is all these things and more; a country of competing values and contradictory habits.

Roger Cohen, writer and *New York Times* journalist, hit the nail on the head when he wrote in a newspaper column in January 2005: 'There are all sorts of countries and then, of course, there is France, or, to put it better, La France, a state but also a being, with its pretensions, its contradictions, its lapses and its loveliness that make us love it or loathe it or, more likely, both at once.'

Indeed. For me, that description helped to explain why, when I was away from France, I always, inevitably, felt like coming back. And why, soon after I returned, I always, inevitably, start to think that maybe it was time I fell out of love with France and moved on.

Epilogue

*You're an expatriate. You've lost touch with the soil.
You get precious. Fake European standards have
ruined you. You drink yourself to death. You become
obsessed by sex. You spend all your time talking, not
working. You are an expatriate, see? You hang
around in cafés.*

The Sun Also Rises, Ernest Hemingway, 1926

I DECIDED IT WAS time we threw a party, to bring together some of the new friends and acquaintances we'd made in Lyon so far, but Michael was less keen. That was because I wanted the party to be a birthday celebration as well — for Michael was about to turn fifty. Michael, though, didn't want to make a big deal about it.

'Can't we just close the curtains, eat in and watch a DVD instead?' he moaned.

'I don't think so,' I replied. 'You know you'll regret it if we end up doing nothing.'

'But we won't be doing nothing,' he said. 'We're going to climb a mountain.'

It was true. I'd ask Michael how he wanted to celebrate his actual birthday and he said he wanted to take time off work and go walking in the Chartreuse Mountains in the Savoie. More specifically, he wanted to climb one of its higher mountains 'just to prove that I can'. It was a guy-turning-fifty thing.

We had recently discovered the Chartreuse, which was about a two-hour drive from Lyon. North of Grenoble, the Chartreuse was part of what was called the French Préalps, a medium-sized mountain range than ran to the west of the actual French Alps. Although they were smaller than the French Alps, the Chartreuse still offered spectacular views along its mountain paths and were a popular destination for French hikers during summer. We also liked to walk there, staying overnight in one of the area's many scenic mountain villages. Both Michael and I had become converts to hiking in recent years: we found it the best way to forget the stresses of the regular week.

We usually chose the low, easier walks. For his birthday, however, Michael wanted to climb a Chartreuse peak called Le Petit Som. At 1772 metres, it was one of the smaller of the Chartreuse Mountains, although it didn't seem that *petit* to me. But the top of the peak was supposed to afford fantastic views of Mont Blanc and surrounding mountains. So with the determination of a Mount Everest expeditionary team, we set off on what would be a 15-kilometre trek in total, on a perfect spring morning in May with a birthday lunch of ham sandwiches and chocolate and a half bottle of champagne in our backpacks.

The plan was to open the champagne at the top, but by the time we got there, we were so tired from the climb that we decided to keep the bottle corked. The views were intoxicating enough anyway. I took a picture of Michael standing next to the cross that marked the top of the peak: he looked happier than I had ever seen him. I still have it on my computer as a screen saver.

What we hadn't figured on, however, was the snow. The walk to the peak had been under a brilliant blue spring sky and through picturesque green fields where cows with big bells around their necks were munching the new grass in glorious oblivion. But the route down the mountain and back to the parking lot took us onto the northern side of the mountain, which, when we looked over from our vantage point on the peak, we noticed was still covered in a blanket of snow despite it being late May.

'Don't worry, we've got a compass and a map, we'll find our way,' Michael said reassuringly.

Michael was keen to complete the walk as it was

described in our guide book. Soon after we started our descent, however, we began to wonder about the wisdom of sticking to the book and not opting to go back the way we came. The snow was soft and deep and covered a multitude of sins like potholes and logs. We needed snowshoes, not walking boots, to negotiate the rather steep descent; I kept tripping and falling and soon found myself completely wet. Michael, having grown up in Canada, was doing better in the snow than me, but I could tell from his face that he was starting to get worried; the path was now completely covered and he was having trouble working out which direction to take through the woods. The sun had dropped behind the peak, and I was starting to shiver.

'I'm not sure I can go on much longer like this,' I told Michael. 'I'm exhausted.' I wasn't sure whether I had the energy now to even retrace my steps and climb back up through the snow to the peak and back down again on the other side, which now seemed to be the wisest option if we wanted to find our way out of the Chartreuse Mountains by nightfall.

It was just then that we heard voices in the distance. Through the trees below us, a group of about thirty people dressed in army fatigues and carrying heavy backpacks were jogging up the mountain towards us. Each was cradling some sort of weapon. It turned out it was the French army on manoeuvres. Suddenly, I had an extra reason to be glad the French hadn't sent their troops into Iraq.

'Are you people OK?' the group leader, a woman, asked when they reached us. She hadn't even worked up a sweat.

'Yes, thanks,' said Michael, 'now that we have run into you. Can you tell us the best way down please?'

We really didn't need to ask — the soldiers' boots had made deep impressions in the snow that even I could follow. 'Just continue on the way we have come up — that's the walking path,' the female captain explained. 'You'll eventually run into another platoon coming up behind us. They'll show you the way from there.'

Two hours later we were back in the car park, exhausted but relieved. We vowed never again to set out on a mountain walk without checking the state of the paths and the weather with the tourist office first. I opened the bottle of champagne we'd carried all the way, and we drank it out of paper cups in gulps.

Before the walk, I'd managed to convince Michael that we should celebrate his birthday with a party the following weekend. We'd already been living in Lyon for more than a year, and had been invited to a few expat parties. It was now our turn.

Both of us have fond memories of parties in France, mostly because, in our case, they tend to bring together a whole lot of expatriates from different countries, which can make for a lively and interesting time.

Epilogue

I've always found expats to be a fun-loving bunch. The writer Mary McCarthy once described them as hedonists — people in flight from the spiritual oppression of their nine-to-five routines at home. 'The average expatriate thinks of his own country rarely and with great unwillingness,' she wrote. She was mainly talking about famous expat writers, such as Ernest Hemingway, Henry Miller and F. Scott Fitzgerald who'd washed up in places like Paris during the 1920s and '30s.

With globalisation changing old horizons, the expatriate life is now an option for more than just the artist. Policemen, lawyers, accountants, teachers, nurses — anyone with a portable skill — can spend some time abroad as part of their careers these days. Regardless, it still seems to have an intoxicating, even liberating, effect on people. It has a lot to do with the fact that expats are far from home, and far from the gaze of family and peers and their potentially disapproving looks. Abroad, you can carve out a different persona for yourself; you can even let your ambitions and inhibitions slip for a while. Anyway, all the expatriates we know seem to love to loosen their ties, kick off their shoes and have a good time.

Not surprisingly, then, some of our best memories of France are of parties, like the cocktail party on the roof of the Australian Embassy thrown for Bob Hawke in June 1989, to which I'd managed to sneak in Michael and two other foreign journalist friends. That night, we saluted the Eiffel Tower with our tinnies of Foster's beer. It marked the end of an extraordinary year that had not only brought me to France for the first time, but had also introduced me to my future husband.

There were also the riotous parties held at my first French apartment on Rue Gracieuse in Paris, which brought together most of the crowd from the Journalists in Europe program, fellow waifs in search of a more meaningful kind of life and just those taking a year out from what they thought was the tedium of their regular lives.

A few years later, we gathered together some of those people again — those who, like us, couldn't get France out of their system and had decided to stay on in Paris — for our second farewell party to France. We held it in the walled garden of our landlord's rambling ground floor apartment in Belleville. At the time, we truly believed that would be our last French hurrah.

Now here we were again, more than decade later, planning to throw another party, this time in Lyon.

It would be no less lively, but the guest list would certainly be more mixed.

There are always quite a number of journalists at our parties, given our background, and several of our old friends from London and Paris said they would fly to Lyon for Michael's fiftieth birthday party. This group included Jean-Marc, one of our former colleagues from the Journalists in Europe program, who now worked for the French state TV channel France–2, based in Paris.

Doug, one of Michael's oldest friends from Canada — they had both manned the picket lines together in a long and legendary strike at the Canadian Broadcasting Corporation in the 1980s — said he would also fly in from Scotland where he now worked as a business journalist.

Also invited were a few of our Australian friends living in London, including Gwen, Emiliya and Pilita who all now worked for the *Financial Times*, plus Pilita's partner Peter who was *The Australian*'s Europe correspondent.

The bulk of our guests though would be Michael's work colleagues at Interpol, many of whom we mixed with out of hours.

There would be quite a few expat police, including John, formerly of Scotland Yard, who'd become one of Michael's closest friends in Lyon. We'd spent a few raucous weekends away with John and his girlfriend, including one at Salles-sous-Bois, our rural haunt, where Michael would try to resurrect (usually unsuccessfully) his skills as a barbecue chef. I was glad when John agreed to give a speech in honour of Michael reaching fifty at the party.

I also intended to invite a few of Interpol's 'civilian' staff whom we'd got to know, including Kate from human resources who'd helped us find our Lyon apartment, and Rachael, Michael's vibrant and competent press officer who was great fun at parties — she'd once enthralled guests at a New Year's Eve do with her wild Shirley Bassey impersonation.

We'd also made friends with Philippe, a clever young Belgian who wrote speeches in English for Interpol's secretary-general, which was all the more remarkable because English was his third language (after Flemish and French).

I also invited my friend Muriel, who headed the French translation at Interpol; she also would be joining us and our out-of-town friends the next day for lunch at a country restaurant. I was turning Michael's birthday into a week-long festival.

As I was compiling the guest list, I realised this would be the first party I'd ever held where cops would outnumber the civilians.

'At least we won't have any problems with gatecrashers,' Michael mused.

The guest list was looking more like a UN of international police: it included Rory, one of Italy's most senior — and well-dressed — policewomen; Jean-Michel, a police superintendent from southern France who spoke a colourful street French; Geoff, a former prime ministerial bodyguard from the Australian Federal Police; and Gwen, an FBI agent from Kansas, who always seemed to impress the single (and married) men at parties with her tales of close calls on the job.

'I've seen some things …' Gwen would say. It seemed a lot of things happened in Kansas.

Anyway, with the guest list sorted, I started to plan the party menu. Including partners, I'd invited about fifty people.

It would be a squeeze in our small apartment. I couldn't seat everyone, so my only option was to provide a light meal that could be eaten standing up.

When it came to catering, there was no better place to be than Lyon, the food capital of France. I headed straight to La Halle de Lyon, the undercover market that sells all kinds of fresh local produce. I must have been walking around the market for about an hour when an elderly woman asked me whether I needed some help. She noticed I'd been staring at the smoked salmon at one of the stalls for several minutes.

'That looks lovely, doesn't it? But it's pretty expensive these days,' the woman said. 'How many people are you buying it for?'

'Fifty,' I replied.

'*Mon Dieu*. You are generous.'

I then explained I was throwing a birthday party for my husband, and I realised I didn't have a clue how to cater for it. She immediately took me under her wing and introduced me to all her favourite *marchands* at La Halle. The stallholders had all sorts of ideas about what I should do.

'We could make you a couple of large pizzas and cut them into small squares for you,' said one. 'What about a platter of tiny *quenelles*?' suggested another.

Claudine — by now my helper had introduced herself — then took me to her favourite *charcuterie,* a special butchery that sold pork and all its accompaniments. The *charcutier*/owner came out to greet me. I told him about the party and that I was partial to the idea of having a large fresh ham-on-the-bone as the centrepiece of my party table, one that guests could have the pleasure of carving themselves.

'What would you like to serve it with?' he asked.

'I'm not sure — what about some tabouli salad or something.' I replied.

He tapped his chin. 'This will be a party attended by a lot of foreigners, right?' he asked. 'Why not serve them something really French? Something they'll remember?'

He then suggested two Lyonnaise salads to go with the ham: one with potatoes and herrings, the other with lentils, bacon and onions. He also recommended I heat the ham before serving, by putting it in a large pot of seasoned broth about 20 minutes before everyone was ready to eat. 'It's always better to eat ham slightly warm,' he said.

By this time, a small crowd of shoppers as well as the *charcutier*'s staff had formed around Claudine and me. Everybody was nodding their heads at the *charcutier*'s suggestions, and added a few more of their own. Only in France could so many people become so animated about a birthday party menu, I thought.

I could hardly reject the butcher's ideas now, so I placed my orders, and bid farewell to Claudine after we exchanged telephone numbers. I then moved on to La Halle's best *patisserie* stall, where I ordered two birthday cakes large enough to hold fifty candles. A final stop at the champagne merchant, and my catering preparations were virtually complete.

On the morning of the big night, I returned to La Halle to pick up all the food — I wanted the party menu to be a surprise, so I left Michael at home. The butcher's assistant helped me load the food into my car, as well as all the party paraphernalia that his boss had now pressed upon me for good measure, like extra bowls and nibblies, broth for heating the ham, platters, carving knives and a useful vice-like contraption to keep my ham upright for carving.

I thanked the young man for his help, and asked him whether he was a student — I presumed his job at the *charcuterie* was only a temporary one.

'No, I'm not a university student, I'm an apprentice — I want to make my career in *charcuterie*,' he said.

'What do you like about the job?' I asked.

'I think the best thing is that you get to meet so many different people.' He then wished me well for the party. 'We'll want to hear all about it later, especially whether your guests like the ham.'

That evening, any fears I had that our journalist friends wouldn't mix well with the Interpol crowd were soon dispelled. Everybody chatted together like old friends. The food was a hit. The speeches were funny. And Michael was pleased he hadn't convinced me that he preferred to spend this birthday quietly and alone.

Even the Secretary-General of Interpol made a surprise appearance bearing champagne and two bodyguards, whom he sensibly left at the entrance to our building. Something for the neighbours to talk about.

The only glitch came when it was time for Michael to blow out the fifty candles on his two cakes.

Naturally, it turned out to be a language problem on my part: I'd gone to the local supermarket the day before and bought fifty *bougies magiques*. Magic candles for a magic night, I thought.

What I didn't realise, however, was that *bougies magiques* actually means trick candles, the type you buy for children's birthday parties as a joke. Every time you try to blow one out, it pops up lit again. It's a funny sight when a little kid is trying to blow out two or three candles on top of a cake; it's hilarious when a fifty-year-old journalist is trying to do the same to a forest of candles refusing to be extinguished.

Michael blew. I blew. Even the Secretary-General tried to blow out the fifty candles, but still they stayed alight. It was fast turning into a Black Forest cake fire. Then clever Emiliya came to the rescue with a bowl of water, into which we dropped the candles one by one. The cakes were saved, but not my dignity. Trust me to get the French wrong again!

Someone then handed me a glass of champagne, and another round of *Bon Anniversaire* was sung. Michael put his arms around me, and made a private toast.

'To you, and to us, and to France,' he said.

Later I walked out onto our tiny balcony and took in the cool May air and the clear night sky.

To France, I thought. To this fascinating country where dogs ride on airplanes and foul the streets with impunity and where the language continually pulls tricks on foreigners. Where, just when you think you've had enough, the street markets are once again overflowing with summer fruits and flowers, and café owners are putting out their tables and chairs under the plane trees on Place Carnot.

France has mesmerised and confounded me since the first moment I stepped off the plane at Charles de Gaulle airport in 1988. Back then, I was more interested in escaping my old life than finding a new life. But a new life I found nonetheless, one in which France has ended up playing a central role. With Michael, I have returned to live here, not once, but twice. We might end up leaving another time, but France, as always, has a habit of upsetting the best-laid plans.

I've come to realise that just like those magic birthday candles my affection for France is going to be a very hard thing to ever fully extinguish.

No matter how hard I try to blow out the flame, it is always going to ignite. Again and again . . .

Afterword

We've since said our '*au revoirs*' to France, yet again. After three years at Interpol, Michael decided to call it quits. He'd had enough of the stress and the constant travel. I, on the other hand, yearned to get back into full-time work. It soon became clear the best way for me to achieve that goal was to move back to the place that knew me the best — and that's Sydney.

So here we are, ensconced in a flat near Bondi Beach with a new cat who doesn't need instructions in French. But our passion for France hasn't been extinguished. I still regularly check French property websites in the hope of discovering that affordable rural gem that might provide us with a French base in our dotage (or sooner), for I know in my heart we'll return one day. We still keep in touch with our friends in Lyon. I also follow the changing political events in France with much interest, particularly the rise of France's so-called new Napoleon — Nicolas Sarkozy. I was surprised that he won the presidency in May 2007 by such a convincing margin.

No one I knew had voted for him. When I lived in France, Sarkozy was scorned by the French media as a thug and neo-conservative. In 2005 when he described young urban troublemakers as 'scum', he was accused of stoking the riots that were then engulfing the low-income housing estates of France. 'Sarko-Fascist' graffiti soon became a common sight in the inner-city areas — my former bourgeois neighbourhood in Lyon included. France's tough guy seemed to be hated in equal measure by the far Right (because Sarkozy wasn't 'pure' French — he's the son of a Hungarian immigrant) and by the far Left (because he was an unabashed admirer of America).

The Socialists, Sarkozy's main opposition, opted for a woman: the elegant Ségolène Royal. She'd managed to capture the Socialist Party's candidacy for the 2007 presidential election from the party's Old Guard: 'Who will look after the children?' one of these dinosaurs sniffed when Ségolène was tipped to run.

As we were leaving France, Ségolène was rating well in the polls. In surveys, the French were saying they were ready for change and were willing to put a woman into the Élysée Palace if that would deliver it. After all, the Germans had elected a woman — Angela Merkel — as Chancellor for the first time in Germany's history and the country was now thriving. Why shouldn't France go the same way? In the end, it's hard to know whether it was her gender or her rather vague policies that were the cause of Ségolène's defeat. My friend Muriel in Lyon thinks it was the former.

'She did very well, but France still isn't ready for a female President,' said Muriel, who'd voted for Ségo over Sarko. 'Sarkozy on the other hand speaks the language of the man on the street. He's anti-immigration and pro-security. He tells them what they want to hear.'

Indeed, Sarkozy's message was particularly well received by older French, like Muriel's mother who voted for Sarko over her daughter's protestations. The 2007 French presidential election's been dubbed the wrinkly landslide: 61 per cent of voters in their sixties and 68 per cent of the over-seventies opted for the man who was also promising change after years of decline. I suspect, though, what these older voters wanted was a return to the old days when France was for the 'pure' French and Islam wasn't the fastest growing religion in the country.

Jean Marie Le Pen's success in linking waves of immigration from North Africa with rising crime — even though there are no statistics to back this up — has changed the political landscape in France. Just as Pauline Hanson dragged John Howard to the Right on immigration — so has the far Right's Le Pen done with Sarkozy in France.

Elderly voters were attracted by Sarkozy's promises to control immigration and tackle crime. He pledged to expel

25,000 illegal immigrants in 2007, stepping up a process begun in 2003 when Sarkozy was Interior Minister. Back then, Sarkozy introduced controversial weekly charter flights to send illegal immigrants back to their countries. The flights were later nicknamed 'Sarkozy charters'.

Taking a tough stand against illegal immigration isn't the only policy initiative the new French leader seems to have pinched from Australia. In January 2007, the Australian Government dumped 'multicultural' from its lexicon and renamed the Department of Immigration and Multicultural Affairs the Department of Immigration and Citizenship — reflecting John Howard's long-stated distaste for the concept of multi-cultures under one southern sky, and his desire for new immigrants to better integrate into Australian society.

As I've said in this book, the French have never accepted the concept of 'multiculturalism'. But the new Sarkozy regime has gone one step further by renaming its Immigration Ministry the Ministry for Immigration and National Identity. This has outraged anti-racism groups with long memories of how the Vichy Government deported French Jews to Nazi death camps during the Second World War under the guise of national unity. They fear the new name for the ministry will only fan greater xenophobia in France.

Respected French historian Patrick Weil is one commentator who sees the re-naming of the Immigration department as an 'ominous' sign. In the past, he says, the right wing in France has resorted to linking immigration with national identity only 'in periods of crisis, to stigmatise certain immigrants'.

'It creates polarisation,' Weil was quoted as saying. 'It justifies racism and xenophobic prejudices because the government — the president — seems to adopt (the same prejudices).' Perhaps a tough new French citizenship test — à la John Howard's — isn't too far away.

Nicolas Sarkozy, though, can count on the backing of much of the French electorate for his tough new immigration regime. Less clear is whether they'll go along with his other promise to usher in a new 'economic revolution' in France. Sarkozy has a clear mandate from the people for change, but as my friend Muriel says, 'The French support change only if it doesn't mean sacrifices for them.'

Indeed, economic reform has defeated many a French leader in the past. Three prime ministers in the Chirac era were forced to abandon reforms in the face of mass demonstrations — the most recent in March 2006 when three million people took to the streets to protest a new flexible job contract for young people. Back then it was Dominique de Villepin — prime minister at the time — who blinked. But Sarkozy's people say it was a lack of support from a weak-kneed Jacques Chirac that was the problem. They say things will be different now that a leader with a backbone is ensconced in the Élysée Palace.

Few would deny that economic reform is needed in France. Since 2005, the French unemployment rate has dropped from just over 10 per cent to 8.3 per cent — yet it's still among the highest in the euro area, and twice the jobless rate of Australia and the United States.

At around 2 per cent per year, economic growth in France is now lagging that of its major rival, Germany — which under Angela Merkel's reforms has managed to transform itself into the standout performer in Europe in recent times. This irks the French, who for years have relied on strong consumer spending and low interest rates to keep its economy growing faster than Germany's.

France is now among the weakest performing economies in the euro zone, with a budget deficit that's blown out to 2.7 per cent of GDP — well above the euro zone average deficit of 1.6 per cent and a far cry from Australia's years of surpluses equaling 1 per cent of GDP. French Governments can no longer throw public money at the problem: Sarkozy instead is promising a stiff dose of Thatcherism.

He's certainly adopted the Thatcher rhetoric. He says he wants to reward the hard workers and crack down on the shirkers. He wants to return France to its glory days. By Thatcher's standards, though, his reforms are modest — his economic agenda includes cutting some taxes, loosening, but not abolishing, the 35-hour week, slashing the bloated French public service and ensuring a minimum of essential services during strikes. Hardly a radical economic and industrial agenda — but one which is sure to inflame every public sector union in the land.

A hint of things to come was played out on election night when Sarkozy's victory prompted a smattering of street riots across the country. In Lyon, my friend Rachael emerged from a restaurant on Terreaux, the main square, on the Monday night after the elections, and walked right into the middle of a mêlée between riot police and young hooded demonstrators who'd just smashed a McDonald's window down the street. 'It was really hairy for a while — bottles were smashing around our heads,' she said. Scores of police in riot gear closed in on the small pack of protesters and the trouble soon passed. In the end, even Rachael thought the protests were mild by 2005 standards when 10,000 cars were torched across France. Since that time, the government has introduced tough new juvenile detention laws that impose jail terms for even minor offenses. That's discouraged many university students from taking to the streets. This time around, says Rachael, 'the only people rioting are those with nothing to lose'.

Isolated outbreaks of unrest are unlikely to intimidate France's tough new cop on the beat. But then you can never underestimate France's desire to mobilise against authority. After all, nearly half the country voted for a Socialist who framed her campaign around long-held notions of French solidarity, protection of the welfare state and rejection of 'barbaric' Anglo-Saxon style capitalistic ways.

Sarkozy was clearly mindful of this 'other' France when he gave his first speech to the nation as president. He abandoned his popularist authoritarian tone, and instead cast himself as a unifier rather than divider, invoking Martin Luther King in the process. He then gave seven of his fifteen Cabinet posts to women, including to one of Arab descent. Imagine a Prime Minister of either persuasion doing that in Australia? In a surprise move, Sarkozy also appointed a prominent Socialist to the post of Foreign Minister.

France wants and needs change. But France is not Britain in the 1970s when Thatcher came to power. Despite how it looks to the outside world, France is not crippled by strikes. Its public services are still among the best in the world; indeed, the British still flock to French public hospitals for surgery. French multinational companies are still leaders in global markets.

The French want France to be great again. They know that means becoming more competitive with the likes of India and China, improving productivity and making the labour market more flexible up to a point. But they don't aspire to the full-blown Anglo-Saxon model with all its inequities. No one wants to say goodbye to the long lunch, or hello to the longer working week. And who can blame them?

How Nicolas Sarkozy can reconcile those two Frances — I have no idea. But as everything with France, it will be an interesting process to watch from the sidelines.

May 2007.

Acknowledgments

This book would have been the poorer without the generous help and guidance of friends and colleagues in Lyon, in particular Muriel Millet, Rachael Billington, Badreddine Touihri, Camilla Patek, Jan Garton, John Newton, Sandrine Collomb, Laurence Lopez, Philippe Lejeune, Roraima Andriani, Stefan Huurman, Magali Laubies and my Friday morning Lyon Bleu French class cohorts — Ilse Gronmeyer, Evgeniya Kostov and Maree Van Hooff — led by our warm and wonderful teacher and friend Janine-Sophie Guimiot.

I'd also like to thank Philippe Le Corre and Michel Moutot in Paris for their frank briefings on French current affairs, and Madeleine Morati-Schmitt for taking the time to explain to me the history of the French women's movement. Bruce and Anne Leonard of La Maison Chaudenay in Burgundy, Bernard Liaudois of Château de Fontblachère in Ardèche and Brent and Rose-Marie Perkins of Le Boomerang in the Bugey hills outside Lyon introduced me to the diversity and generosity of French country living, while Australians in Paris Ralph Heimans and Martin Grant showed me how expats could survive and succeed in a foreign country.

Speaking of Australian expatriates, I'd also like to express my gratitude to my London friends — Gwen Robinson, Pilita Clark, Peter Wilson, Emiliya Mychasuk and Michael Fry — for encouraging me to embark on a book project in France when I should have been out there finding myself a real job, and for turning up to our Lyon police parties on short notice.

In Sydney, thanks must also go to Margaret Connolly, Amruta Slee and Lydia Papandrea for helping me turn my ideas into a story, and then helping me to sharpen it into a book.

This book however would not have been possible without the loving guidance of my best friend, Michael Rose, who devoted much of his little free time in Lyon to reading, re-reading and editing my manuscript, when he should have been working on his own.

Finally, I could not have managed to live the life I've always wanted without the support and love of my family back home who have always been there for me, particularly during the many years I've lived abroad. So here's an overdue thank you to John, Elsie, Gary, Sue, Carolyn and Luigi. And to my nieces and nephew — Lucy, Juliette and Jordan — my apologies for seeing far too little of you because of *My French Connection*.

Walkley Award–winning journalist SHERYLE BAGWELL has worked in print and television in Australia and Europe for more than twenty years. She wrote the ground-breaking 'Corporate Woman' column for *The Australian Financial Review* in the 1990s, and was the newspaper's European correspondent based in London from 1998 to 2001. In 2003, she moved to Lyon in France with her husband where she continued to work for a variety of media. The couple divide their time between Australia and France and in early 2006 returned to Sydney. They currently live in Bondi Beach.

PHOTO: STEFAN HUURMAN